WHEN THE SMOKE CLEARED

WHEN THE SMOKE CLEARED

THE 1968 REBELLIONS AND THE UNFINISHED BATTLE FOR CIVIL RIGHTS IN THE NATION'S CAPITAL

KYLA SOMMERS

THE
NEW
PRESS

NEW YORK
LONDON

Published in the United States by The New Press, New York, 2023
Distributed by Two Rivers Distribution

LIBRARY OF CONGRESS CATALOGING-IN-PUBLICATION DATA

Names: Sommers, Kyla, author.
Title: When the smoke cleared : the 1968 rebellion and the unfinished
battle for civil rights in the nation's capital / Kyla Sommers.
Other titles: 1968 rebellion and the unfinished battle for civil rights in
the nation's capital
Description: New York : The New Press, 2023 | Includes bibliographical
references and index. | Summary: "A history of the uprisings and
protests in Washington, D.C., following the murder of Martin Luther King
Jr. in 1968"-- Provided by publisher.
Identifiers: LCCN 2022040111 | ISBN 9781620977477 (hc) | ISBN 9781620978108
(ebook)
Subjects: LCSH: Race riots--Washington (D.C.)--History--20th century. |
African Americans--Washington (D.C.)--Social conditions--20th century. |
African Americans--Civil rights--History--20th century. | Washington
(D.C.)--History--20th century.
Classification: LCC F200 .S66 2023 | DDC
305.896/07307530904--dc23/eng/20220830
LC record available at https://lccn.loc.gov/2022040111

The New Press publishes books that promote and enrich public discussion and understanding of the issues vital to our democracy and to a more equitable world. These books are made possible by the enthusiasm of our readers; the support of a committed group of donors, large and small; the collaboration of our many partners in the independent media and the not-for-profit sector; booksellers, who often hand-sell New Press books; librarians; and above all by our authors.

www.thenewpress.com

Composition by Bookbright Media
This book was set in Minion and Trade Gothic

Printed in the United States of America

10 9 8 7 6 5 4 3 2 1

For my family
&
the friends who make DC home

Contents

Introduction

Rev. Dr. Martin Luther King Jr.'s assassination on April 4, 1968, ignited centuries of grief and anger at American racism. An incalculable number of Black Americans took to the streets to protest this injustice in more than one hundred cities across the United States. The rebellions in Washington, DC, were the largest in the country. The capital endured $33 million in property damage ($238 million adjusted for inflation) and fifteen thousand federal troops occupied the District. Enraged crowds started more than one thousand fires. But what happened after the city stopped burning?

As the activist and future DC mayor Marion Barry declared at a DC City Council hearing in May 1968, the rebellions "created a vacuum and an opportunity." Something would have to be done to reconstruct portions of DC, but it remained to be determined what would be rebuilt and whose interests would be served in the process. Would DC seize the chance to rectify the structural inequalities that motivated the uprisings?[1]

This book tells the stories of the Washingtonians who ambitiously grasped this "opportunity" to rebuild the capital as a more just society that would protect and foster Black political and economic power. The majority-Black city's populace aided their communities during the uprisings and responded with resiliency and determination in the aftermath. DC's government, community groups, and citizens loosely agreed on a reconstruction process they believed would alleviate the social injustices that were the root causes of unrest.

The rebellions challenged the same powerful institutions that generations of moderate and militant Black activists had previously picketed, boycotted, and sued. Most often, people attacked the most accessible representations of white people's power over Black communities: white-owned and/or -operated stores, commuter highways, and "occupying" police forces. Black Washingtonians had confronted these manifestations of white political power as they demanded freedom, economic opportunities, good education, accountable policing, voting rights, and political power for over a century. Even though the tactics used by protesters were different, the rebellions predominantly targeted the same groups that Black people had long pressured to change.

After the uprisings, Black Washingtonians and parts of the DC government emphasized the idea that the rebellions were the result of legitimate anger at systemic racism and the government's failure to address it. Building on this understanding of the upheaval, DC leaders adopted an ambitious plan to resolve many of these long-standing inequities. This project incorporated the government programs and principles created by President Lyndon B. Johnson's Great Society, a series of legislative measures that aimed to eliminate racial injustice, end poverty, and reduce crime. The Civil Rights Act of 1964, the Voting Rights Act of 1965, and the laws that created Medicare and Medicaid were all passed as part of the Great Society. It also included the Economic Opportunity Act of 1964, which established the Office of Economic Opportunity (OEO) to combat poverty nationwide, in part by creating community-based organizations called community action agencies. The federal government mandated "maximum feasible participation" from low-income citizens in creating and managing these programs. The effort to rebuild DC seized upon the idea that the people who were most affected by government initiatives should have some control in how those programs were administered.

Three elements of the city's plan demonstrate how Black Washingtonians used the concept of citizen participation to demand economic and political power. First, after the uprisings the DC City Council held public hearings to listen to the community to determine how it should respond to the rebellions. A group of Washingtonians coordinated with each other to present a clear, compelling narrative of the problems that Black people faced in the capital and the reforms they desired. These solutions included policies that explicitly benefited and even favored Black residents as a way to compensate for the historical discrimination African Americans in DC had endured. The DC City Council adopted most of these suggestions into its blueprint for responding to the rebellions.

Second, Black Washingtonians lobbied for a role in police oversight. Harassment by police officers was one of the biggest issues facing Black people in DC. After police officers killed two Black men in the summer of 1968, Black people protested and demanded action from the city. After a government commission studied the issue, the DC City Council passed legislation that limited when a police officer could fire a gun and created civilian review boards to grant Black community members a guiding role in police hiring and discipline.

Finally, DC incorporated citizen participation into its rebuilding plans for Shaw, a 90 percent Black neighborhood that had been the center of Black Washington since the end of the Civil War. More than 50 percent of Shaw residents were surveyed to ask how they wanted their community to be rebuilt. The ensuing plans eschewed private development and instead tasked nonprofit groups with building new housing in partnership with the DC government. Black businesses and workers would design and build the residences as well as public amenities like libraries and schools.

This response to the rebellions was very different from the reactions of white and conservative Americans, who considered the events after King's assassination to be an apolitical crime spree that demonstrated the need for stronger police forces. Washington suburbanites had complained about DC crime for more than a decade. Some had demanded more police even when crime rates were low. Politicians had stoked these fears and used DC crime as a platform to oppose civil rights and encourage larger, more powerful police departments. But after the uprisings, the concern over crime in the capital reached new heights. Some suburban residents refused to even enter the District, and others called for the military to permanently occupy the capital to control crime.

The fears and demands of white suburban Americans greatly affected American politics in the aftermath of April 1968. While President Johnson had previously emphasized large government programs to combat poverty and racial injustice in response to urban upheaval, the president now foregrounded anticrime policies like the Safe Streets Act that ballooned police department budgets and permitted more electronic surveillance. Richard Nixon made crime in DC a core issue in his 1968 presidential campaign. Once elected, Nixon used DC to experiment with different anticrime measures including mandatory minimum sentences and "no-knock" warrants. As other local and state governments modeled these measures, they disproportionately harmed Black Americans and other people of color.

Richard Nixon's agenda also limited DC's efforts to rebuild. He destroyed the government programs that made DC's reconstruction plan possible, slashed funding for urban housing projects, and discouraged citizen participation programs. Development companies were allowed to bid on rebuilding projects, shutting out local nonprofits.

Nonetheless, the plans and efforts of a majority-Black city to rebuild and reform itself deserve consideration, especially as Americans continue to grapple with the crises of racial inequality and police brutality. From the June 2020 protests for racial justice to the insurrectionist attack on the U.S. Capitol on January 6, 2021, recent events have demonstrated that the histories of protest, policing, racial inequality, and self-governance in Washington, DC, are timely and consequential. The 1968 uprisings and the 2020 protests in DC that followed the murder of George Floyd were not comparable in terms of scale—fewer than five hundred people were arrested in connection to the DC protests in 2020, while more than six thousand were arrested in 1968.[2] Still, this history of the 1968 uprisings in the capital helps to explain our current tumultuous moment and offers historical insights on how previous generations have responded to ongoing systemic racism.

Popular and historical accounts of the 1968 upheaval often emphasize its physical damage and largely overlook the thousands of Washingtonians who responded with a strengthened commitment to address structural inequality. According to many histories, the rebellions pushed a city already in decline off the precipice. Crime skyrocketed, the white and Black middle class abandoned the city in droves, and the damaged neighborhoods became urban wastelands.[3]

The narrative of urban decay is reproduced in much of the public understanding of the civil disturbances. The *Washington Post*'s interactive piece on the fiftieth anniversary of the upheaval, "A City Destroyed by Riots, Then and Now," contrasted photos of damaged buildings with contemporary images of bustling streets.[4] In "Everything Was on Fire," the DC-based news web-site WTOP recounted the rebellions and their impact on the city: "After the riots, crime spiked in Washington—and most other urban centers nationwide—sparking white flight out of America's cities, including the District. . . . Crumbling storefronts and vacant lots pockmarked the cityscape for years."[5]

While the story of crime and decay constitute one understanding of the impact of April 1968, it is certainly not the only legacy.[6] There is more to the story of the rebellions than burned-out buildings and white backlash. The personal narratives and oral histories interwoven throughout this book show the disparate ways people experienced and thought about the uprisings. The efforts to help those harmed by the upheaval offer inspiring stories of community building instead of destruction. Countless Washingtonians were willing to answer surveys and attend community hearings to help create the best city possible in the aftermath of the rebellions. In anticipation of the fiftieth anniversary of the 1968 uprising, historian Marya McQuirter launched the "dc1968 project"—a digital storytelling undertaking in which McQuirter created daily posts showcasing activism, art, and everyday life in 1968 Washington. "Part of the reason why I came up with this project is because I wanted to push back against what I call a single story or narrative that we have about 1968 in D.C.," McQuirter explained. The year 1968, in her view, should not just be understood as a "moment of rupture or fracture in this city. . . . I think 1968 has to be seen as a year of activism and a year in which people woke up."[7]

A closer look at the capital's history reframes our understanding of the rebellions of April 1968 so that the events are no longer primarily associated with violence and despair, but also activism and awakening.

WHEN THE SMOKE CLEARED

1

"We Want to Free DC from Our Enemies"

BLACK ACTIVISM IN THE CAPITAL

WASHINGTON, DC, IS UNLIKE ANY OTHER AMERICAN CITY. IT IS not part of any state, and for most of its existence its residents were unable to vote for president. To this day, Washingtonians have no representatives in Congress who can vote on legislation. DC's unique government and history is rooted in the United States' long legacy of anti-Black racism and fear of Black political power. The racial disparities and undemocratic practices in the capital—and the ways Black Washingtonians challenged this oppressive system—help explain why the 1968 rebellions happened and how leaders responded.

Washington's Founding to the Second World War

America's founders selected a plot of land along the Potomac River, forged from the slaveholding states of Maryland and Virginia, for the new nation's capital city in 1790. While Northern states had lobbied to seat the government permanently in Philadelphia, Southerners believed that plan would give too much power to abolitionists. They threatened to leave the union unless the capital was moved south, and they got their way. The federal government moved to DC in 1800 and, almost immediately, Washingtonians lost the ability to self-govern. Congress passed the Organic Act in 1801, which placed DC under the control of Congress and the president. They would establish DC's laws similarly to how a state passes legislation. The Organic Act also prevented Washingtonians from voting for president or congressional representatives, almost entirely disenfranchising the populace. Washington City, the central downtown portion of the capital, was allowed to create a municipal government with a presidentially appointed mayor and a dual-chamber city council elected by white men.[1]

This city council imposed the first Black codes, laws imposing specific rules and fines for African Americans, in 1808. The city added more codes that restricted Black people's freedom when white Washingtonians felt the most threatened: during the War of 1812, amid calls for the abolition of slavery in the capital in the 1820s, following the 1831 rebellion of enslaved people led by Nat Turner in nearby Virginia, and after DC's Black population grew by 70 percent in the 1840s.[2]

White Washingtonians also enforced white supremacy through extrajudicial violence. After an enslaved person allegedly attempted to kill his enslaver in 1835, a white mob destroyed symbols of Black success: a church, a school, and a restaurant owned by Black businessman Beverly Snow were attacked. The so-called Snow Riots were followed by even tougher restrictions on Black life including a law that barred Black people from owning a business (other than driving carts) and required every Black resident to have at least five white people testify they were of good character.[3] Despite these racist laws, free Black people comprised nearly 25 percent of the total population of Washington in 1840, and by 1860 DC had the largest Black population per capita of any American city.[4]

In 1861, Southern states seceded from the United States, sparking the Civil War. With the absence of Southerners in Congress, Radical Republicans—the staunchly antislavery wing of Abraham Lincoln's Republican Party—were powerful enough to legislate reforms in the capital. In 1862, Congress abolished slavery in DC, making it the first place south of the Mason-Dixon Line to emancipate its enslaved population. Most of white Washington and the press, however, criticized emancipation and pushed for more oppressive Black codes.[5]

After the end of the Civil War in 1865, Radical Republicans focused their reform efforts on the capital because they directly governed the District and it had no legislators to object. Some legislators even believed forging the capital in a radical, Northern image was "beautiful, poetic justice" that punished the former Confederacy. While most white residents opposed Black enfranchisement (in a local referendum, only thirty-six out of 7,339 white people supported it), more than 2,500 Black Washingtonians signed a petition to lobby Congress for suffrage. In 1867, Congress overrode President Andrew Johnson's veto and granted African American men in Washington, DC, the right to vote in local elections, even before the Fifteenth Amendment extended this right nationwide.[6]

DC's Black population nearly quadrupled during the Civil War, from eleven thousand to forty thousand people, and, shortly thereafter, in the 1868 DC mayoral election, nearly 50 percent of registered voters were Black men. They were instrumental in electing local leaders who pushed for school integration and passed antidiscrimination laws. The Equal Services Act of 1872 barred businesses such as restaurants, barbershops, and hotels from refusing service based on race. Another Equal Services Act, passed in 1873, required proprietors to serve "any well-behaved and respectable person" at the same price and in the same manner as any other customer. Violating the ordinance resulted in a $100 fine ($2,395 adjusted for inflation) and the loss of one's business license.[7]

This postwar period, called Reconstruction, also birthed

many of the civic and cultural institutions that shaped Black life in DC for decades to come. In 1867, Congress chartered Howard University and located its campus in the neighborhood that is today called Shaw. The Freedman's Bureau, a government agency created to aid newly free African Americans, built a hospital nearby and converted wartime barracks into housing. Newly free people settled in tenements, alleys, and homes throughout the city, often close to the Union army camps they inhabited during the war.[8]

Reconstruction and the Black political power that accompanied it were short-lived, however. In 1871, Congress turned DC into a territorial state and appointed Alexander "Boss" Shepherd, a well-known business leader, as the governor. After Shepherd's ambitious physical improvement projects incurred debt nearly twice the city's legal limit, Congress dissolved the territorial government in 1874 and replaced it with an appointed three-member board of commissioners that would run the city government. Most white Washingtonians supported the plan, in part because Congress would fund 50 percent of DC's budget, alleviating the city's debt and inability to fund itself through municipal taxes. They also believed that Congress, no longer controlled by Radical Republicans, would be more favorable to their interests than the pro-civil-rights city council elected during Reconstruction. The Black male franchise had existed for less than a decade in the capital, and white Washingtonians were so opposed to it that they were willing to give up their right to vote so that Black people would no longer have a voice in DC's governance. Under the new system, Congress could pass laws for the city without any input from its residents. The Organic Act of 1878, part of the compromise that officially ended Reconstruction, made the commissioner structure permanent, and all DC residents lost the franchise for nearly one hundred years.[9]

Despite this undemocratic system and its racist roots, the hope of federal employment, quality education, and middle-class life brought many Black newcomers to the capital in the following decades. In 1883, the federal government created a civil service system that democratized job access and, subsequently, the number of Black civil servants in DC tripled. Although Black employees were often limited to menial jobs and passed over for promotions, federal employment provided long-term job stability and formed the core of Black middle-class DC.[10] Washington's public schools were relatively well-funded because DC law required education funds to be distributed proportionately to Black and white schools based on population. DC attracted the best teachers in the nation, and in 1899 students at one Black high school scored higher on their examinations than students from the two white high schools. [11]

By 1900, DC boasted the largest African American population of any American city.[12] DC was also the political and cultural center of Black America. Washington contained the largest number of Black homeowners in the country, and Black newspapers across the nation carried stories describing the fine lifestyles and parties of the Washington upper crust. Prestigious Howard faculty members and elite clubs such as the Bethel Literary and Historical Society further cemented DC's status as the center of Black culture.[13] The DC elite also included Black entrepreneurs who believed Black businesses would foster community solidarity and prosperity. Nicknamed Black Broadway, the business district in Shaw along U Street NW was the heart of African American Washington. In 1880, there were fifteen Black-owned businesses around U Street. By 1920, there were more than three hundred.[14] For every successful Black business owner and bureaucrat, however, there were many more domestic workers and day laborers living in poverty.[15] At the turn of the twentieth century, nearly 25 percent of Black Washingtonians lived in one- or two-room shacks in the alleys behind the homes of the middle and upper class.[16]

The lives of both elite and working-class Black people worsened as DC institutions were increasingly segregated during the Progressive Era. In the early twentieth century, Presidents Theodore Roosevelt and William Howard Taft both reduced the number of federal job appointments reserved for African Americans. During the 1920s, President Woodrow Wilson, a Southern racist, segregated the federal workplace after his wife learned that white women worked next to Black men. He also drastically reduced the number of Black people employed in the federal government and banned Black people from federal office lunchrooms and bathrooms.[17] Endorsing segregation became "the thing to do," and local government offices and businesses followed the Wilson administration's example. White Washingtonians demanded laws that would segregate public transportation and bar having mixed-race children. Black people were no longer welcome members of the Washington Board of Trade (BOT), the city's primary commercial association founded in 1899. In the absence of an elected local government, the BOT had significant political power as it often effectively lobbied Congress to pass policies it supported.[18] Through this influence, the BOT indirectly functioned as a governing body.

Many Black Americans resolved to resist and fight worsening discrimination, a phenomenon referred to as the "New Negro Movement." Some federal employees challenged workplace segregation. In 1912, DC started its own branch of the National Association for the Advancement of Colored People (NAACP), the foundational civil rights organization, and many Black women campaigned for civil rights and women's suffrage.[19] Such activism only intensified at the close of World War I as Black Americans, especially veterans, pushed the United States to instill the democratic values it fought for abroad into civil rights policies domestically. Threatened by the New Negro Movement and the assertiveness of Black veterans, many white people were determined to maintain white supremacy. This resulted in riots that damaged Black communities across the nation and a surge in lynchings from 1917 to 1919.

After several white women in Washington were allegedly raped by a Black man, newspaper headlines were so evocative that the local NAACP chapter warned the press that more "inflammatory headlines and sensational news articles" would result in race riots. They were right: in an era when white mobs lynched Black men for merely flirting with white women, the furor over the alleged assaults resulted in a posse of more than one hundred white men, most of whom were in the military, beating random Black men. To destroy visible signs of Black success, the white mobs attacked many Black-owned businesses along U Street.[20] Some Black Washingtonians fought back and purchased over five hundred guns to guard their streets and homes. While nearly all postriot reports concluded that white mobs instigated the violence and Black people acted in self-defense, only eight or nine of the roughly one hundred people arrested during the riots were white. In the riot's aftermath, virtually no action was taken to alleviate white racist hostilities.[21] The worsened racism and living conditions during this era deterred migration to the capital, and by 1930, DC's Black population was proportionally the lowest since the Civil War.[22]

The Great Depression during the 1930s exacerbated hardships across Washington. A 1938 survey found DC's unemployment and welfare needs were the greatest in the country. To make matters worse, racist Southern congressmen tried to block aid from going to DC's Black residents, the federal government gave many jobs normally reserved for African Americans to white people, and some Black people were fired from their jobs and replaced by white workers.[23] The city's population also grew by 36 percent in the 1930s, resulting in major housing shortages that disproportionately affected Black people since the surrounding suburbs refused to rent or sell to them. The government also displaced Black Washingtonians as it bulldozed their neighborhoods to build new offices and housing for federal employees.[24]

Housing issues for DC's African Americans only worsened with the start of World War II. The federal government demanded a massive increase in Washington-area housing, but it was intended for soldiers and government workers instead of low-income families. In 1943, the District's housing agency was reorganized as the National Capital Housing Authority (NCHA), and it proposed building affordable housing to alleviate the housing shortage. Home builders' organizations and the real estate industry opposed the plan because they preferred for-profit construction built by private industry. Citizens associations, all-white neighborhood groups that were dedicated to maintaining segregated neighborhoods, opposed the plan because it would create housing for Black people too close to their communities. Despite the clear support for public housing from civic associations (Black community groups that paralleled, but often opposed, all-white citizens associations), the District constructed scant affordable housing and private industry built new residential developments.[25]

Underlying many of these issues was the fact that Congress's unique power over DC allowed Southern segregationists to impose their racist beliefs on the capital. Senator Theodore Bilbo (D-MS), for example, declared that he wanted to be on the Senate DC Committee so he "could keep Washington a segregated city." The House and Senate committees on the District of Columbia almost always had to approve any legislation regarding DC before it could advance to a floor vote in the respective legislative chamber. In other words, these committees controlled which policies affecting the capital had even a chance of passing. From 1945 to 1947, Bilbo chaired the Senate DC Committee, giving him considerable control over appropriations and what legislation made it to the Senate floor. When Senator Bilbo won reelection in 1946, the *Washington Post* commented that the former Confederacy clutched DC as a "helpless pawn."[26]

The issues of inadequate housing, job discrimination, and segregationist leaders did not end with the conclusion of World War II. In Washington, a generation of activists worked to alleviate the hold of structural racism on the capital. From 1945 to 1968, Black activists faced the same problems and adversaries, but their tactics shifted over time. Increasingly, African Americans pushed for not just an end to discrimination based on race, but also on proactive policies that would rectify the impact of centuries of American white supremacy. Black Washingtonians challenged this endemic inequality, often self-consciously invoking "Black Power" to demand increased "citizen participation."[27] While the meaning of Black Power is debated by scholars, I refer to the term's connotation in the late 1960s: a call for "racial solidarity, cultural pride, and self-determination" often paired with a "militant posture."[28] "Citizen participation" is the idea that people affected by government policies and programs should have a say in the formation and administration of such initiatives. Black Washingtonians demanded access to jobs, quality education, and housing. They also demanded the ability to elect their own leaders, to craft and implement urban development policies, and to control government-funded anti-poverty programs.

The Lost Laws and Desegregation

The antisegregation laws passed during Reconstruction, the Equal Services Acts of 1872 and 1873, disappeared from the official city register in 1929. But the statutes were never formally repealed. When the prominent civil rights attorney Pauli Murray was a law student at Howard University in 1944, Murray and other students discovered these "lost laws" with the help of a librarian.[29] Later, Murray's work would influence Supreme Court Justices Thurgood Marshall and Ruth Bader Ginsburg. "Elated over these preliminary findings," Murray wrote, "I went around the law school waving the statute and arguing that the old civil rights legislation was still in force."[30] To test if the laws could still be enforced, Murray and other students, many of whom were associated with Howard University's chapter of the NAACP, led a lunch counter sit-in at Thompson's Cafeteria, a popular segregated restaurant in downtown DC. Howard students trickled into Thompson's in small groups until there were fifty-five of them reading books as they waited to be served. Outside, other Howard students formed a picket line. After four hours and the loss of 50 percent of its normal clientele, the chain's headquarters called and instructed the restaurant to serve the Black students.

The victory, however, did not last. As the students prepared to hold another demonstration, Mordecai Johnson, the first African American president of Howard, banned off-campus protests by university organizations. Howard received 60 percent of its funding from the federal government, and Johnson worried the students' activism could jeopardize those resources.[31]

While the Howard students' campaign was curtailed by their own school, later that decade, activists continued what Murray had started. To resurrect the lost laws and ensure their enforcement, twenty-six citizens formed the Coordinating Committee for the Enforcement of the DC Anti-Discrimination Laws in 1949 and appointed Mary Church Terrell as chairperson. Terrell was in her eighties and had been a leader in the civil rights movement for decades. She was one of the first two Black women to earn a master's degree, was a charter member of the NAACP, and had been a prominent voice for Black women's suffrage. The committee's strategy to dismantle segregation combined legal challenges, protests, boycotts, and lobbying. First, the group needed a test case for a lawsuit. In 1950, Terrell and an interracial group went to Thompson's Cafeteria, the same place Murray had protested in 1944, and attempted to get lunch together. After the group took their food trays, a manager asked them to leave, citing city law and company policy that barred serving African Americans. This incident was the basis of *District of Columbia v. John R. Thompson Co., Inc.*, a case brought by DC's local government against the restaurant's owner in 1950. The Washington Board of Trade, which had long supported segregation, offered legal aid and wrote an amicus brief in support of Thompson's.[32]

The *Thompson* case garnered national attention, and organizations, government representatives, and concerned citizens wrote amicus briefs in support of enforcing the antidiscrimination laws. These briefs often emphasized the importance of DC desegregation to national security and the American image abroad. The solicitor general of the United States, Philip Perlman, posited, "the existence of racial discrimination in the Nation's Capital constitute[d] a serious flaw in our democracy" that was especially important because "the United States is now endeavoring to prove to the entire world that democracy is the best form of government yet devised by man."[33] DC was uniquely important because "the eyes of the world [were] upon it": it received the most international press coverage and it was where most foreign diplomats formed their impression of the United States.[34] Perlman echoed a report from President Harry Truman's administration on American race relations called *To Secure These Rights*. Washington, it asserted, "should symbolize to our own citizens and to the people of all countries our great tradition of civil liberty. Instead, it is a graphic illustration of a failure of democracy."[35]

As the case wound its way through trial and appeals, the

Coordinating Committee for the Enforcement of the DC Anti-Discrimination Laws convinced some businesses to desegregate using protests, boycotts, and negotiations. Volunteers visited nearly one hundred restaurants and lunch counters to determine if they served Black patrons, and the committee published a list encouraging Washingtonians to patronize the desegregated restaurants. The committee also lobbied business owners to integrate; if businesses refused, it organized pickets, boycotts, and letter writing campaigns to company leaders. The protests were frequent and creative; the group picketed Hecht's department store three times a week for six months and had Santa Claus lead the line at Christmastime. Using these tactics, the committee convinced some businesses to desegregate before the *Thompson* case was decided.[36]

The Supreme Court eventually ruled in the committee's favor in 1953, holding that the "lost laws" barring discrimination still applied. The ruling effectively barred segregation at DC restaurants, hotels, barbershops, and other businesses. The next year, the Supreme Court's ruling in *Bolling v. Sharpe*—a DC-specific lawsuit that was decided in parallel with *Brown v. Board of Education*—desegregated schools. By 1954, de jure segregation (discrimination by law) was illegal.

Citizen Participation and Control

These victories did little to alter the distribution of power in the capital, however, and did not tangibly improve many Black people's lives. Southern segregationists on the Senate and House DC committees still controlled the District and blocked any bill that would allow its residents to elect their own leaders, Black people still struggled to find affordable housing, and many employers would only hire African Americans for the most menial jobs.

The militant firebrand activist Julius Hobson worked tirelessly to alleviate each of these issues. Hobson was a Black man, a decorated World War II veteran, a government statistician, an atheist, and a "Marxist Socialist." Hobson got his start in DC activism when he joined the parent-teacher association at his son's school in the early 1950s. From 1961 to 1964, Hobson led the DC branch of the Congress on Racial Equality (CORE), a pacifist organization founded in 1942 that used nonviolent direct action to battle white supremacy. He was famous for his confrontational politics, including holding "rat-catching rallies" and threatening to release the creatures in the wealthy Georgetown neighborhood after city commissioners were slow to respond to the central city's rat infestation problem.[37]

In the early 1960s, Hobson worked with CORE to lobby employers to implement antidiscrimination hiring practices.[38] If discussions failed, CORE launched pickets and boycotts to encourage people to shop only in stores with Black salesclerks. Hobson and CORE effectively pressured large department stores and smaller retailers to hire more African American Washingtonians in a wider variety of positions, producing five thousand jobs.[39]

But Hobson felt these gains were insufficient. In 1964, he denounced picketing and marching campaigns and instead urged civil rights organizations to "concentrate on the problems of poverty which affect the masses of Negroes who are more concerned about jobs, good housing and fair treatment from the police than they are about 'integration.'"[40] Hobson created a DC chapter of Associated Community Teams (ACT), an activist organization recently created in 1963 that focused on abolishing oppressive and exploitative institutions. Hobson called for greater participation of low-income Black people in new anti-poverty programs created by the Economic Opportunity Act of 1964, part of President Lyndon Johnson's Great Society initiative. Community action agencies, created by the Office of Economic Opportunity (OEO) to aid those living in poverty, were mandated to include the "maximum feasible participation" of low-income citizens in running these programs.

Hobson and ACT seized upon this requirement for citizen participation and argued that the United Planning Organization (UPO), the agency responsible for administering OEO funds in DC, was too far removed from the concerns of low-income Washingtonians. ACT brought Black people in poverty to UPO offices to demand their opinions be heard. Hobson filed a lawsuit claiming the lack of poor people on UPO's board meant it violated the OEO's requirement for residents' input and participation. By 1968, over fifteen hundred low-income people served on DC community advisory boards and even the UPO board of trustees, thanks in part to Hobson's advocacy.[41]

Hobson and others also fought for better education for Black children. Predominantly Black schools received less funding and were more crowded than predominantly white schools, so Hobson sued the DC school superintendent over the ongoing discrimination. In 1967, Judge J. Skelly Wright ruled in *Hobson v. Hansen* that the DC school board "unconstitutionally deprive[d] the District's Negro and poor public school children of their right to equal educational opportunity with the District's white and more affluent public school children." The policies determining where students went to school caused de facto segregation so severe that the judge determined they "violated plaintiff's constitutional rights."[42] While the court stopped short of saying that the school board practiced de jure (by law) segregation, the decision asserted that it was "impossible not to assume that the school administration is affirmatively satisfied with the segregation which the neighborhood [school] policy breeds."[43]

Black Washingtonians did not just want equal educational

opportunities; they also demanded more control over the content of children's education. ACT coordinated a school boycott in March 1967 to protest "for academic excellence through integrated schools."[44] A flyer for the march demanded "quality education" which included "more Negro and Puerto Rican principals," and that "Negroes be taught their history and culture in school." "No responsible person or leader can be opposed to these demands," the flyer asserted, "unless he is a field hand for the plantation bosses at city hall and the board of education."[45] After the school board appointed a new superintendent in 1967 without citizen input, Hobson was incensed and pushed for increased citizen participation in school board decisions.[46]

As activists organized to gain more control over federal antipoverty programs and education, they also worked to challenge DC's glaring lack of self-governance. Washingtonians had not been able to elect their leaders for almost one hundred years, and instead the board of commissioners ran the DC municipal government. Under this system, Congress exerted enormous power over DC, which allowed Southern segregationists to enforce their racism in the capital. Even though DC home rule (self-governance) was popular among members of Congress, the House and Senate committees on DC would not let legislation move forward.

Underlying this undemocratic position was anti-Black racism and fear of Black power. The number of African Americans in the capital doubled from 1910 to 1940. By 1957, African Americans constituted more than half of the District's population. White support of home rule declined as this percentage grew.[47] According to those who testified in congressional hearings, many white Washingtonians feared that "if we get home rule, the Negroes will take over the city" and that "minority groups would control local elections here."[48] In response to a *Washington Post* survey on home rule in 1966, white DC residents clearly articulated the racism behind their opposition, saying such things as it "isn't right that the Nation's Capital would be all colored" and "they don't have the right education to do the right job." One rejected the idea "because a colored fellow would be mayor—no other reason."[49]

The Senate passed home rule legislation four times in the 1950s. The House of Representatives, however, never even voted on these bills because Southern segregationists would not let them advance from the House DC Committee to the House floor. After President Johnson pledged his support for home rule in an address to Congress in 1965 and members of both parties backed proposed legislation, many were hopeful that home rule would finally be approved. A slew of DC organizations—including the Washington Home Rule Committee, the DC Democratic Committee, and CORE—lobbied for the bill's passage, but efforts were stymied when Southern segregationists on the House DC Committee again refused to bring the bill to a vote.[50]

After this failure, local activists intensified their efforts to achieve self-governance. Hobson and ACT filed a lawsuit alleging DC residents' inability to elect their leaders violated the Fifteenth Amendment granting African Americans the right to vote, but the District Court found the legal reasoning unpersuasive and rejected the suit.[51] Martin Luther King Jr. gave speeches on home rule's importance, and the DC Coalition of Conscience, an organization of religious groups, gathered signatures to show citizen support. More than four thousand people attended a 1966 rally for home rule. The rally and other efforts often chastised the business community, especially the Washington Board of Trade, which had immense political power under the existing system and staunchly opposed home rule.[52]

Marion Barry and Walter Fauntroy, two Black men active in the civil rights movement, worked to undermine the BOT's antidemocratic position. Today, Barry is primarily known for his tenures as DC's mayor from 1979 to 1991 and 1995 to 1999. Barry came to DC in 1965 to lead the local chapter of the Student Nonviolent Coordinating Committee (SNCC, often pronounced "snick"), a civil rights group started in 1960 in the wake of several sit-in campaigns. In the second half of the 1960s, SNCC became a leading militant group and was associated with the Black Power movement. Barry quickly became a well-known figure in local politics with campaigns such as the 1966 boycott of the Capital Transit Company.[53] After the company proposed bus fare hikes, Barry and SNCC launched a one-day bus boycott on January 24, 1966. Ridership decreased by 75,000 people and the boycott successfully prevented the increased fares.[54] The next year, Barry and others created Pride, Inc., which provided Black boys and young men with jobs. Funded by the Department of Labor, Pride, Inc. aimed to empower young people through economic opportunities and career training.[55]

Walter Fauntroy led the Washington Bureau of the Southern Christian Leadership Conference (SCLC), a civil rights group founded and led by Dr. Martin Luther King Jr. Fauntroy had helped organize both the 1963 March on Washington for Jobs and Freedom and the 1965 marches from Selma to Montgomery. An outspoken critic of urban development policies that displaced Black people, Fauntroy had created the Model Inner City Community Development Organization (MICCO), a coalition of 150 community groups and churches, to advocate for more equitable city planning. He was a minister and led the DC Coalition of Conscience.

In 1966, Barry and Fauntroy formed Free DC, a home rule advocacy group that believed it could lessen the BOT's resistance by pressuring its individual members. Free DC insisted that businesses sign a petition to support home rule, lobby federal officials, display a sticker in their store window making it clear that they supported the policy, and donate money to the organization itself to support its efforts on an institutional level. If a business refused, Free DC urged the community to boycott it. Some in Congress were so angered by the monetary demands that they called for an investigation into the legality of the approach, and subsequently the group dropped its request for funds. Free DC initially focused on H Street NE and later expanded to Fourteenth Street NW. Both streets were lined with businesses owned by white people that served a predominantly Black neighborhood and clientele. Three hundred and fifty out of roughly four hundred stores along H Street displayed orange and black stickers that read "Free DC" below an image of broken chains. Free DC also picketed big businesses deeply ingrained in the BOT, such as Hecht's and Kann's department stores. While the Free DC organization only lasted six months, it succeeded in increasing interest in home rule among Black Washingtonians and positioning the BOT and the individual businesses that made up its membership as key obstacles.[56]

These home rule campaigns consistently confronted the white business community and other "establishment" figures. At one community meeting, people cheered Hobson as he criticized the power of conservative whites and middle-class Black people. The crowd booed William A. Press, the vice president of the BOT, when he asserted unemployment was not a real problem in DC. A resident claimed that the BOT's membership "was composed of merchants who exploited the poor by marking their goods at astronomical prices, owners of slums, and employers who pay low salaries and oppose a minimum wage law."[57] Barry connected businesses to general inequality when he said, "We want to free D.C. from our enemies—the people who make it impossible for us to do anything about the lousy schools, brutal cops, slumlords, welfare investigators who go out on midnight raids, employers who discriminate in hiring and a host of other ills that run rampant throughout our city."[58] Black activists in the capital understood how DC's lack of democracy empowered those who were hostile to alleviating racial and economic inequality.

After the Senate and House DC committees again blocked home rule legislation in 1966, President Johnson pursued another strategy. Johnson proposed to Congress a plan to restructure the DC government so that the executive branch would appoint a nine-person city council and a mayor-commissioner to govern the capital. DC residents would be able to vote for their school board. Since the House DC Committee would not allow the bill to leave committee and go to a vote on the House floor, the bill advanced through the House Judiciary Committee and passed in 1967. Johnson appointed Walter E. Washington, a Black native Washingtonian and the former director of the agency that governed DC public housing, as mayor. Members of the House DC Committee viewed Mayor Washington as an illegitimate leader appointed to usurp their power. Congressman John McMillan (D-NC), the chairman of the House DC Committee, insisted that "communist sympathizers" backed DC home rule and was so opposed to Washington's appointment that he sent the African American mayor a wagon of watermelons after he submitted his first budget to McMillan's office.[59] Other committee members refused to refer to Washington as "mayor," instead calling him a commissioner.[60]

Johnson selected mostly moderate Black civil rights leaders and liberal businesspeople for the DC City Council. Fauntroy became the council's vice chairperson. While this was an improvement from the previous system, Washingtonians still had almost no ability to choose their leaders and Congress retained substantial power.

From education to anti-poverty programs to governance, Black Washingtonians worked to reduce racial inequality, often by demanding a role in making the decisions that affected their communities. Julius Hobson, Marion Barry, Walter Fauntroy, and countless others used a variety of tactics to challenge institutionalized racism. Their activism extended to another significant problem for DC's African Americans: finding a place to live.

Displacement and Housing Discrimination in DC

In 1945, Congress created the Redevelopment Land Agency (RLA) to purchase "blighted" urban lots, bulldoze them, and then sell them to private contractors for redevelopment. As part of a federal urban renewal program, the RLA launched a massive plan to gut and rebuild the Southwest quadrant of DC in the early 1950s. The RLA's aim was to create a modern city that could ebb the tide of white flight—white people moving from the city to the surrounding suburbs—that started after World War II ended in 1945 and accelerated once schools desegregated in 1954. The RLA selected DC's Southwest quadrant (also known simply as Southwest) for redevelopment because it believed the neighborhood had poor housing conditions and "a central and almost strategic location" close to major office buildings and recreation areas.[61] The quadrant's inhabitants were predominantly African Americans, many of whose ancestors moved to the neighborhood after the Civil War because it was close to industrial jobs along the Potomac River waterfront. Southern migrants to Washington also settled in Southwest and used the community networks there to adjust to their new life in the city.[62]

Redevelopers, the RLA, and the city government heralded urban renewal as a triumph of modernity and beauty over blight and despair. A 1956 city report praised the redevelopment and claimed that razing slums allowed DC to better live up to its role as the nation's capital.[63] The *Washington Post* architecture critic

Wolf Von Eckardt celebrated the project in 1961 for combining "suburban wholesomeness with urban stimulation."[64] A 1967 RLA guide to the neighborhood proclaimed that "the old Southwest died" with the bulldozer and the "radical change" of urban renewal resurrected a vibrant, modern community.[65]

Southwest residents and community groups, however, protested the RLA plan. One Black neighborhood leader said it constituted "mass eviction."[66] In the lawsuit *Berman v. Parker*, redevelopment opponents contended that urban renewal violated the equal protection clause of the Fifth Amendment. In 1954, the Supreme Court ruled that the Redevelopment Act, the legislation that created the urban renewal program, was constitutional. The court determined that beautification was an acceptable use for eminent domain, the process by which the government seizes private land for its own use.[67]

Through the Southwest project, 99 percent of the buildings in the 550-acre redevelopment area were demolished in the 1950s and 1960s. It displaced thousands of Southwest residents, 76 percent of whom were Black and most of whom were considered low income. Yet of the 5,900 new units of housing built, only 310 qualified as moderate-income housing and just one apartment complex offered low-income housing. Unable to afford the new housing in Southwest, more than one-third of those displaced relocated to public housing. Two thousand families moved into private rental housing, often in Shaw and the surrounding area as well as in the Anacostia neighborhood in Southeast Washington.[68] Only 391 displaced families were able to purchase their own homes, none of which were in their previous Southwest community. This forced relocation destroyed many of the African American social networks that had developed in the Southwest neighborhood. For example, in a survey of displaced Southwest residents taken five years after they relocated, one-fourth of respondents said they had not made a single new friend in their new neighborhoods. By 1972, Southwest was 80 percent white and half as populous as it was prior to urban renewal.[69]

Those who were displaced encountered stark housing segregation as they relocated. Residential discrimination was rampant in DC and had only worsened over time. From 1900 to 1962, the suburbs flipped from roughly one-third to only 6 percent Black. During the same period, DC's Black population rose from 25 percent to more than 50 percent of the city.[70] Housing discrimination forced the concentration of Black people in select urban neighborhoods like Shaw.[71] Only eight out of 211 apartment complexes in the District would rent to Black people.[72] The Federal Housing Administration (FHA) and private lenders encouraged segregation through "redlining," a practice in which lenders denied home loans in Black neighborhoods and almost exclusively granted them in white neighborhoods. Lenders rarely approved mortgages in areas west of Rock Creek Park, the nearly two-thousand-acre park in Northwest DC that acted as a barrier between Black Washington and white wealthy neighborhoods. In upper Northwest DC, racial covenants (legal contracts written into property deeds that barred the future sale of a home to a Black person) and tradition informally banned African Americans.[73] Citizens associations, whites-only neighborhood groups, also prevented integration. According to a report on segregation in Washington, "In the drive to exclude the Negro, the Citizen's Associations have functioned as the front-line shock troops, completing his encirclement by a network of mutual defense pacts, or agreements not to sell, erected all around the inner zones of the city."[74] The racial divide was so stark that one Washingtonian compared the park to the Berlin Wall in Germany and the DC border to the Great Wall of China.[75] Using more violent imagery, another Washingtonian testified in a 1962 congressional hearing on housing discrimination that the border was a "white noose around the black core, with Negroes heavily in the center of the city and the white noose of suburban American around this core."[76]

Black Washingtonians, some residents of the surrounding suburbs, and civil rights organizations mobilized to protest housing discrimination. For example, DC's branch of the Congress of Racial Equality picketed DC residential buildings owned by segregationist Morris Caffritz, the suburban real estate development giant Levitt and Sons, and Federal Housing Administration offices that used racist redlining loan practices. In 1963, a coalition of the local CORE, NAACP, and SCLC chapters organized a march that drew nearly four thousand Washingtonians to protest housing and job discrimination. These efforts had limited success. Although DC adopted "the most sweeping" fair housing regulation in the country, which banned racial discrimination in the sale or rental of housing in 1964, the regulation changed little because the Human Relations Council, the agency that processed complaints about unfair housing practices, had no power to punish those who broke the law.[77]

Some Black residents tackled housing issues by seeking to prevent new urban renewal projects from further displacing them. After the completion of the Southwest urban renewal project, the RLA planned the largest redevelopment project in the United States in an area of DC named Northwest #1, which included the historically Black Shaw neighborhood. U Street NW, the long-standing center of Black culture and business, and the Fourteenth Street NW shopping strip were part of the redevelopment area. Northwest #1 also included eight blocks of Seventh Street NW, a major artery lined with small stores that served predominantly Black patrons. The neighborhoods that surrounded Northwest #1—Columbia Heights, Pleasant Plains, LeDroit Park, and Mount Vernon, for example—were also majority-Black neighborhoods that were considered DC's "inner city." This area was where the "white noose" of housing discrimination had forced much of DC's Black population to live.

Initial designs would destroy and rebuild 80 percent of the area and relocate the same percentage of its mostly African American population. Shaw residents showed up en masse at RLA Neighborhood Advisory Council meetings and demanded community involvement in planning, employment opportunities from the project, and the rehabilitation of buildings instead of bulldozing and reconstruction. It was during this process that Walter Fauntroy created the Model Inner City Community Development Organization, a coalition of 150 community groups and churches, to utilize the RLA's provision for citizen input in planning and demand that redevelopment occur on the terms of the community. "We have taken urban renewal, a tool often used to destroy black neighborhoods," said MICCO member Reginald Griffith, "and fashioned it into an instrument by which the people can preserve and upgrade their own community. We shall not be another Southwest."[78] MICCO and the residents of Northwest #1 showed that Black people wanted control of their neighborhoods and were willing to organize to make it happen.[79]

But urban renewal wasn't the only federal program that risked displacing thousands of Black people from their homes. Originally, the National Capital Planning Commission (NCPC)—the government agency tasked with guiding federal development projects in the greater Washington area—planned to build a DC highway system through the Cleveland Park and Georgetown neighborhoods. In the early 1960s, the affluent white people whose homes would be destroyed by this proposed highway used legal action and their Capitol Hill connections to derail this plan. Congress placed a five-year ban on freeway construction in these wealthy communities. The planners then redesigned the highway system to go through the inner city and force tens of thousands of people—80 percent of whom were Black—out of their homes. In 1965, activist Sammie Abdullah Abbott formed the Emergency Committee on the Transportation Crisis (ECTC) as a coalition between white and Black Washingtonians that aimed to stop the construction of the highway system and instead build a mass transit subway. The ECTC intentionally foregrounded racial justice and Black voices and characterized the proposed highways as "White Man's Roads . . . thru Black Man's Home!"[80] Abbott sought out Black people to lead: construction worker and activist Reginald H. Booker was the chairman, and Marion Barry was a vice chairman. Simultaneously, Abbott recruited white leaders to the cause, such as Peter S. Craig, a lawyer who was instrumental in blocking the highway through Cleveland Park and Georgetown. While the highway issue was unresolved at the time of Martin Luther King Jr.'s assassination, the ECTC was an important organization that connected community control to racial justice and Black power.[81]

Even after desegregation, Black Washingtonians had a significantly harder time than white people finding a job and a place to live, earning a decent wage, and getting a good education. Many were agents of change who resisted federally imposed policies that they found unsatisfactory, demanded control over their communities and government, and used varying strategies to achieve their goals. They built on decades of activism and new government programs that emphasized citizen participation to demand not only access to basic rights, but also power to make decisions for themselves and their communities. Hobson and others used "citizen participation" requirements to win poor people some control over anti-poverty programs. Barry used Department of Labor funds to provide jobs to young people. Fauntroy's MICCO developed a plan to reshape a neighborhood using citizen input and African American laborers. Groups like Free DC campaigned for Washingtonians' ability to select their own leaders through home rule.

But segregationists in Congress, joined by white citizens groups, the DC police department, and the business establishment resisted these demands for equality and power. These groups used one central strategy to do so: they associated Black people with crime.

2

"The Nation's Capital Is in a Sweat"
CRIME, POLICING, AND RISING TENSIONS

AFTER DESEGREGATION IN THE CAPITAL, POLITICIANS AND THE police used exaggerated fears of Black crime to limit civil liberties in the 1950s and 1960s. They stoked alarm over urban crime and decline to rally white voters, undermine liberal efforts at civil rights reform, and push policies with dangerous consequences for communities of color. This tactic, combined with incidents of police harassment and brutality, led to increasing confrontations between law enforcement and Black communities.

DC schools were one of the earliest targets of this Southern strategy. Most schools, especially those in the South, were slow to comply with the 1954 *Brown v. Board of Education* Supreme Court decision that mandated integration. Not so in Washington, thanks to the prodding of President Dwight D. Eisenhower. To the president, DC was the perfect place to earn credibility with civil rights groups without upsetting states' rights advocates since DC was under federal control.[1] DC integrated in the school year immediately following the *Brown* decision and its schools were soon thrust into the national spotlight by those trying to safeguard segregation.

Southern segregationists in Congress, fighting a desperate rearguard action to stave off integration in schools back home, tried to use Washington's experience to make the case that school integration had been bad for the city and would be equally bad elsewhere. While Eisenhower argued that Washington, DC, was a positive "model for the rest of the country," Congressman James Davis (D-GA) charged that the District was actually a cautionary tale with "tragic results which come from the breakdown of segregation and substitution of an integrated public-school system."[2]

In 1957, the House DC Committee created a special subcommittee to investigate integration in DC schools. The subcommittee's chief counsel, William Gerber, asked school administrators and teachers leading questions to suggest that integration had destroyed Washington's schools. He repeatedly riled up racist fears about interracial sex to suggest integration would corrupt innocent, naive white children.[3] Some educators who testified blamed behavioral issues on racist stereotypes such as bad parenting, absent fathers, and community crime as well as "kid glove" treatment in place of harsh discipline.[4] To Clarence Mitchell, head of the NAACP in DC, the hearings relied so heavily on distorted data and racist tropes that he called them "unhooded clan meetings"; for its part, the *Washington Post* slammed the hearings as a "hatchet job."[5] Although many teachers defended desegregation and the DC school district's assistant superintendent called it a "miracle of social adjustment," the subcommittee sent hearing transcripts and distorted reports to schools in the South in the hopes that they could use this purported information on the "dangers of integration" as an excuse to delay its implementation at home. In a speech to the segregationist States' Rights Council in 1956, Congressman Davis charged that DC's model of desegregation had failed and was instead a cautionary tale:

> I have seen there the tragic results which come from the breakdown of segregation and substitution of an integrated public-school system. The same thing can

happen, and will happen [in the South], if the people meekly accept wrongful usurpation of power, and a Supreme Court dictatorship, as they did in Washington.[6]

The Southern distortion and weaponization of events in Washington went beyond integrated schools. For example, in 1957, the famous columnist Willie Snow Etheridge, a white woman, was mugged in DC right off Connecticut Avenue—a location that was generally considered a "good" part of town due to its location west of Rock Creek Park and wealthy residents. "It is a disgrace that the citizens of these United States can't walk the streets of their Capital . . . without being mugged by hoodlums," she wrote in a national magazine.[7] Members of Congress similarly bemoaned the "terror" of DC crime, fretting that it was unsafe to go out at night and dramatically claiming that lawlessness in the capital city disgraced the entire country. The solution, according to some members of Congress and white community groups, was stronger anticrime laws.[8]

This sensationalized concern over crime, however, was just as disconnected from reality as the narrative about DC school integration. At the time of the Etheridge incident in 1957, the DC crime rate was one of the lowest in the country, and 10 percent lower than it had been the previous year. Yet the narrative of a crime-plagued city stubbornly persisted. In 1956, after DC crime decreased by nearly 20 percent over three years, all-white citizens associations continued to ask Congress for more police because residents said they were afraid to go out after dark.[9] In 1963, Congress convened joint congressional hearings on "the increasingly serious crime situation in the District of Columbia." At these hearings, the chairman of the House DC Committee, John McMillan, asserted, "We all know we have this problem [crime]. We don't feel it is necessary to have any further investigations. What we want to do [is] try to help the law enforcement officers in the District of Columbia solve this increasing crime problem."[10] Despite McMillan's certainty, crime in Washington was actually down in 1961 and 1962 and consistent with national averages.[11]

Why the contradiction? Worry about crime was a cover for racist fears.[12] As the District became a majority-Black city in 1957, it was no coincidence that white Washingtonians reported feeling less safe and believed that the District was one of the most dangerous cities in the country. This stems from the deep-seated, pervasive, and racist American inclination to associate Blackness with danger and crime. This false narrative was also politically useful to integration opponents in the wake of *Brown*. Southern lawmakers claimed that crime in DC was the outcome of integration and proved that African Americans were dangerous and thus less deserving of rights. For instance, in 1956, Congressman Davis bluntly stated that "Negroes" were responsible for the high crime rate in DC.[13] In 1959, Senator Olin Johnston (D-SC) made speeches in Congress almost daily connecting integration and crime because he claimed newspapers failed to report the "chronic ailments that accompany forced integration."[14] Senator Allen Ellender (D-LA) asserted in 1963 that DC crime proved "his contention that Negroes cannot govern themselves."[15] "The vision of Washington as a hotbed of rapine and bloodshed has been disseminated by congressmen who view the crime rate as the predictable and deserved reward of racial desegregation," concluded journalist J.W. Anderson of the *Washington Post* in 1964.[16] These baseless racist statements rejected not only racial equality but also the fundamental American principle of democratic self-rule.

The heightened concern over DC crime also provided a platform to criticize recent Supreme Court decisions. In 1957, the Supreme Court ruled in *Mallory v. United States* that confessions obtained by law enforcement during a person's unlawful detention could not be admitted in federal courts. The police claimed such court rulings that granted citizens more rights made their jobs impossible and would result in rampant crime (in fact, research showed that the *Mallory* ruling did not impact DC crime rates).[17] In 1963, the DC police chief, Robert Murray,[18] insisted the police department did not need new officers, only fewer restrictions and new powers such as preventative arrests.[19] Many in Congress agreed. "The Bill of Rights should not be used as a legal haven for the unsavory criminal element who today is depriving the law-abiding men, women, and children of another right: the right to walk the streets of the Nation's Capital city without fear of bodily harm," said Senator Alan Bible (D-NV).[20]

Such statements created a different version of rights in response to the civil rights movement: there was also "the right" to safety, much as segregationists asserted "the right" to associate with whom one wanted as a way of resisting desegregation. "I am here merely as a humble member of at least that portion of the Washington public which is becoming conscious of the frightening loss of certain rights hitherto regarded as unalienable—the right to walk in safety on the public streets of this city and the right to security in our homes or places of business," remarked a member of an anticrime group in 1962.[21] To rectify the imbalance of "rights," the courts needed to have "as much responsibility in protecting the community as it has in protecting the rights of the individual. And it is out of balance."[22]

According to law-and-order advocates such as Chief Murray, the "balance" could be restored if criminals had fewer rights and received harsher punishments, and if police officers had more power. If white people, coded in other white people's speech as "law-abiding citizens" or the "community," lacked rights, then "criminals" were privileged as the courts and society purportedly treated them with "kid gloves."[23] Congressmen advocated "law-and-order" measures such as building more prisons, establishing reform schools, criminalizing vagrancy, instituting mandatory minimum sentences, and administering "tough love." Senator Olin Johnston and Congressman Omar Burleson (D-TX) recommended that two companies of U.S. Marines patrol DC.[24]

By 1964, crime (mostly nonviolent) did rise in DC. Republican presidential nominee Barry Goldwater made DC crime a campaign issue that year, blaming it on liberal court decisions and poor White House leadership.[25] Congress continued to politicize DC crime and to advocate for increasing the power of law enforcement and reducing citizens' rights. In 1966, both the House of Representatives and Senate passed a DC crime bill that, among other provisions, allowed evidence to be admitted in court that was obtained during unreasonable periods of detention. President Lyndon Johnson vetoed the bill, however, because he believed it violated Americans' civil liberties.

Black newspapers and activists emphasized the racism embedded in the crime panic and criticized police overreach. An editorial published in 1959 by the Black newspaper the *Washington Afro-American*, for example, noted a double standard in how crime was treated depending on its location in the city and how it could be used politically: all the crime that members of Congress and the police really cared about was crime with white victims.[26] Other editorials in the same newspaper examined the irony of blaming civil rights leaders for crime increases when Southern leaders had recently refused to desegregate schools in defiance of the Supreme Court's *Brown* decision: "The philosophy of disobeying laws they deem to be unjust . . . has been followed with complete immunity for years by Southerners."[27] Black activist Julius Hobson meticulously documented the police department's hiring discrimination and threatened to sue in an attempt to get them to hire more Black people.[28] In the mid-1960s, DC's chapter of ACT, the militant civil rights organization Hobson led that was dedicated to abolishing exploitative institutions, distributed fifteen thousand questionnaire forms to DC residents inquiring about police misconduct. The responses revealed overwhelming "resentment against the police department" because of how often Black people were mistreated by officers.[29] For example, after observing a busy Shaw intersection on a Saturday night, Hobson said he saw police wantonly stop and question Black people who were merely standing or walking on the street. Police would swiftly, and sometimes violently, arrest people who made even the slightest objection to this surveillance. While congressional leaders fretted about crime rates, Black people wanted to be protected from this type of police harassment and violence.[30]

Two incidents demonstrate the power and racism of the police and their defenders in the 1960s. First, in 1965 four Black boys were taken into police custody for merely playing football in an alley, something that was not usually an arrestable offense.[31] As the children were held at the Tenth Precinct a few blocks away, a crowd of one hundred people gathered outside to protest their arrests and detention. Further confrontation was avoided after a representative of the NAACP convinced the crowd to disperse. The head of the Community Relations Division of the DC police department blamed the incident on the "poor judgement" of the officers. "I don't mind their busting up the football game, but I am critical of their insisting on taking the kids to the station," he explained. "There is no question in the world that this is the type of thing that is going to get us into trouble, if trouble ever comes."[32] Many in the police department were incensed that a police officer had publicly criticized other officers. West Virginia Senator Robert Byrd—the Democratic chairman of the Senate DC Committee and a staunch advocate for law and order and the DC police—conducted interviews with all officers involved, insisted they did nothing wrong, and shielded them from punishment.[33]

In an editorial, the *Washington Afro-American* argued that the boys would not have been arrested if they were white.[34] Julius Hobson led a march against the police and called for the removal of the arresting officers. "All we've had are . . . words and more words," he asserted. "If [the police chief] is sincere about police abuse, then he ought to move the men responsible for it. He ought to treat the brutal policeman like the criminal that he is." Hobson warned that future police misconduct could result in urban rebellions and specified H Street NE, U Street NW, and Fourteenth Street NW as likely hotspots due to the frequent "targeting and misconduct he saw when he watched police activity."[35]

Tensions between the DC police and Black Washingtonians rose once again in August 1966 in Northeast DC when a group of Black teenagers assembled along Kenilworth Avenue NE, ostensibly to fight another group after an earlier confrontation. When the other side failed to show up, the nearly two hundred youths decided to "raise hell anyway" by throwing projectiles at passing cars and setting small trash fires. Police and firefighters were greeted with rocks as they arrived on the scene. Captain Culpepper, a white officer from the Fourteenth Precinct, sealed off the area from traffic and ordered his officers away from the group. He then called community and religious leaders and asked them to persuade the youths to disperse; they came and convinced the teenagers to go home.[36]

Most of the local press and civil rights leaders praised both Culpepper and the Fourteenth Precinct's generally good track record in dealing with the community.[37] Senator Byrd, however, excoriated Culpepper on the Senate floor and went to the precinct to personally berate him for being "derelict in his duty" because he did not arrest the teenagers. He urged stationing the military in

DC to "curb unruly mobs."[38] A *Post* editorial charged that Byrd's resistance to police restraint endangered the community:

> Senator Robert Byrd undoubtedly has the power, although hardly the moral right, to play with dynamite in the explosive atmosphere of this city's current racial tension. But he ought to understand that his interference in the operations of the Washington police department present the gravest imaginable danger to human life and public order. He has been engaged in nothing less than the encouragement of mutiny and the incitement of violence.[39]

Byrd and white Washingtonians who rejected any criticism of the police increasingly blamed crime on those who sought reform and accountability. When DC residents called for an investigation after police officers killed an unarmed Black man in 1967, Byrd chastised activists because he thought their demands for justice hurt police morale. After conducting interviews with DC police officers, Byrd charged that "there is almost to a man the feeling that many of the problems of the Police Department are generated, compounded and multiplied by . . . civil rights organizations." Byrd was even upset when President Lyndon Johnson's Crime Commission urged the department to ban officers from using racial slurs or calling Black men "boy."[40]

Officers and politicians insisted that any effort to hold police accountable or restrict their power would backfire and result in higher crime rates. In a 1967 report, DC police asserted that their low morale was because of "diminished respect for the police by extravagant charges of brutality and misconduct."[41] When five detectives were indicted for taking bribes, several officers did not want them to be prosecuted, believing the public's perception of the police was already too damaged.[42] Even though police were rarely disciplined for misconduct, officers reported that they were hesitant to arrest Black people because they feared they would be charged with brutality.[43] Congressman Joel Broyhill (D-VA), who had previously introduced a bill to turn over control of the DC police to Congress, charged that investigations would make the District government look weak and "engulf the city in a wave of lawlessness."[44]

Police officers' spouses also defended their partners against criticism. After the *Post* called for police restraint, seventy police wives went to the newspaper's offices to demand better treatment of their husbands. "Specifically, the wives complained that news media play up stories that result in demonstrators and lawbreakers being 'pampered,'" the *Post* reported, "but fail to give adequate attention to the problems and indignities suffered by Washington policemen." "How come nothing is printed about how bad our husbands are hurt?" the wives asked. "They always say how bad the Negroes are hurt." In an op-ed in the *Post*, the group of wives called for more police power and greater use of force, including shotguns and canine units to stop crime.[45]

This characterization of crime and policing was simply wrong, and many rejected the notion that citizens owed law enforcement uncritical support. "One reason for the low state of police-community relations here (and the resultant lack of citizen cooperation in law enforcement) is the fact that too few Washingtonians have been able to feel that the police force was their own," William Raspberry, an African American columnist for the *Washington Post*, contended. "Too many policemen live outside the city; too many citizens have viewed the police as an occupying army; there being no local self-government, the citizenry has no effective means of determining what men—or what type of men—head the police force."[46] The *Post* editorial staff asserted that broad calls for police support actually silenced and oppressed Black Washingtonians: "The slogan, 'support your local police,' has been taken over in a curious way by people who seem to mean by it 'support your local police against the community'—or at least against its poor people and its colored people, who, given the discriminatory character of educational and employment opportunities in recent decades, tend to be the same."[47]

Julius Hobson also challenged the notion that police lacked power or support and illuminated the sharp divide in the perceptions of policed populations and the police themselves: "These men have raised a continuing cry for more authority, more right to make arbitrary arrests, to turn more dogs loose in the poorest and most oppressed neighborhoods and the right to hold and question suspects until they, the police, decide that the suspect should have legal counsel." Yet, despite this nearly unchecked power, many in Congress were preoccupied with expanding police power and inoculating officers from any criticism or oversight. "Congress leads a chorus of cries for more protection by the police," Hobson concluded, "while the poor plead for protection from the police.[48]

The city did adopt small but entirely insufficient changes to try to alleviate the deep frustrations with law enforcement in the Black community. For example, in 1967 the DC police department adopted an affirmative action policy to hire more Black officers. Still, in 1968 the police force was 80 percent white in a city that was nearly 70 percent Black.[49]

Anticipating Unrest in the Capital

The Black community's frustration with policing was not unique to DC. Neither were incidents of police brutality nor fears of urban uprisings.

By early 1968, multiple major cities had been rocked by urban upheaval, including Detroit, Michigan; Newark, New Jersey; and New York City. The federal government had devoted considerable resources to try to understand rebellions and prevent them. After the civil disturbances in the Los Angeles suburb of Watts in 1965, President Johnson created the McCone Commission that authored a report, "Violence in the City—an End or a Beginning?" The commission reinforced racist stereotypes as it concluded the uprising was the result of a ghetto pathology that included absentee fathers, crime, and single-mother-headed homes. After the rebellions in Detroit and Newark in 1967, Johnson created another commission to study urban uprisings, the Kerner Commission. The commission's report, released in February 1968, reached a different conclusion than the McCone Commission had: civil unrest was the result of unequal economic opportunity and racism. To prevent further uprisings, the government needed to intervene to curtail discrimination and create better social services and job programs.

In response to the new report, Walter Fauntroy stated he was "happy to see as responsible a group as this [Kerner Commission] . . . [define] racism as the heart of the problem. . . . This is another of those reports that is a clear handwriting on the wall."[50] To Fauntroy and others, avoiding urban upheaval necessitated government action to foster social equality. Julius Hobson praised the Kerner Commission's report as the "first official admission that the fountainhead of black problems in America emanates in the white community where oppressive power comes from."[51] Hobson thought it was inaccurate to view uprisings as a product of a criminal pathology or random outbursts in response to economic inequality. He argued the root of these social problems was institutional racism and considered the events "rebellions" or political protests to overthrow structural discrimination.

The "long, hot summer" of 1967 not only led to a reevaluation of why urban uprisings occurred, but it also reshaped how the military and DC officials approached their response to urban uprisings. In Detroit, at around 3:45 a.m. on July 23, 1967, the police raided an unlicensed after-hours bar (called a "blind pig") and arrested most of the eighty-two people inside. Onlookers protested the arrests and looted nearby stores. After the demonstrations and destruction escalated the following day, Governor George Romney—Senator Mitt Romney's father—mobilized the Michigan National Guard. Romney gave the commanding officer permission to "use whatever force necessary" and the Guard fired mounted machine guns, rifles, and tear gas at civilians. Two days after the protests of police power began, Romney requested federal aid, and President Johnson ordered federal troops into the city. By the time the army completely withdrew July 29, forty-three people were dead. The majority were shot by National Guard troops or police officers.[52]

According to historian Barrye La Troye Price, "Detroit was a watershed that brought riot control to the forefront within the Johnson Administration and U.S. military."[53] A military after-action report found that both the federal troops and Michigan guardsmen needed better training to handle and apprehend people looting and starting fires. The Department of the Army launched a task group to study how to better control uprisings. The group made sixty-six recommendations, and the military subsequently created the Department of the Army Civil Disturbance Committee to implement the suggested policies and plan for future urban upheaval. By December 1967, the military had acted on all sixty-six recommendations, developed better training programs, and coordinated with police, National Guard units, and city governments. The army created a riot training course for senior officers, designed minimum training requirements for all units in August 1967, and developed a mock city at Fort Gordon, Georgia, for training exercises.[54]

The army task force also created a specific action plan for potential disorder in Washington, DC, called Operation Cabin Guard, which used military units that were highly trained and experienced with sensitive missions. The 503rd Military Police Battalion from Fort Bragg, North Carolina, previously served in Oxford, Mississippi, to allow James Meredith admittance to the University of Mississippi and in Selma, Alabama, to protect Dr. King and his followers as they marched for voting rights. The Third Infantry from Fort Myer, Virginia, and the Ninety-First Engineer Battalion from Fort Belvoir, Virginia, stifled demonstrations against the Vietnam War at the Pentagon in October 1967. Further, as part of the preparations, military units were assigned to police precincts in DC. Many commanders had toured the precinct they were responsible for in early 1968. Such preparations led *Washington Post* reporter Ben Gilbert to conclude that the units had been "trained thoroughly in the latest riot-control techniques, which emphasized restraint in the use of physical force."[55]

The Washington police and government also prepared to handle disorder with restraint. After Patrick Murphy was appointed DC's public safety director by the Johnson administration in 1967, he consulted with the chief of DC's Metropolitan Police Department, John Layton, and together they created a full-time position dedicated to "the function of the planning and training for disorder prevention and control."[56] Murphy was critical of how police had handled recent American uprisings, alleging that "police had demonstrated an unexpected depth of incompetence, insensitivity, and lack of preparedness in dealing with these civil disorders; and despite all this, there was unfortunately no indication that the bottom of the barrel had been plumbed."[57]

Instead of stockpiling weapons to prepare for potential violence, Murphy focused on "minimizing a department's potential contribution . . . to heightened racial tension, and its occasional proclivity toward pointless exercises in brutality and other forms of macho-policing."[58] In a *Washington Post* article from March 26, 1968, Murphy indicated that the city's police force could "prevent any serious disorder in the city this spring and summer" and was "prepared for any eventuality."[59] Chief Layton said the police needed to carefully avoid inflaming uprisings "even if demonstrators egg them on."[60] In a study of the city's response to the civil disturbances done by the Brookings Institution, an influential DC think tank, the researchers found that the city preplanned to use "police restraint and the notion of a massive show of military strength" by federal troops.[61]

The DC police were certainly prepared, however, to also make a "massive show of military strength" if desired. After the 1964 uprisings in Harlem, a Black neighborhood in New York City, which took place after a fifteen-year-old Black boy was shot and killed by a police officer, Congress passed President Johnson's Law Enforcement Assistance Act of 1965. The bill created the Office of Law Enforcement Assistance (OLEA), which supported experimental surveillance programs for police serving urban areas.[62] After the upheaval in Watts, California, in 1965, the OLEA funded the modernization of police departments with "advanced weapons and technology" including military-grade rifles, riot gear, tanks, helicopters, and bulletproof vests.[63] The DC police department received $1.2 million from Congress to increase the size of its force and outfit it with modern technology and weapons including computers and walkie-talkies.[64] The police developed "so-called sophisticated tools of riot control" including chemical mace, a machine that sprayed sticky foam to stop people in their tracks, and even a "banana oil" technique with which the "police would smear the streets with banana oil so rioters and looters would fall down."[65] The problem, of course, was that the oil would also make the police slip. Johnson's OLEA created larger, federally

subsidized police budgets and militarized departments, two phe-
nomena that police-accountability activists are still working to
reverse today. Congress also passed the 1967 District Antiriot
Bill that created harsher punishments for crimes associated with
rebellions.[66]

Despite these federal initiatives, the city's acknowledgment of
the need to avoid aggravating protesters and practice restraint
earned praise. On March 4, 1968, exactly one month before
Dr. King's assassination and the unrest that followed, African
American *Washington Post* columnist William Raspberry wrote
an article commending DC's preparations for potential uprisings. "City officials seem to be making most of the right moves
to deal with possible summer violence, at least as far as the police
end of it is concerned," he wrote. Washington was "not turning
to armed vigilantes" or ordering "the menacing police tanks or
.50-caliber machine guns or Stoner rifles that can rip a four-inch
hole in a man." Instead, "the plans rely heavily on snuffing out
rumors before they can work their mischief, on moving quickly
to make arrests when they have to be made (and just as quickly
quitting the scene), on tempering firmness with restraint." Raspberry credited this policy to Mayor Walter E. Washington, who
understood "ghetto unrest"; the "remarkable" director of public
safety, Patrick Murphy; and the easy availability of federal troops
in the capital. "Study after government funded study" indicated
people rebelled because of economic and racial inequalities, but
"still we try to deal with the problem either by insisting that poor
people remain docile or by shooting them down. . . . There is, in
the attitude of local officials, a glimmer of hope that Washington
may have the wisdom and the courage to try another way."[67]

As the federal and District governments prepared for potential
unrest, two developments in 1968 made many in Congress, the
national media, and the Federal Bureau of Investigation (FBI) fret

that mass violence would indeed erupt in DC. First, Stokely Carmichael, the former national chairman of the Student Nonviolent
Coordinating Committee whose name was nearly synonymous
with Black Power and radicalism, moved to DC. Carmichael first
came to the capital to study at Howard University in 1960, where
he quickly became extremely active in the civil rights movement.
He went on Freedom Rides to desegregate interstate transportation, registered people to vote in Mississippi during the Freedom
Summer of 1964, participated in activist Gloria Richardson's campaign to desegregate Cambridge, Maryland, and more. Famously,
Carmichael coined the phrase "Black Power" in 1966 at a protest
in Mississippi.[68]

Six months after announcing his plans to settle in DC, Carmichael arrived in January 1968 and created the Black United
Front (BUF), a coalition of moderate to militant Black leaders. The
BUF aimed to expand "the lines of communication between, and
affecting togetherness among, all the Black people in the District
of Columbia in order to obtain a rightful and proportionate share
in the decision making councils of the District, and rightful and
proportionate control of the economic institutions in the Black
community."[69] In other words, it would coordinate Black activist efforts to influence and hopefully dominate DC's governance.
Nearly one hundred Black leaders attended the first meeting to
organize the BUF, and members included Marion Barry, Walter
Fauntroy, Julius Hobson, and Reginald H. Booker of the Emergency Committee on the Transportation Crisis, the group formed
to oppose a highway that would displace thousands of Black
Washingtonians.[70] Even though many of the BUF's members such
as Walter Fauntroy did not agree with all of Carmichael's militant
stances, they joined the organization hoping it could have a big-
ger impact than previous campaigns for Black rights. Carmichael
believed this umbrella organization would lessen infighting

between Black groups and leaders. DC was one of the few places in the country with a majority-Black population, and this provided a unique opportunity to control the District's governing institutions. Carmichael aimed to orchestrate a "Black takeover" of the police department, schools, and welfare department.[71]

Second, Martin Luther King Jr.'s Poor People's Campaign (PPC), led by his Southern Christian Leadership Conference organization and set to begin on April 15, also stoked fears of violence. After presenting a list of legislative demands to Congress and executive agencies, a multiracial coalition of thousands of self-proclaimed poor people would set up camp on the National Mall to lobby Congress to pass anti-poverty legislation. King thought this demonstration in the heart of the capital would force politicians to think about those living in poverty and the problems they faced. While King threatened civil disobedience to disrupt the government, including tactics like blocking highways and bridges, he also assured people that those coming to DC were trained in nonviolent tactics.[72]

Both Carmichael's presence and King's impending campaign created alarm. "Stokely Carmichael says he's coming, and the nation's capital is in a sweat," reported the *Wall Street Journal.* "Other segments of the white community here fear the Carmichael brand of 'black power' may provide the germ to an epidemic of trouble."[73] In a March 1968 letter to the Washington Board of Trade, an insurance company urged business owners to "develop [their] own riot protection plan."[74] That same month, a local news station argued that demonstrators should have to pay bonds to cover any potential costs they might "thrust upon the public."[75] To quell the concerns over the impending Poor People's Campaign and Carmichael's continued presence, Mayor Walter E. Washington delivered a televised interview to encourage DC residents not to "overreact." When asked about Carmichael, Washington said the militant was operating in "an orderly fashion" to "unify many of the black residents who have turned to unity" as a political strategy.[76]

DC police and the FBI saw things differently and worked to sabotage Carmichael and King's activism. As part of the Counterintelligence Program (COINTELPRO)—a series of FBI projects that aimed to surveil, infiltrate, disrupt, and discredit political groups—the FBI had closely watched Carmichael and his associates for years.[77] For example, an FBI memo written mere hours before Martin Luther King Jr.'s assassination summarized Carmichael's involvement with SNCC and promotion of Black Power. The report concluded that SNCC was "of such potential danger [to qualify] for counterintelligence consideration," and that the "primary individual target would be Stokely Carmichael."[78] DC police infiltrated PPC planning meetings in Atlanta to gather intelligence about the nonviolent campaign and assess the likelihood it would lead to urban unrest. The Washington field office of the FBI launched a covert campaign to "foster disunity" in the BUF, discredit Stokely Carmichael in the Black community, paint King as a "hypocrite," and mitigate King's PPC fundraising campaign.[79]

In a report assessing the likelihood of rebellions in DC, the FBI downplayed the Black community's activism and their frustrations. Simultaneously, the report panicked about King and Carmichael's presence in the capital. DC's "racial record had been comparatively peaceful," but "danger signals [had] arisen as a result of Stokely Carmichael's present efforts to create a Black United Front in Washington and Martin Luther King's plans for a massive civil disobedience demonstration in the Nation's Capital this spring. Were it not for Carmichael and King," the report argued, "Washington could probably look forward to another year of comparative racial peace."

Although "Carmichael's current organizing activity and King's scheduled demonstration bode ill" for DC, the FBI thought the District was less volatile than other cities because it had a "responsible middle class" who would prevent urban unrest. Additionally, the city's design would prevent uprisings because the city's "Negro ghettos are spread out and interspersed with pleasant neighborhoods." Recent reforms, including the appointment of Walter E. Washington as mayor, "evoked a generally favorable response among the Negro population, giving ghetto residents hope for a more satisfying future."[80] But the FBI analysts were wrong. A mere month after the memo was written, the capital burned in the wake of King's assassination.

3

"They Take This Nonviolent Man and Kill Him Violently"

APRIL 4, 1968

YVONNE BASKERVILLE WAS DRIVING NORTH ON FOURTEENTH Street NW to her home in Columbia Heights when a radio news bulletin announced that Dr. King was shot outside of his hotel in Memphis, Tennessee. "I thought I was going to have a stroke," she recalled. "I mean I was just devastated. . . . You didn't know that he was dead, you prayed that he wasn't dead, but you just knew everything that he'd worked so hard for, everything he had planned and prayed for was just gone." Once home, she sat in the car to collect herself before she went inside to be with her children and great-grandfather. Born in 1872, the elderly African American considered King a "saint" and was devastated by his assassination: "He just really lost it. He was so pained that this could happen in America, that someone could really kill him, you know, not an accident, not lightning or anything unusual, that someone could plan and plot and kill such a man of peace was just unbelievable. So that night we didn't sleep, we couldn't sleep."[1]

"Everybody in my house was crying . . . my uncles, my aunts, my mother, my father, everybody," reflected Elizabeth Williams Frazier, an African American DC native.[2] Bonnie Perry, a thirteen-year-old in 1968, witnessed "people upset everywhere . . . crying and holding one another and fussing and cussing and walking up and down the street. It was like confusion everywhere." To Perry, the sadness was coupled with a profound sense of hopelessness: "It was like there was no hope for the future. He was the person that was most prominent as a Black leader at that time, and now he's gone. So it's like what do you have to live for?"[3]

Some Washingtonians were eating at Ben's Chili Bowl, a Black-owned restaurant on U Street NW, when they learned King was shot in Memphis. According to Virginia Ali, who owned and operated the diner with her husband, Ben, the patrons anxiously wondered, "What's happening? What's happening? What's happening?"[4] Just a block and a half away at the intersection of Fourteenth and U Streets NW, large crowds congregated on the sidewalks after radios and television programs broke the news at 7:30 p.m.[5] Fourteenth and U, located in DC's Shaw neighborhood, was one of the busiest intersections in the city and a critical juncture for Black Washington. The U Street bus line was one of the few routes that transported people from Northwest to Northeast DC. The Fourteenth Street line funneled people from the "inner city" to offices and shops downtown. Abundant takeout eateries, liquor shops, and drugstores allowed commuters to run errands on their way home from work. The primary shopping destination for the city's African Americans was just a few blocks north along Fourteenth Street in the Columbia Heights neighborhood. Shoe and clothing shops, grocery stores, and car dealerships lined the road. The area was also the city's "nerve center" for civil rights activism. The Southern Christian Leadership Conference, founded and led by King, had its Washington, DC, office above the Peoples Drug Store at Fourteenth and U. The DC branches of the NAACP, the Student Nonviolent Coordinating Committee, and the Congress on Racial Equality were all located within a couple blocks.[6]

People gathered on the street below the SCLC office to seek the guidance of the organization that King led, and some went into the office in search of news from Memphis. Betty Wolden, a white

NBC reporter on location, said Fourteenth and U felt "ominous—like before a hurricane strikes."[7] Police closely monitored the crowd but did not disperse it because "the mood of the group was . . . one of shock and dismay rather than of anger," and the department believed it would be "futile and probably an incensing dispersal of the assembly."[8]

Police officers used a similar tactic to quell a disturbance at the same intersection two evenings prior. A group of three hundred young Black people gathered at the Peoples Drug Store the night of April 2. A month before, the store hired security guards to deter shoplifters, and tensions over the decision persisted. After white police officers appeared, the teenagers threw bottles and stones at them. Firefighters arrived to put out a small fire started in a tree. Believing the visible police presence further inflamed the situation, a lieutenant removed uniformed officers from the area. Activist Stokely Carmichael was moving furniture from the old SNCC office into its new building when he encountered the confrontation. Carmichael urged the crowd to "go home," and people eventually dispersed.[9] The assembly on April 4 was much larger, however, and this time it would not be tamed.[10]

At 8:20 p.m., a news bulletin over the radio announced that King was dead.[11] At the Washington Hilton, Vice President Hubert Humphrey broke the news to the DC politicos gathered at a Democratic Party fundraiser. King's assassination "stunned the participants and plunged them into a mood of immediate, gloomy concern."[12] Not everyone, however, was saddened. One lobbyist in attendance smiled and remarked, "Of course I'm from the South and I'm glad." A congressman "grumbled that he saw no reason to adjourn the dinner 'just because of this.'"[13] All speeches and President Lyndon Johnson's appearance were canceled, and the "filet mignon dinner was barely consumed before the event was ended."[14]

A mile away at Ben's Chili Bowl, religious music played over the radio as people in tears came into the restaurant. "People are talking about it," recalled the Chili Bowl's co-owner Virginia Ali. "This was a gentle man. This was a man that didn't believe in violence. And look how violently he dies." Beyond the grief, she remembered the disbelief: "It's not real. We don't believe this . . . and then you turn on the TV, you turn on the radio and you hear that this is really for real. It's just really for real."[15] WOL, a popular "soul" music radio station, played organ music as DJ Bob Terry pleaded, "This is no time to hate. Hate won't get you anywhere. And let me tell you something too, white man. Tomorrow before you get back in that car and go out to the suburban house, you better say something nice to that black man on the job beside you. You'd better stop hating too."[16]

To many Black Americans, King was an exceptional figure who embodied their hope for freedom and equal rights. His assassination extinguished that hope and laid bare the ugly reality that many Americans opposed that dream. "Here's a man who's tried his best nonviolently to get more jobs and better living facilities and bring equality to all people . . . and they take this nonviolent man and kill him violently," reflected Virginia Ali. "The kids just couldn't understand that, the kids just got mad and they reacted not just in Washington but across the country."[17] "What was so hurtful was that Martin Luther King was assassinated," said Washingtonian Betty May Brooks-Cole. "I immediately labeled the person as a coward because here was a peaceful guy, a nonviolent guy, that was only trying to promote freedom and equal rights for everyone, which we really needed because, as a white person you would not understand how it impacted us on a daily basis, being discriminated against."[18] Native Washingtonian Reuben Jackson discussed this sense of disillusionment in an oral history interview:

Martin Luther King had a speech where he said . . .
we just want America to be true to what you have on
paper.[19] . . . I think what the assassination said was that
there were people who were not interested in saying
the premise on which this country was based, that
they weren't really interested in seeing it carried out
for everyone. . . . So I think that this was confirmation
that there were and are forces who just said no, we're
not having this. . . . It's just like someone tapping you
on the shoulder saying, "Well, but it's not like that."
And yet I think that just bothered people. . . . I just
think there was just this anger, like, "How? How could
you?" You know, "Here we go again."[20]

In this moment of hopelessness and anger, many blamed King's
death on white people in general. African American *Washington
Post* columnist William Raspberry wrote that the uprising started
with the outrage that a white man killed King and, "in a matter of hours, the victim had become, in the eyes of too many of
us, all black people; and the murderer was no longer one stupid,
hate-filled white man, nor even bigoted white Southerners. It was
that generic Whitey." Some felt "that Whitey had shown his true
colors, Whitey had killed the one man who had given black people
hope that non-violence could work; that Whitey had killed the
man who merited the title 'Negro leader' if anybody ever deserved
that overused term; that Whitey had declared war on black people."[21] As Washingtonians responded to King's death, some acted
upon their anger at overarching white racism.

Back at Fourteenth and U NW, many people's initial shock
evolved into bitterness and rage.[22] By 8:30 p.m., just ten minutes
after the crowd learned of King's death, officers requested another police wagon to "control [the] crowd throwing bottles."[23] At

the SCLC office overlooking the intersection, Rev. Arnold Davis called Walter Fauntroy, head of the local chapter of the SCLC and vice chairman of the DC City Council, to inform him of the angry crowd gathering below. Fauntroy agreed to attempt to calm them.[24]

A few minutes later at 8:52 p.m., Stokely Carmichael left his nearby office to ask stores to close. "They took our leader, so, out of respect, we're gonna ask all these stores to close down until Martin Luther King is laid to rest," he declared. "If [Senator Robert] Kennedy had been killed, they'd have done it."[25] As Carmichael went from shop to shop, a crowd followed him and shooed customers out of the stores.[26] Most shopkeepers easily complied with the request. As the group entered the Peoples Drug Store at about 9:00 p.m., President Johnson's address played over the radio: "I ask every citizen to reject the blind violence that has struck Dr. King, who lived by nonviolence. . . . We can achieve nothing by lawlessness and divisiveness among the American people. Only by joining together and only by working together can we continue to move toward equality and fulfillment for all of our people."[27]

Fauntroy similarly urged peace as he met Carmichael at Fourteenth and Wallach Place NW, a block south of U Street, at 9:15 p.m. While the two men differed ideologically, they had interacted for months as members of the Black United Front. Grabbing Carmichael's arms, Fauntroy pleaded, "This is not the way to do it, Stokely. Let's not get anyone hurt. Let's cool it." "All they were doing," Carmichael assured Fauntroy, was asking stores to close. Fauntroy left convinced this was a "useful channeling of the frustration." Carmichael resumed his mission and the crowd following the militant grew larger, at one point stretching almost a full block behind him.[28] Street corners all along Fourteenth Street were increasingly crowded as people grappled with their shock and anger.[29]

As Carmichael traversed the streets, he subdued some calls for violence. As someone yelled that they would "kill whites," Carmichael turned around asked, "Are you ready to kill? How you gonna win? They got guns, tanks. What do you got? If you don't have your gun, go home. We're not ready. Let's wait until tomorrow. Cool it."[30] When a woman broke a window at the Belmont TV and Appliance Store five blocks north of U Street at Fourteenth and Belmont, SNCC workers blocked people from taking television sets. Carmichael grabbed two children trying to get past, took a gun out of his waistband, and shouted, "If you mean business, you should have a gun. You're not ready for the 'thing.' Go home. Go home."[31] After hearing what sounded like gunshots (it actually was glass breaking), Carmichael wrestled a firearm from a man and demanded that people "Go home, go home, go home. None of this. None of this, we're not ready. . . . You won't get [a leader] like this. You'll just get shot. Go home."[32] In an interview the following day, Carmichael insisted he did not mind people breaking windows, but he thought it was unsafe to be on the street without guns because Black people would be shot in confrontations with the police.[33] People should go home to stay safe. Many of his followers did not heed this advice.

There was no one definitive event that ignited the pattern of window-breaking, looting, and arson that erupted that night. *Washington Post* reporters believed the first incident of property damage occurred at the Republic Theatre on U Street when a boy punched his hand through the glass and took a bag of popcorn at 9:37 p.m.[34] The police department, however, first reported window-breaking and looting at 9:30 p.m. at a Safeway grocery store a few blocks north of U Street.[35] In an oral history interview, Virginia Ali asserted that a brick thrown through a store window at Fourteenth and U sparked the upheaval.[36] According to the *Washington Post*, at roughly 9:54 p.m., some men at

Fourteenth and U kicked and broke a window, and a man threw a trash can through the storefront of the Peoples Drug Store before throwing a bottle through a liquor store window.[37] Lillian Wiggins, a reporter for the *Washington Afro-American*, witnessed people taking liquor, clothing, and electronics from stores when she arrived at Fourteenth and U at about 10:00 p.m.[38] The fire department received its first call at 10:50 p.m. after two cars were set ablaze at Fourteenth and Belmont, five blocks north of U Street.[39]

The consistencies in each account reveal the essential story of how the disturbances began. After the news broke that King was shot, crowds congregated at the intersection of Fourteenth and U, and more people assembled after they learned King was dead. Stokely Carmichael began asking stores to close shortly before 9:00 p.m., and the crowds following him grew as he went store to store. After 9:30 p.m., there were scattered instances of window-breaking and minor looting. Shortly before 10:00 p.m., the uprisings began in earnest as more and more people broke shop windows.

SNCC workers could no longer block people from entering stores, and "youths with television sets, electrical appliances, clothing, shoes, and other items began streaming past Carmichael at 14th and U." Realizing the situation was beyond his control, Carmichael got into a Ford Mustang and left the area at 10:40 p.m.[40] Reporter Lillian Wiggins saw "whiskey in large quantities . . . being lifted from the store through the broken plate glass windows. Televisions were being carried from a T.V. repair place and clothing was being stripped from the windows. Mannequins, colored and white, were scattered from one end of the street to the other." One man approached Wiggins and remarked, "They shouldn't have done this. Killing Dr. King was the worst thing the white people could have done."[41]

Law Enforcement and the First Night

Local and federal government leaders immediately prepared for civil unrest in Washington after they learned King was shot. President Lyndon Johnson, Mayor Walter E. Washington, and officials at the Central Intelligence Agency, the Federal Bureau of Investigation, the 116th Army Division, and the Army Command Center at the Pentagon were all briefed on developments in Memphis and the reaction in DC and across the country.[42] The 116th Division, a military unit responsible for surveilling civilians, went on "Lantern Spike" alert after King's assassination, and 120 agents were called to its headquarters. The division dispatched teams to report disturbances and surveil potential Black militants in DC.[43] Military leaders traveled from their homes to the Army Command Center to prepare for the possibility of sending troops into Washington.[44] The mayor's office, the police department, and the Civil Defense Unit (CDU), a four-hundred-person rapid-response police unit that had undergone intensive riot-control training, established immediate contact to closely monitor the mood of the city.[45] Public Safety Director Patrick Murphy left his home to go to Fourteenth Street less than ten minutes after he heard the news from Memphis.[46] Plainclothes police officers went to Fourteenth and U Streets NW as early as 8:45 p.m. to gather intel. Some officers were even in the group following Carmichael.[47]

After observing the crowds around U Street, Murphy discussed strategy with another officer at Sixteenth and U Streets at 9:00 p.m. The earliest police reports, as well as their own observations, indicated that the gathering citizens were nonviolent. As Murphy left the area at about 9:30 p.m., he allegedly told a reporter, "We've giving it the light touch. There are no great numbers of [police] visible."[48] While Murphy would later deny using the phrase "light touch,"[49] the police's actions matched this statement.

The department justified this "light touch" In its after-action report: "In view of this early non-violent attitude of the crowd on U Street, it was the judgement of police officials that it would be unwise to engage in what would likely be a futile and probably an incensing dispersal of the assembly."[50] In other words, the police believed a visible presence only risked public outrage and escalation, so they stayed on the fringes and instead put units on alert and activated intelligence sources. This strategy was understandable considering the tensions between the Black community and police in DC and the police's recent success with deescalating situations by reducing their visible presence. Walter Fauntroy thought the presence of uniformed officers would provoke the crowd and discouraged a robust police presence in a conversation with a officer that night.[51] As of 10:00 p.m., there were virtually no uniformed police officers around Fourteenth and U.[52]

Once people started breaking into businesses, however, the police quickly increased their presence until it was unsafe and impractical to stay. At 10:10 p.m., an officer reported the first incident of property damage over police radios and requested more officers: "Plainclothes cruisers requested; breaking windows at 14th and U Sts., NW."[53] Uniformed officers moved to confront the crowds but were "heavily outnumbered." Police radioed that people were throwing stones at them, and Murphy subsequently ordered the police to pull back "while reinforcements were summoned and equipped." With each new "frantic call" reporting harassment, Murphy emphasized that the police officers should back out if in danger. The retreating police attempted to seal off Fourteenth Street to "confine the disorder to already damaged blocks" while they waited for backup.[54] Meanwhile, police officers rushed to their headquarters downtown to get riot gear, and the CDU mobilized before heading to the Fourteenth Street corridor. Officers cordoned off the area and began making arrests by 11:15 p.m. A rain shower and the increased presence of law enforcement cleared the streets, and at 11:28 p.m. police reported there was "no rioting in Northwest Washington."[55]

They were too optimistic. The downpour was short-lived and the streets quickly refilled as crowds moved north up the Fourteenth Street hill to the central shopping district in Columbia Heights. "Enforce the law vigorously for any violation and make arrests," Deputy Chief Raymond Pyles instructed police over the radio.[56] The fire department, led by Chief Henry Galotta, mobilized its entire squad at 11:51 p.m.[57] At 12:30 a.m., the first large fire started at Fourteenth and Fairmont Streets.[58] As firefighters arrived to extinguish the flames, people taunted them and threw stones and other projectiles.[59] Police launched one hundred baseball-size canisters of tear gas to disperse the crowd and allow the firefighters to work. This was the first large-scale use of tear gas during the disturbances, but it would be far from the last. In total, 150 stores were damaged, seven buildings were burned, and nearly two hundred people were arrested that Thursday night.[60]

Although Fourteenth Street was not fully quiet until about 4:00 a.m., around midnight Murphy and Police Chief Layton determined that the police could sufficiently quell the outbreak and did not require outside help.[61] At 3:00 a.m. on April 5, Murphy met with officials from the Army Command Center at the Pentagon. The men chose not to call up federal troops because the police had successfully contained the disturbance and they believed further upheaval was unlikely during the daytime.[62] Nevertheless, the city still prepared for the possibility of renewed unrest. The DC National Guard was ordered to assemble in uniform at the DC armory for potential deployment Friday night. The CDU was sent home at 5:30 a.m. with instructions to report at 5 p.m. Friday and to be prepared for several days away from home. The police department canceled planned leave and days off for all officers. The Pentagon instructed the Third Infantry at Fort Myer to be ready to head into Washington, DC. With preparations made and the city calm, Mayor Washington toured the city's streets before finally arriving home at 4:30 a.m.[63]

4

"You Just Can't Expect People Not to Act This Way"

UNDERSTANDING THE REBELLIONS

As dawn broke, street cleaners sprayed white foam to wash the glass and debris down the Fourteenth Street hill as burglar alarms still rang "in an unsettling chorus."[1] Flags flew at half-mast at the request of Mayor Washington.[2] Washingtonians opened their copy of the *Washington Post* to read the headline "Dr. King Is Slain in Memphis."[3] A *Post* editorial urged peace: "It would be the last and final and ultimate repudiation of everything for which Martin Luther King stood if it were to arouse racial hatred and excited the kind of violence that he deplored. Then, indeed, the grave would have its victory."[4] An article in the *Washington Daily News* suggested further rebellions could be worse than the murder of the Nobel Peace Prize winner: "The assassin, perhaps worst of all, has given stature to those other fanatics who cry, 'Burn, baby, burn.' Among those to whom Dr. King was a symbol of peace, the message of violence will now seem less extreme."[5]

Many Washingtonians went to their jobs as usual hoping the upheaval had passed. Traffic was congested as drivers slowed to view the destruction.[6] Some store owners assessed the damage and began repairs with plywood.[7] The owner of a hair salon that had been looted the night before kept her hair appointments for that morning.[8] Many parents still walked their children to

school.[9] Although the courts worked through the night to process those arrested, judges were determined to stick to "business
as usual."[10]

It was soon apparent, however, that Friday, April 5, would not
be governed by "business as usual." By 8:45 a.m., people were
already removing goods from a grocery store in Northwest DC.[11]
The Civil Defense Unit informed the Department of Corrections
at 8:57 a.m. that the police expected a "major disturbance."[12] By
11:00 a.m., people once again crowded around Fourteenth and U
Streets and other intersections along Fourteenth Street.[13] Sensing
a potential resurgence of disorder, the police sent parole officers to
potential trouble areas.[14] People began breaking windows along
Fourteenth Street at roughly 11:45 a.m., and the first fires erupted around 12:15 p.m. The situation quickly escalated, and the
fire department confronted "mass fires along 14th St up to Park
Road"—more than a mile north of Fourteenth and U Streets—by
the early afternoon.[15]

Simultaneously, schoolchildren became increasingly unruly.
It was a contentious decision to even hold classes that day. The
Student Nonviolent Coordinating Committee and the DC public
school system teacher's union wanted the schools to close. The
school board, however, decided to keep the schools open so children would stay off the streets.[16] As chaos spread through the city
on Friday, citizens and leaders debated if schools should stay open
to prevent students from participating or close to honor King and
allow students to get home safely. Parents called asking for their
children to be released, SNCC continued to demand closures, and
principals reported an unusually tense and restless atmosphere.
But the police department asked schools to prohibit students from
leaving for lunch since some campuses were as close as one block
from Fourteenth Street. School officials thought keeping children
inside would be impossible. Sterling Tucker, executive director

of the Washington Urban League, called Deputy Superintendent Benjamin Henley to ask him to keep the schools open because closing them was "the worst thing that could happen." "We can't hold these kids," Henley replied, "you don't know how they have been acting." By noon, over half of Cardozo High's seventeen hundred students had left and groups from McKinley High in Northeast DC had departed to go to Howard University.[17]

As Fourteenth Street erupted again, many reporters were nearby at a press conference with Stokely Carmichael at the New School for Afro-American Thought, a newly founded Black educational and cultural center that was located two blocks north of Fourteenth and U Streets.[18] The 11:00 a.m. presser was scheduled to address SNCC President H. Rap Brown's upcoming trial for allegedly inciting a riot in Cambridge, Maryland, in July 1967. Carmichael's remarks instead centered on his reaction to King's assassination.[19]

First, Carmichael specifically blamed white Americans for King's murder and asserted the assassination signaled a fundamental change for the Black community:

> As for Dr. King's murder, I think white America made its biggest mistake when she killed Dr. King last night because when she killed Dr. King last night, she killed all reasonable hope. When she killed Dr. King last night, she killed the one man of our race that this country's older generations, the militants and the revolutionaries and the masses of black people would still listen to. When white America killed Dr. King she opened the eyes of every black man in this country.[20]

Carmichael stated that King's assassination was uniquely egregious because King was nonviolent. He "was the one man in our race who was trying to teach our people to have love, compassion and mercy for what white people had done."[21]

To him, the assassination was white America's declaration of war on Black people, and Carmichael was ready to lead the charge to retaliate and fight:

> When white America killed Dr. King last night, she declared war on us. There will be no crying and there will be no funeral. The rebellions that have been occurring around these cities and this country is just light stuff to what is about to happen. We have to retaliate for the deaths of our leaders. The execution for those deaths will not be in the court rooms. They're going to be in the streets of the United States of America. . . . There no longer needs to be intellectual discussion. Black people know that they have to get guns. White America will live to cry since she killed Dr. King last night.

"What do you say to black people who have to die to do what you say?" asked a reporter. "That they take as many white people with them as they can," Carmichael responded. "We die every day. We die in Vietnam for the honkies. . . . We die cutting and fighting each other inside our own communities. . . . We die in your jails. We die in your ghettos. We die in your rat-infested homes. We die a thousand deaths every day. We're not afraid to die, because now we're gonna die for our people." It was "crystal clear," he believed, that "today the final showdown is coming" and "the only way to survive is to get some guns." Asked what the confrontation would accomplish, Carmichael voiced a pessimistic but bold answer: "The black man can't do nothing in this country. Then we're going to stand up on our feet and die like men. If that's our only act of manhood, then Goddammit we're going to die. We're tired of living on our stomachs."[22] Despite Carmichael's strong rhetoric, neither Carmichael nor other Washingtonians killed white people in the rebellions.[23] In his biography of Carmichael, historian Peniel E. Joseph concluded that King's assassination "exposed contradictions, both politically and personally, within Carmichael. He alternated between serene calm and passionate anger."[24] While he urged people to go home on Thursday night, on Friday morning he called for retaliation for the death of King. "Let me make clear what happened last night," he asserted in his Friday morning press conference, "last night we led all of those youngsters up and down the street to close the stores in memory of Dr. King. . . . We weren't stopping them from kicking in a few windows—we were stopping them from coming out on the streets without guns. When they come out on the streets we want them to have guns. . . . The only way to survive is to get some guns."[25] Later, however, he obtained special permission from the police for Ben's Chili Bowl to stay open during the curfew so community leaders would have a place to plan how to restore peace.[26] Carmichael was a man both deeply saddened and enraged by the death of a man who had a "powerful hold on him personally and politically."[27] His actions and rhetoric reveal a man oscillating between preserving peace and ordering war.

While very few other Black leaders condoned "war" as Carmichael did, many African Americans similarly saw King's assassination as a "final straw" and sympathized with those who were looting and burning. ACT leader and firebrand activist Julius Hobson declared, "I say that the next white man that comes into the black community preaching non-violence should be dealt with violently." "You just can't expect people not to react this way," said Edward J. MacClane, president of the Negro Federation of Civic Associations, the governing body of DC's Black civic associations.

"The city has been heading this way for a long time."[28] A member of the traditionally nonviolent NAACP's DC branch stated that "We are sitting in a 'state of shock.' No one can be blamed for the consequences that may occur. . . . A lot of leaders are not coming out tonight because they are afraid of becoming irrational themselves."[29] Others echoed Carmichael's belief that King's assassination revealed a larger truth about the fate of African Americans and the cruelty of white people. Lester McKinnie, chairman of the DC branch of SNCC, asserted that "We can see by this act of aggression what is in store for all of us—the African people in America."[30]

Others criticized any violence as a disgrace to King's legacy. Maxine Boyd, a local government official who had participated in the 1965 Selma march, claimed that "The greatest tribute we could make to Dr. King would be to implement his philosophy of nonviolence in spite of the Black Power Movement." "I hope and pray that what Dr. King lived for will prevail and that the black people of America will not riot and cause violence," wished Benjamin Alexander, an African American member of the DC Board of Education.[31] Walter Fauntroy traveled from news outlet to news outlet urging people to stay peaceful. He requested "restraint, calm and nonviolence" and begged people to "handle your grief the way Dr. King would have wanted it." Fauntroy believed those who acted violently did "dishonor to the life and mission of Dr. King."[32]

Two ceremonies held at Howard University on Friday morning reflected the wide range of responses to King's assassination. Howard University canceled classes, and its president, James Nabrit, led a memorial service at the university's biggest auditorium. Simultaneously, militant students held their own ceremony outside. Nabrit memorialized King as "a man of love, of non-violence—a black man, an American." Students outside set up a loudspeaker and took turns giving speeches. Some pulled down the American flag and replaced it with the black and red banner of Ujamaa, a Black-nationalist organization based on campus. As the crowd inside the auditorium sang the civil rights anthem "We Shall Overcome," students on the courtyard carried a bloodied effigy wrapped in white.[33] Although many students made "vehemently" anti-white speeches at the rally, white *Washington Post* reporter John Anderson said he never felt in danger: "I was standing there, very conspicuously white, and yet hardly anyone as much as glanced at me. I never had the sensation of being in danger. The hostility was directed at an abstraction that was white, and powerful, and downtown; it was not toward a specific white man standing in the crowd in the middle of the Howard campus."[34]

As the "eulogy type program" ended, Carmichael arrived at Howard after his press conference.[35] According to the FBI, Carmichael held up a gun and declared "tonight bring your gun, don't loot, shoot."[36] The *Washington Post*, however, reported Carmichael held up a gun and said, "Stay off the streets if you don't have a gun because there's going to be shooting." Carmichael only briefly stayed, and the assembly dispersed soon after his departure. Although the rally at Howard was heavily covered by the press and many believed it spurred Friday's upheaval, Fourteenth Street was already on fire when Carmichael arrived.[37]

The Height of the Upheaval

Friday, April 5, was the height of the upheaval. Washingtonians started over five hundred fires, and two hundred were burning simultaneously late that afternoon.[38] Eleven buildings were already aflame on Fourteenth Street when the blazes were set on Seventh Street NW at 1:00 p.m. By roughly 3:00 p.m., H Street NE was also on fire.[39] By 10:50 p.m., the three streets were "burning for one solid mile."[40] Law enforcement received a call reporting a rebellion-related incident every eight seconds Friday night.[41] By midnight, the fire department had been dispatched to 280 fires.[42]

Across DC, the attacks on businesses conformed to a general pattern. Once masses gathered, young people broke store windows and pushed aside glass before entering. Other teenagers followed, then young children, and finally adults went into the businesses and emerged with merchandise. Once a store was mostly cleaned out, someone—normally an older teenager or adult—would set the store ablaze.[43] On Seventh Street NW, two hundred to three hundred people crowded each block in the early afternoon before fires started.[44] The fire department believed there was a "definite relationship between disorderly crowds and [the] number of fires occurring."[45] The fires were often started by one person working along one stretch. For example, on H Street, witnesses saw one man burn building after building down the block. He took a soda bottle from under his coat, lit the Molotov cocktail, and threw it to engulf the store in flames.[46]

Before order was restored, the District endured $33 million in property damage ($238 million adjusted for inflation) and over one thousand fires. One thousand three hundred and fifty-two businesses were harmed, nearly five thousand people were displaced from their jobs, and two thousand people were left homeless.[47] The destruction was concentrated in three business districts located in predominantly African American neighborhoods: Fourteenth Street NW, Seventh Street NW, and H Street NE. Focusing on statistics and property damage, however, cannot fully convey events that were chaotic, dramatic, cathartic, and occasionally joyful for some. "Tear gas fill[ed] the eyes and throat" as police in masks and riot gear moved in "combat-type formations" down the city streets "filled with broken glass, pieces of mannequins, and troops."[48] "The street was crisscrossed with firehoses, some of them propped untended on chairs, pouring water into the smoldering ruins of what had been a Safeway, a pawn shop, a liquor store," reported *The Hatchet*, George Washington University's student newspaper.[49] "Mustard and catsup oozed past burst boxes of cake mix" in grocery aisles.[50] Two men pushed a grand piano down an alley next to a music shop. A furniture store owner rocked in his chair with a shotgun in his lap as he smoked a cigar.[51] One woman had "so many hams in her arms that she kept dropping them and when she tried to pick one up another one would roll out of her arms."[52] "I really chuckled to see people coming out of [stores] with speakers that were as big as that glass," recalled Jaqueline Rogers Hart, a Black Washingtonian. "People were running out of grocery stores with half a cow on their back. So it was a lot of ridiculous sort of things that was happening."[53]

During this period of upheaval, some African Americans felt less fear than their white acquaintances and colleagues. Faith Davis Ruffins was at school when she learned of the chaos across town. A student at National Cathedral School, a private school in upper Northwest DC, Ruffins was the only Black pupil in her class. Her classmates were concerned about how she would get home and she realized "they're afraid because they're white. It didn't seem to me that I was really in any great danger. . . . It seemed to me that I would actually be in more danger in a predominantly white area."[54]

To many, the mood on the streets Friday was a joyous "carnival atmosphere." *Washington Afro-American* journalist Ruth Jenkins observed a "laughing quartet of young people run against the traffic light pushing shopping carts of looted goods."[55] "It was sort of carnivalesque," recalled Ruffins. "That might be a word that a cultural studies person would call it today. . . . It was kind of funny, actually."[56] Robert Allen of *The Hilltop*, Howard University's student newspaper, asserted that "By the second night of violence . . . rage had faded and had been replaced by that much deplored 'carnival atmosphere.'"[57]

But some Black Washingtonians did not feel safe or find humor in the situation. "Cameras were showing what was going on, places were on fire, people were afraid. . . . Older women were crying," recalled Betty May Brooks-Cole, a Black Washingtonian who was twenty-four years old during the rebellions. As she sat on her porch in the Capitol Hill neighborhood, she saw young boys steal clothes from the dry cleaners she used. "God, please give me my clothes!" she yelled. But the boys did not stop. Brooks-Cole reflected that "it was a terrible, terrible situation. I never experienced anything like that in my entire life. It was quite scary."[58] Mrs. Howard, a Black woman who worked as a cleaner, was feeding her grandchildren dinner when she heard an explosion in the liquor store below her apartment. "I just stood there and saw everything burn down," she said. "I didn't get out nothing, not one thing. . . . I just stood there, knowing all I had was going down."[59]

Kenneth Tolliver, a thirteen-year-old Black student, felt a range of emotions as he journeyed home after his school closed Friday. As the bus went down Georgia Avenue, some Black men got on and attacked the white bus driver. Farther south, at Florida Avenue and Seventh Street, the bus had to stop because the streets in front of it were ablaze and impassable: "I can remember we finally got down to [Florida] Ave and the 7th St bus had to turn there because the block in front of us was ablaze. It was like in a movie, like a battle scene in a movie. . . . I can remember my clothes, I can remember the heat, the searing heat you know, from the fire." Tolliver also recalled the looting, and to him it seemed to be "a ball. . . . It was funny." As he wandered the streets, he saw his father with a case of liquor. They went home together, and there his brother had "about a half a side of cow" in a crate on his shoulder. Still, Tolliver was "frightened because my mother, she's the domestic one and she hadn't gotten home, and it took her forever to get home and . . . that was most of my fear, concern."[60]

Workers downtown panicked and fled Friday afternoon as news outlets reported the chaos in Washington. Some could see smoke and looting from their office windows.[61] Petrified, white workers left their downtown offices to return to the suburbs and neighborhoods in upper Northwest Washington. Some fleeing were city employees needed to coordinate the District's response. "One of the most distressing things to me was the fact that many of our department heads could not be found on Friday," said a key member of the mayor's team. "They were so frightened that they simply fled the city."[62] Even those tucked away in the suburbs panicked, and many flocked to grocery stores to stock up on food. "It's worse than a Saturday afternoon," one grocer claimed. "It's like they're expecting a three-foot snow."[63]

This mass exodus resulted in one of the worst traffic jams in DC history.[64] Buses and cars could not travel many routes because of the fires and crowds. The city advised motorists to avoid using "7th, 13th, 14th, and all adjacent streets" at about 3:15 p.m.[65] These closures meant the available routes were even busier.[66] "The delays were exacerbated because street lights and buses were not yet on the rush hour schedule and the police were too busy to direct traffic.[67] To help, some civilians got out of their cars to try to "untangle the hopelessly snarled" vehicles.[68] Many commuters experienced delays of "monumental proportions" that added hours to commutes.[69] People crowded airport and train terminals as they rushed to leave the city.[70]

Some suburban commuters seeking to flee were confronted as they drove home through Black neighborhoods. Young people targeted cars driven by white people and threw rocks and bottles at them.[71] In a few cases, some boys rocked cars that were stopped at intersections, including along Fourteenth Street, on Friday afternoon. In one rare instance, youths pulled a white teenager out of a car and beat him until a priest intervened.[72] Others dropped rocks and bricks onto cars from the bridge over Kenilworth Avenue NE, nearly five miles southeast of Fourteenth and U Streets.[73] The WOL radio station, whose primary audience was Black Washingtonians, instructed drivers to keep their lights on during the day "in honor" of King. "Thousands of cars, taxis, transit buses, police cruisers . . . all with their lights on during the day," wrote the *Washington Afro-American*. "It's the 'soul brother' insignia, and it has a smashing impact."[74] "I heard that anybody who didn't have his lights on in memory of King would be subject to exposure to violence," said Walter Fauntroy.[75] While Fauntroy believed this was just a "rumor," reporters from the *Washington Afro-American* on the streets Friday witnessed several incidents of youths selectively targeting cars based on their lights.[76]

Understanding the Rebellions

Most participants were not affiliated with radical groups or "professional robbers, arsonists, and thieves," as Democratic Senator Russell B. Long of Louisiana claimed. According to the DC Bail Agency, the "typical suspect" arrested during the disturbances had no prior record.[77] "Reporters and photographers on the streets during the disorders described the typical looter as inexperienced and, in some cases, unsure about what to do next," wrote *Washington Post* reporter Ben Gilbert.[78] William Raspberry of the *Washington Post* described the average participant as "mainly bewildered types who, for the first time in their lives, saw a chance to get something for nothing—and got caught."[79]

At least two extremely small fringe groups stated that they systematically started fires. The groups claimed to have stockpiled flammable materials such as kerosene, dynamite, and gasoline prior to King's assassination.[80] They targeted white-owned shops such as carryout restaurants and liquor stores that they considered to have taken advantage of or discriminated against the Black community.[81] None of these radicals, however, claimed to have instigated the disturbances nor did they claim to be a large, popular movement. "There were very, very few organized groups doing things . . . in the street" insisted John Smith, an employee of the DC government who spoke candidly on the condition of anonymity during an oral history interview. Most participants were "just angry people. . . . Your average citizen was out there. Not setting the fires, but looting the stores . . . These people [pointing to a photo of a crowded street during the disorders] weren't part of any group or anything."[82] "The majority of the places that were burned were burned by the mass of black people," a member of an anonymous radical group told a *Washington Post* reporter in 1968."[83] While these radicals hoped for a mass revolution, they acknowledged that their small groups did not start the rebellions nor did they influence most who participated.

There were certainly people who took advantage of the lack of police presence to take items with little thought to Dr. King's death. "By the second night of violence," wrote Robert Allen of the Howard *Hilltop*, "rage had faded. . . . No targets of political significance were hit."[84] For some, taking items was simply practical or an economic opportunity. One woman told a reporter that she was "looting" a store because she shopped for groceries every Friday night and there was nowhere else to go.[85] In another store, a mother told her son, "Don't grab the groceries . . . grab the book." As one reporter explained, "The book, of course, was where the accounts were kept" and taking it would erase the merchant's records of customer's debts.[86] Some took items and later sold them to make money.[87]

To some people, looting articulated a political message. "I don't see nothing wrong in stealing from those white men," said a young Black man. "I have been looking for a job for over a year now, but I can't find nothing. . . . What you see out here ought to teach white people a lesson. They got to stop going around killing Negroes."[88] When asked by a reporter why he looted, an anonymous man replied, "I'm doing this because they killed Martin Luther King. This is my way of getting them."[89] For others, harming businesses or taking goods was an act of rebellion that flipped the normal order on its head. As former Black police officer John Jackson put it: "Man, they were trying to get even with all these things that they thought people were, that they perceived people were doing to them over all these years. And they were turning the tables. They were having some fun."[90] "The rebellions were largely apolitical except to the extent that 'reclamation' (i.e. looting) is a political act and rage is a political emotion," wrote Robert Allen of the Howard *Hilltop*. "Despite the personal motivation of individual looters, however, the significance of the rebellions should not be overlooked. The mere fact that so many ordinary Black People are willing to take to the streets, if only to 'reclaim' a color TV set or a fifth of Johnny Walker Red, is clearly one of the most significant political facts of this decade."[91] "This idea of burning, man, was to destroy what this white man stood for," said former Pride, Inc., leader and activist Rufus "Catfish" Mayfield. "I might have had the impulse to burn; a man can just restock his store and raise his prices a little bit if it's just looting."[92]

Participants mostly harmed businesses that possessed merchandise. The National Capital Planning Commission's survey of the damage concluded that "looting and burning were aimed at commercial establishments."[93] One thousand three hundred and fifty-two businesses sustained damage, and many were shops with attractive, expensive merchandise.[94] In total, "About 95% of the [damaged] business establishments were in retail trade and services."[95] While 439 residential units were damaged, only twelve were single-family residences. Over 50 percent of housing units harmed were along Seventh Street where many people lived above businesses.[96] Almost no one attempted to damage government buildings. Only eight public properties (less than .1 percent of the damage) were affected.[97]

The targets of the destruction suggest that some Washingtonians participated in the uprisings as an act of rebellion against "the system" of white power. White-owned businesses were long-standing opponents to desegregation and home rule as well as the most accessible manifestation of white institutions in Black neighborhoods. While incidents of physical violence against white people were rare, when they did occur, they occurred where whites "invaded" Black neighborhoods: suburbanites commuting to work on inner city roads and a few people in Black neighborhoods that were deemed "not to belong." For some, harassing police officers, soldiers, and firefighters was a rebellion against what many viewed as an "occupying force" and communicated a willingness to challenge the enforcers of white institutions. People thus attacked the closest junctures that represented white people's power over Black communities: white-owned and/or -operated stores that demonstrated a sort of colonialism in their communities, commuter highways that exemplified white people abandoning the city for the suburbs while still extracting resources from it, "occupying" police forces, and (rarely) white people who they identified with the larger "whitey" who assassinated King. Ibrahim Mumin, a DC resident reflecting on the rebellions in an oral history in 2012, summarized this political sentiment. He commented that commercial corridors were attacked because:

People were, in some respect, striking out at where they
considered the power structure was. In many instances
they felt that . . . people . . . were making money and it
wasn't them. You know, it's one thing to be in poverty
and you're surrounded by everybody else, but many of
the merchants were considered the people who were
making money but taking it out of the neighborhood.
They were not reinvesting in the neighborhood. . . . It
was anger and I think people were striking out at what
they considered the enemy. And people who they had
access to were the other merchants who were in the
neighborhood.[98]

Additionally, Washington activists had targeted these manifestations of the "power structure" for decades as they demanded
freedom, economic opportunities, good education, accountable
policing, voting rights, and political power for over a century. The
Coordinating Committee for the Enforcement of the DC Anti-
Discrimination Laws, Julius Hobson, CORE, and ACT all mobilized Black Washingtonians against white businesses to oppose
discrimination, gain employment opportunities, and obtain
home rule. Free DC directly urged Washingtonians to boycott
small white-owned businesses that refused to back home rule in
Shaw and along H Street. Organizations including the Emergency
Committee on the Transportation Crisis, the Model Inner City
Community Development Organization, and others criticized
city planning by white outsiders that bulldozed Black neighborhoods to create amenities for white Washingtonians. Citizens had
also long demanded police accountability and an end to police
brutality. "We want to free D.C. from our enemies," Marion Barry
said before the upheaval, "the people who make it impossible for
us to do anything about the lousy schools, brutal cops, slumlords,

welfare investigators who go out on midnight raids, employers who discriminate in hiring and a host of other ills that run rampant throughout our city."[99] At least some participants in the civil disorders wanted to "free DC" from these "enemies."

Acknowledging the political aspects of the upheaval does not suggest that everyone who participated was doing so as a protest of the white power structure. Many participants were, by their own admission, primarily motivated by opportunism amid chaos. While many white businesses were targeted, some Black businesses also suffered damages. Virginia Ali was proud that Ben's Chili Bowl was spared, but she also thought racial solidarity only went so far in protecting Black-owned establishments. Although "community support" kept Ben's from being burned, Ali believed that for "clothing stores, I don't think it really mattered what color [the owners] were. If they wanted to go in those clothing stores, [they did]."[100] As noted by BUF member Calvin Rolark, "Some businesses that are truly equal opportunity employers were destroyed."[101] Although Washingtonian Reuben Jackson believed the disturbances were politically motivated for many, he acknowledged the other aspects of it: "Yeah, one can say there were some opportunists who just took things. It was a good time to get a good TV or something."[102] In other words, while there were political dimensions to the disturbances, people participated for a variety of reasons. As concluded by the *Washington Afro-American*, "There is no single reason covering individual motivation of participants."[103]

Regardless of the reasons that people participated, law enforcement was completely overwhelmed by the chaos on Friday afternoon. Hundreds of businesses lost merchandise, and the DC police were unable to restore order. The DC fire department did not have the capacity to respond to the twenty-five to thirty new fires started every hour.[104] It was time for the federal government to intervene.

5

"Helmeted Troops Cast Long, Fierce Shadows"

THE MILITARY'S OCCUPATION OF DC

On Friday afternoon, the city and federal government mobilized outside help. General Ralph E. Haines Jr.—the vice chief of staff for the army and the commander of the military's response to the disorder called Operation Cabin Guard—and Public Safety Director Patrick Murphy toured the city that afternoon and at about 2:45 p.m. decided to start moving troops toward Washington. To communicate this command, they needed to use a pay phone, but the phone lines were so jammed they had to drive from gas station to gas station until they finally found a phone with a dial tone. At one gas station, Haines was hit by a rock as he got out of the car. Eventually, Haines and Murphy found a working pay phone, and at about 3:00 p.m. Haines instructed the Pentagon to move the first troops into the city. Around 3:30 p.m., troops from the Sixth Armored Cavalry left Fort Meade, in Maryland, and the Ninety-First Combat Engineers left Fort Belvoir, also in Maryland, toward the capital. Additionally, the Pentagon ordered three thousand troops to be ready to move to Washington on thirty minutes' notice. Shortly after, they doubled the number of soldiers on alert to six thousand.[1] At about 4:00 p.m., President Johnson formally ordered federal troops into Washington to quell the—in his words—"hell-raising."[2]

Overwhelmed as twenty-five to thirty new fires broke out every

hour, the DC fire department requested aid from nearby suburban firefighters at 4:30 p.m., and the first reinforcements arrived
forty-five minutes later. Seventy-two fire engines from DC and
sixty from the surrounding suburbs worked to limit the destruction. Despite the additional help, there were so many fires that the
department could only reduce the flames to embers before moving to the next blaze. Under normal circumstances, firefighters
were required to completely extinguish a fire.[3] "It's been one con-
tinuous nightmare," remarked one firefighter. "Some of the fires
we fought on 14th St and Seventh St would ordinarily have been
four-alarm fires. But the force could only spare one pumper to
fight them." Another firefighter was so exhausted he proclaimed,
"I couldn't even tell you what day it was." Over that weekend,
many in the fire department worked sixteen-hour days as they
evacuated people from buildings and extinguished flames.[4]

Finally, at 5:15 p.m., Mayor Washington instituted a state
of emergency in DC and established a citywide curfew from
5:30 p.m. to 6:30 a.m. The mayor's proclamation banned the sale
of alcoholic beverages, gas and flammable liquids (unless the
gas went directly into a car), and firearms.[5] According to May-
or Washington, "ninety-nine per cent of the staff was against"
imposing the curfew across the entire city, presumably because
they felt that only parts of the city were under siege. Nevertheless,
the mayor believed a uniform policy was necessary because if it
was only implemented in parts of the city, people could simply
travel to areas exempt from the curfew and loot there. Further,
Washington feared a selective curfew would further anger Black
Washingtonians and worsen the civil disturbances: "The affected areas which were practically totally Negro, if we slapped it on
there, it would have been taken as a racial act, with racial over-
tones. Certainly, it would, no doubt, have reacted."[6]

As the troops traveled into the city, the traffic jams delayed their arrival.[7] Phone jams also slowed the activation of the DC National Guard. Relying on a phone tree to contact each member, it took the Guard hours to reach its soldiers.[8] Federal troops first arrived in DC around 5:00 p.m.[9] By 5:11 p.m., five hundred troops stood guard in front of the White House and surrounded the Capitol building not long after with "their machine guns out of place against the marble and majesty of the nation's shrines and monuments."[10] Many of the armed forces were sent to the most damaged areas: Fourteenth Street NW, Seventh Street NW, and H Street NE.[11] Troops urged people to go home, assisted police, protected firefighters, guarded some buildings, and cordoned off streets. By 9:00 p.m., two seven-hundred-strong troop battalions "occupied and sealed off" the north and south ends of Fourteenth Street. Soldiers also blocked off eight blocks of Seventh Street.[12] Troops used a similar strategy to get H Street NE largely under control by 10:00 p.m. *Post* reporters observed that "the troops had effectively placed clamps on the three main trouble areas," which made it easier for police to "catch and arrest hit-and-run looters." Soldiers also detained people carrying looted goods until police could arrive at the scene to make arrests.[13]

As the three major disorder areas were contained, sporadic flare-ups persisted across the city, especially in shopping centers in the Anacostia neighborhood in Southeast Washington.[14] Stores in Anacostia were first attacked around 5:00 p.m. on Friday, and in total about fifty businesses were damaged. One hundred fifty troops from the DC National Guard occupied the far northeastern section of Anacostia, and seven hundred soldiers from the Ninety-First Engineers patrolled the far Southeast by Friday night.[15]

Throughout the capital, troops and police dispersed crowds so that the fire department could work without harassment.[16] "We don't mind fighting the worst kind of fire," commented one firefighter, "but it's kind of unnerving to have to dodge bricks and bottles from bystanders, and I'll confess we were worried about being badly hurt."[17] Numerous accounts from newspapers, memos to the president's Situation Room, and records of the Office of Emergency Preparedness confirm that firefighters faced verbal harassment and some violence across the city. A fire truck at Fourteenth and Girard Streets "took a battering from hurdled bottles, bricks, and stones," and a block south, crowds stoned firefighters Friday afternoon.[18] At Fourteenth and Columbia Streets in Columbia Heights, firefighters were setting up a fire hose when a group pushed them aside and warned, "We didn't build the goddamned fire for any white people to put out."[19] Children and adults cut fire hoses at several locations along Seventh Street.[20] In a few instances, firefighters felt so threatened that they fled.[21]

Police officers and troops also faced targeted violence. Robert Allen of *The Hilltop* noted that "there was open hostility to the cops."[22] Officers were attacked at Eighth and H Streets NE Friday afternoon.[23] After someone threw a tear gas canister into a police cruiser, two officers were hospitalized.[24] Reporter Lillian Wiggins was on Fourteenth Street Thursday night when she saw "six policemen . . . holding ground with a group of about fifty hecklers. They were cursing the officers and in general creating a very unpleasant scene." Near Fourteenth and Euclid Streets NW, Wiggins was "caught in the middle of a glass, rock throwing session and had to duck into a D.C. Transit bus for cover to avoid the glass and tear gas." "Young militants" used "guerilla type warfare against the officers," and in response, police "rushed in completely armed with helmets, gas masks and gas guns."[25]

Many working to restore order were not harassed, however, and very few were injured. Firefighter Austin Gibson reported that he "didn't have too much trouble with looters. They were too busy with the stores."[26] Some Black Washingtonians helped the firefighters by holding fire hoses and bringing them coffee and chairs.[27] "Only the teenagers harassed us," said soldier Jack Hyler, "and that really didn't seem to be racial, just against authority." When children threatened the military, Hyler claimed, adults emerged from their homes and "told the kids to go away and leave us alone—that we just had a job to do. The kids dispersed and there was no trouble."[28] The mayor's report on the disorders, co-authored by the police and fire departments, found that "police and fire forces working along the line of 14th Street were subjected to a great deal of verbal abuse and were the targets of some thrown missiles." Despite some harassment, no firefighters were seriously injured. Although "interference to firefighters from civilians was great at [the] start," it decreased once "troops were able to secure [the] fire area."[29]

Restraint and Its Limits

The military followed its preestablished policy created in the wake of the Detroit uprisings and encouraged troops to practice restraint.[30] Federal soldiers were ordered to "assist the civilian law enforcement authorities to restore law and order, and in accomplishing this mission, to do so with the minimum use of force."[31] A memo from General Haines ordered:

> Minimum force, consistent with mission accomplishment, will be used by both military and civilian personnel. Moreover, commanders and their personnel will avoid appearing as an invading, alien force rather than a force whose purpose is to restore order with a minimum loss of life and property and due respect for the great number of citizens whose involvement is purely accidental.

Further, Haines instructed personnel to "be civil; the use of epithets and degrading language will not be tolerated."[32] In one incident when police officers used the barrels of their loaded weapons to move unresisting citizens, Public Safety Director Murphy and Deputy Chief Jerry Wilson stopped the police and ordered them to "request" people to move instead.[33]

Murphy deliberately avoided any scenario that risked the use of police firearms. In several instances on Thursday night and Friday afternoon, he ordered officers to retreat because they were outnumbered. While this tactic was later denounced by many conservatives, Murphy and others defended it as an effective strategy to sidestep the potential escalation of violence. If police did not have enough officers to control a situation, they might resort to excessive force for self-protection. "If I had not withdrawn them," Murphy said in reference to a confrontation between police and citizens in a heavily looted area, "it might have been necessary to discharge their firearms to protect themselves." "Once we start shooting," said another officer, "the other side is liable to start shooting back." When police officers were sufficiently concentrated in an area, the preponderance of force present "discouraged fighting back and subsequent retaliatory violence by police."[34]

The thousands of troops in Washington held unloaded rifles, although they did carry ammunition. Soldiers were not allowed to load their guns unless commanded to do so or under an imminent threat. Troops were banned from using warning shots, and if they did fire a weapon, they had to intend to wound rather than to kill. To reinforce these restrictions, each soldier carried a card that, in part, read:

2. I will BE COURTEOUS in all dealings WITH CIVILIANS to the maximum EXTENT POSSIBLE UNDER EXISTING CIRCUMSTANCES.

3. I will NOT LOAD OR FIRE my weapon EXCEPT WHEN AUTHORIZED by an OFFICER IN PERSON, when authorized IN ADVANCE BY AN OFFICER under certain specific conditions, or WHEN REQUIRED TO SAVE MY LIFE.

4. I will NOT INTENTIONALLY INJURE OR MISTREAT CIVILIANS, including those I am controlling, or those in my custody NOR will I WITHHOLD MEDICAL ATTENTION from anyone who requires it.[35]

As opposed to the 156,391 rounds fired by the military in Detroit, troops fired only fourteen rounds in DC.[36]

The police also were instructed to avoid using their service revolvers when interacting with civilians.[37] Famously, Murphy insisted that he would resign from his position as public safety director before he would order police to shoot people who looted.[38] In one instance, police under fire from a sniper in the woods refrained from "spraying bullets around the area" and instead "tossed in tear gas and moved in to arrest three men."[39] "We didn't shoot and they didn't shoot," reported one police official. "With all the guns that we know the people have out there and with all the guns that we have, I believe a miracle has occurred."[40]

This policy received immediate backlash. Gladys N. Spellman, the white chairman of the board of commissioners in Prince George's County, authorized the police to shoot looters to prevent property damage.[41] Spellman believed that protesters did not come to Prince George's County (which borders DC) because "we displayed force. . . . I made it clear that I did not want a single policeman to stand by if looting began."[42] For his part, Senator Robert Byrd called the White House on Friday, April 5, to say "he wanted to be on record as believing . . . the looters should be shot, if they are adults (but not killed, just shot in the leg); that he feels the time for restraint is ended."[43]

Soldiers and officers did use escalating force to remove people from damaged areas. The mayor's after-action report found that "resistance to the clearing operation was difficult to overcome in view of the buildup of the crowd which involved persons from very young children to very old adults."[44] "We asked people to go home," said Sargent Edward Dera. "If they didn't react immediately, we would walk toward them with our rifles and they usually would move." If people did not move, the troops "warned them we would use tear gas if they didn't. After I warned them again, we put on our masks and I'd throw the gas."[45] From April 4 until the end of the state of emergency on April 15, the police fired eight thousand canisters of tear gas and the military used 5,258 CS grenades (the military's version of tear gas).[46] To keep people out of buildings, troops sometimes threw tear gas into stores because it made it very painful to enter. The chemical irritant could linger for hours in open air and for days or even weeks in buildings. "CS has a strong burning sensation that attacks your eyes, nose, and even your skin. . . . All you want to do is get out so you can breathe," reported a Sixth Calvary officer.[47] "I know what it feels like to have tear gas in your face," recalled Virginia Ali. "It's like you can't open your eyes. It's just burning. . . . It's horrible."[48] One firefighter reported his exposure to tear gas impaired his vision for days.[49]

The policy of restraint did not mean that officers were lenient or unbiased. According to Murphy, police were told to make "all arrests that were humanly possible."[50] The police sometimes took advantage of this power and enforced the law in racist ways. In drafting the curfew regulation, the DC Office of the Corporation Counsel and Mayor Washington did not specify an extensive list of exceptions and instead expected "judicious enforcement" by the police department. While the corporation counsel intended that arrest for violating the curfew to be used only as a "last resort" if someone did not leave when asked, the police "made use of the curfew as a mass arrest device for controlling the civil disorder and charged defendants with curfew wholesale because this was a convenient way of clearing the streets."[51] Many officers were "frank to admit that a black violator was much more likely to be arrested than a white violator."[52] For example, "carloads of homeward-bound, Negro paper handlers from the Washington Post, dressed in their work clothes, were more than once brusquely ordered out of their automobiles, made to lean against the hood of their cars, and frisked." The white journalists dressed in suits, however, were rarely asked to leave their cars if stopped during the curfew.[53]

Some officers expressed racist resentment both on the streets and back at their precincts. As police returned to their stations after completed shifts, they used "racial epithets and [made] strong complaints about the order for restraint that Murphy had given them." Their words suggested that many "still harbored strong resentment toward the Negroes they saw in the streets." The Washington Post reported that some police taunted citizens, calling them "welfare people" and other "thinly veiled racial epithets."[54] Any person who gave "back talk" was likely to be arrested by police officers. In one egregious instance, a Black firefighter was arrested by white police as he wearily rested while walking home from work. Officers said he was "surly" when they talked to him. Eventually, a judge dropped the firefighter's case because he had a reason to be on the streets because he was leaving his job.[55] In another instance, a police officer arrested a man sitting on his own front porch because he reportedly "sassed" the officer. Other officers said that "dress and general appearance" were used to determine who was a "troublemaker." Finally, some law enforcement officials arrested "everything that moved," including people walking their dogs, a man taking out his garbage in front of his house, and even a man rushing across town to take his girlfriend in labor to the hospital.[56]

Some officers and soldiers did threaten violence, despite the policy of restraint. One sergeant, for example, instructed soldiers that "if they give you any bullshit, smash them in the face with the butt of your rifle." After a car passed through a checkpoint without stopping, twenty soldiers surrounded the vehicle and ordered the car's occupants to stand against the car as they searched it. The young Black couple stood with the points of unsheathed bayonets against their backs until the troops let them go.[57] In one instance, a *Washington Post* reporter moved through a crowd to ask what happened as several African Americans were arrested and a white police officer with a gun drawn ordered the citizens to "get out of here. You are going to be shot." Other journalists witnessed officers firing into stores or in pursuit of people with merchandise. Others witnessed police unnecessarily use tear gas.[58]

Additionally, the police were still guided by the same policy on the use of firearms that had been in place since 1954.[59] Under such provisions, police officers shot and killed fifteen-year-old Thomas Williams and twenty-year-old Ernest McIntyre.[60] According to police accounts, Williams raced past Officer David L. Thompkins, who was holding a different person at gunpoint. When Williams ran by, he allegedly hit the officer's revolver, causing it to fire and fatally wound him.[61] Officer Albert Lorraine intentionally shot McIntyre because, according to Lorraine, McIntyre "approached the officer in a threatening manner" with a "shiny object."[62] Lorraine fired one shot immediately and two more as McIntyre ran away. Both Thompkins and Loraine were cleared after a federal grand jury declined to bring charges. Many were outraged that the officers would not be prosecuted and demanded greater police accountability.[63] Both shootings occurred in Anacostia, where officers were not warned to avoid using firearms, unlike in other sections of the city.[64]

Most deaths resulting from the disturbances were the unintentional result of fires. Three people burned to death, two were killed by smoke inhalation, one died after a three-story brick building on H Street collapsed on him, and one man was murdered close to Cardozo Senior High School.[65] In total, thirteen people died during the disturbances.[66]

The city burned, buildings crumbled, and thirteen perished. Many compared DC to a war zone. "You think that you're in a war because the whole city around you is burning," reflected a Black Washingtonian who was a young man during the rebellions. "Sirens are going off everywhere. People are running. You heard things that sound like shots. Some of them were."[67] The destruction reminded a firefighter of pictures of the ongoing war in Vietnam.[68] "I guess it was like how I always imagined Berlin must have looked after World War II," said a twenty-one-year-old private, "Everything was burned, gutted, and crumbling."[69] The *Washington Daily News* reported that "flames leaped to the sky and the helmeted troops cast long, fierce shadows as they marched in the light of the blazes."[70]

Soul Brother and Selective Targeting

Amid the chaos, Ben's Chili Bowl was one of the only establishments permitted to stay open despite the curfew. According to Virginia Ali, Stokely Carmichael got special permission from the police for Ben's to stay open late so that police officers and members of the community working to restore peace would have a place to eat and talk and plan.[71] "He went to the precinct," Ali recalled, "because he said and other officials said we needed some place to meet to strategize to try to see what we could do to calm the violence, and they chose this place."[72] While Ben's was not damaged, it was in the epicenter of the upheaval. One customer, for example, asked to exchange looted bottles of Courvoisier liquor for a cheeseburger. Ali was convinced that Ben's survived because it was well known and respected in the community. "There were all types of rumors like someone said, 'I heard [they're] burning U Street, man I hope they don't touch Ben's.' So we had that kind of neighborhood respect, maybe."[73] The fact that Ben's was open during the height of the upheaval also meant that it was unlikely to be destroyed.

Some business owners opted to guard their businesses to avoid damage. A white man who owned a takeout store on Seventh Street protected his business with a pistol. When a group came by and threatened to burn the place, the owner pulled out his gun and threatened to shoot if they touched anything in his store. The youths ran away.[74] However, relatively few business owners remained to guard their stores and instead closed on Friday afternoon and went home. The curfew made it difficult for many to guard their establishments overnight.

Other business owners adopted different strategies to attempt to avoid theft and arson. Black-owned businesses wrote "soul brother" or "soul sister" in soap on shop windows in hopes racial solidarity would spare their stores.[75] "Somebody came out and said, 'You've got to identify your business as a black business.' So we write a big old [sign saying] 'Soul Brother' across the window," recalled Virginia Ali.[76] Some white-owned businesses wrote "soul brothers and sisters work here" or "Soul Brother Managed" in attempts to use Black employees to save them.[77] Other businesses wrote "Soul" on windows without any credible justification other than protection and were spared. "An Esso pump with 'soul' scrawled on it just doesn't make any sense," commented a *Daily News* columnist.[78] As the *Washington Afro-American* journalist Ruth Jenkins noted, the signs became ubiquitous:

> "Soul brother" signs proclaiming "I'm of the black race. Please don't hurt or damage me." Car lights in broad daylight make the same appeal.... "Soul" scrawled on almost every window that's left. Sometimes, written on the inside, it looks backward from the street. "Soul" in five-foot letters on the glossy doors of a luxury apartment building. "Soul" at the flower shop overshadows the Easter decorations. "Soul" tied to a magnificent tree in a well tended front garden. "Soul" scribbled on Fords and El Dorados alike.[79]

Business owners were right to think that their relationship with the African American community impacted their fate during the disturbances. Although some "Soul Brother" businesses were damaged, certain stores were targeted during the disorders because Black Washingtonians believed they "shortchanged" their community. "Veteran Negro newsmen claim that in many instances rioters and looters spared establishments that were either owned by Negroes, treated Negro employees favorably or were owned by 'White soul brothers,'" noted the *Daily News*.[80] "A few black businesses were destroyed probably by accident but most remained intact," *The Hilltop* reported. "The direction of the fires was unquestionably against white power."[81] A government engineer wrote in his diary that he was told "practically every Safeway store was attacked by mobs because of the higher prices these stores charged for their food in ghetto areas."[82] The white-owned Esso gas station with "soul" written on it survived without damage.[83] Public Safety Director Patrick Murphy believed there were certain unexplainable "instances where some stores were deliberately avoided and others hit."[84] Many people were motivated to lash out against the white businesses they believed hurt their neighborhoods.

By midnight Friday, 6,600 troops roamed the streets of Washington and five thousand more joined them by Saturday morning. At his 1:20 a.m. news conference, Mayor Washington described the city as "quite calm" despite some sporadic looting and untamed fires.[85] The next morning, John Hechinger, a white business owner and chairman of the DC City Council, reported that "troops have quelled the disturbance and the worst is over; [the] City should be able to get back to normal."[86] While the worst was indeed over, Saturday was still chaotic. "Saturday, April 6th, was a story of old fires rekindling as new fires were lit," reported the fire department in its after-action report.[87] Arsonists started 120 fires throughout the day, and "major" looting persisted in scattered locations away from heavy troop concentrations.[88] The Army Command Center dispatched additional troops to Washington throughout the day, and by that evening 13,600 active duty troops and 1,800 National Guard soldiers occupied Washington.[89] Government employees began to clean up and assess the damage. Crews surveyed street conditions, inspected fire damage, and cut off damaged water lines.[90] By 11:00 p.m. on Saturday night, Cyrus Vance, the special Pentagon representative in charge of coordinating the city and federal government's civil disorder response, announced in a televised address that the city, with help from federal troops and the curfew, was "secure."[91]

6

"You Have a City in Flames. . . . And so Some People Will Have to Languish in Jail"

THE ADMINISTRATION OF JUSTICE

ON THE MORNING OF FRIDAY, APRIL 5, A GROUP OF JUDGES MET to determine how to operate the DC Court of General Sessions— the closest equivalent to a state lower court in DC that handled misdemeanor criminal cases—that day. Chief Judge Harold Greene led the meeting of General Sessions judges, several of whom were recent appointees to the court as part of a reform measure to select jurists more sensitive to individual circum- stances and less inclined to automated justice.[1] The judges decided to maintain "business as usual" that day because they incorrectly thought the city would not erupt in chaos again.[2] Judge Greene set up a special assignment court to process the nearly two hundred people arrested Thursday night.

By early afternoon, judges smelled smoke from their chambers, and some witnessed people looting downtown shops from their office windows. Around the courthouse "there was a touch of tear gas in the air and the wail of police-car sirens."[3] Judge Greene ventured out to observe the ongoing damage but retreated after hearing shouts that a crowd was coming up the street throwing rocks and bricks.[4]

Amid this upheaval, the judiciary tackled an enormous task. From Thursday, April 4, to Sunday, April 7, approximately 4,200 people were arrested for looting, rioting, and curfew violation.[5] In those four days, the court filed as many felony and misdemeanor charges as it normally did in six weeks.[6] To handle the crisis, the courts ran nonstop from Friday, April 5, to Monday, April 8. The District Court postponed scheduled criminal cases so that attorneys and judges could help with disorder cases in the Court of General Sessions.[7] Despite the efforts to increase efficiency, the flood of prisoners created confusion and delays as the legal system strained to process all detainees.

Processing this influx of people required a small army of lawyers. Judge Greene hesitated to make a general appeal asking for lawyers' help because he did not want to admit publicly that "the court was in serious trouble."[8] He failed to consult with the Washington Bar Association, DC's Black lawyers' organization, but did approach John E. Powell, the president of the mostly white DC Bar Association. Greene requested that Powell ask lawyers to volunteer as defense attorneys, but Powell refused because he was afraid volunteers would sue the DC Bar Association if they were injured.[9] Seeing no alternative, Greene put out an unattributed call for volunteer lawyers over the radio and television on Friday. More than 250 DC attorneys responded.[10]

The volunteers tasked with representing those arrested sometimes exacerbated problems because many were "uptown lawyers" who dealt primarily with corporate or civil law and were inexperienced with criminal cases.[11] Many "knew nothing about how the Court of General Sessions operated" and "didn't even know where the cellblock was," according to one veteran criminal law attorney. They were left "sitting on their hands for hours without being assigned a defendant."[12]

But the lack of knowledge of some volunteer attorneys was just one issue that delayed processing defendants. By the time Judge Greene instructed judges to maintain "business as usual" Friday morning, the Court of General Sessions was already significantly behind schedule. Completing and keeping track of the forms needed to charge and identify defendants "caused the biggest tie-up in the smooth administration of justice" during the upheaval.[13] Since many police officers who made the arrests went home without completing their paperwork Friday morning, the prosecutors did not have enough information to charge some of the accused.[14] The problem only worsened on Friday and Saturday as the number arrested and the subsequent backlog grew. Those arrested came to court in large groups with little paperwork and usually without the arresting officer so that as many police officers as possible could be on the streets.[15] A single marshal was responsible for matching people who had been arrested with their documents while he also answered phone calls. The U.S. deputy marshal reported Saturday morning that while he had 150 signed complaints and 150 detainees at the courthouse, "none of the complaints matched any of the prisoners."[16] By the afternoon of Saturday, April 6, only twenty-five out of 225 prisoners in the courthouse cellblocks had been formally charged with a crime.[17] Judge Greene recognized that many people were imprisoned for extended periods without charges and "warned the US attorney's office and the police that he [could not] hold people for any substantial period of time without charges."[18]

Suspects could not have a hearing until their paperwork was complete, so those arrested were held for hours or even days in cellblocks not intended for overnight or extended stays.[19] Some arrested on Thursday night were still imprisoned and had still not been charged with a crime on Saturday afternoon because of the "serious delay[s]" preparing documents.[20] That evening, twenty to thirty people were released because they had been detained for over forty-eight hours without being charged. "No trace" or record of their crimes could be found.[21] In one of the most extreme cases, Robert Skelton, an African American postal clerk, was detained for more than four days before he was finally released. He was arrested and charged with looting on Friday, April 5, and he had a hearing the next day. His bond was posted but no one could find him to release him. Skelton was finally found in the DC jail on April 10.[22]

To reduce the paperwork delays and confusion, the courts adopted a less formal method of charging the accused beginning Saturday afternoon. The arresting officer no longer personally swore to the complaint, and officials collected only the bare minimum of information for each charge.[23] The police department shifted schedules to allow officers the time to come in to fill out the required forms and encouraged officers to do paperwork directly after they completed their shifts.[24]

The police and courts also adjusted their approach to curfew violations on Saturday to expedite processing. After Mayor Walter E. Washington imposed the curfew Friday evening, over one thousand people were arrested for violating it that first night.[25] At first, judges held hearings for those accused of violating the curfew and set bail.[26] As the backlog grew, Police Chief John Layton recommended that the curfew violations be considered a different class of offense. Beginning Saturday, the courts processed those accused of violating the curfew who already spent the night in jail under Title 7 of the 1967 DC Omnibus Crime Bill. This specified that people arrested could be released if they were issued a citation requiring a later court appearance. The 2,532 people arrested for violating curfew were then booked at a police precinct, photographed, and held overnight at a jail. The next day, they were driven back to the police precinct, given a citation like a traffic ticket, and released without being arraigned. Judges believed this policy was a middle ground between holding defendants until they appeared before a judge (which normally would not occur until the morning after arrest) and immediate release with a ticket.[27]

As the judiciary adapted to the mayhem and arrests tapered off on Sunday, the courts were able to catch up with processing defendants. By 4:00 p.m. on Sunday, April 7, the courts had reduced the number of detainees from 1,550 to 400. By 12:00 p.m. Tuesday, "virtually all" of those arrested on Monday night and Tuesday morning had been arraigned.[28] In total, 1,675 people appeared before a judge over the weekend.[29]

The U.S. Attorney's Office, Judges, and Bail Policy

When these 1,675 citizens appeared in court, the only significant ruling at the initial hearing was setting bail.[30] Recent legislation established new guidelines for how judges should determine a defendant's bail. Passed by Congress in 1966, the Bail Reform Act specified that judges could only consider a defendant's "likelihood of reappearance for trial" when setting bail. The severity of the crime could only be factored in as it related to the chances the accused would return for trial.[31] The act also mandated that people could be released on personal recognizance instead of monetary bond. This meant that the defendant was released on their promise to return for trial instead of demanding bail in the form of property, cash, or a purchased bond. If the defendant did not reappear, they faced a $500 fine and up to a year in prison. The DC Bail Agency was responsible for gathering information to make a bail recommendation based on "considerations of employment, length of residence, past record and family ties."[32] The Bail Reform Act was intended to prevent individuals from remaining in jail for minor offenses due to their inability to raise money for the bond.[33]

Some, however, thought that this law should be ignored during the rebellions. While the judge processing people accused of disorder-related offenses initially set bail in compliance with the

Bail Reform Act and released most defendants on personal bond, things changed after a Friday evening meeting with U.S. Attorney for the District of Columbia David Bress, Chief Judge Greene, and other judges. The U.S. Attorney's Office encouraged the judges at the DC Court of General Sessions to not only consider if the defendant would return for their trial, but also if they would commit another crime in the uprisings. Bress asked the judges to set monetary bail for those accused of disorder-related crimes because the U.S. Attorney's Office feared the defendants would leave the courtroom to go further participate in the rebellions.[34]

After the conference with Bress, Judge Greene called another meeting with judges working these cases and asked that they set bail at $1,000 for those accused of looting unless a "responsible person" was in court to vouch that the accused would reappear for trial and not return to the upheaval. Greene, either directly or through a clerk, pushed restricted release on each judge handling disorder cases until Sunday, April 7. By then, the city was calm enough that Greene felt the policy was no longer necessary.[35] Contrary to the rumors that initiated this policy on Friday, only one person was rearrested that day, and he was rearrested on the court steps for scuffling with a police officer. In total, out of the 6,230 adults arrested during the upheaval, only six were rearrested for serious crimes that contributed to property damage.[36]

Most judges were willing to deviate from the Bail Reform Act and were more willing than normal to ignore the DC Bail Agency's recommendations. While judges normally adhered to the agency's recommendations 90 percent of the time, during the uprisings the court only followed the agency's suggestion in 60 percent of cases. The court released 25 to 30 percent fewer defendants who were recommended for release on personal recognizance than it usually did.[37] Judges adopted a "loose" standard of $1,000 bonds for felony cases, and they frequently used the "emergency situation" as justification.[38] On Friday evening, a judge set monetary bond in thirteen out of fifteen cases because it was the "unanimous view of all the judges" that "nobody involved in looting is to be released on their personal bond."[39] While setting bail, another judge remarked, "You have a city in flames and there are certain facts you deal with. You deal with the facts in the order of their priority and so some people will have to languish in jail."[40]

Judge DeWitt S. Hyde made the policy of restricted release the most explicit on Saturday, April 7, to allow for the possibility of an appeal. "Because of the emergency situation in the city," Hyde proclaimed, "of riots and widespread arson, and because of the fact that it has been reported to us that many people released on bond when they were in trouble originally, have started to return to the streets and engage in the same activities, and because of the representations made by the United States Attorney for the district of Columbia, this Court feels obliged to set bond in this case. Bond will be set at one thousand dollars."[41,42]

Ignoring the Bail Reform Act caused significant hardships because it was consistently difficult for defendants to make bail. Nearly 50 percent of those denied personal bond spent three or more days in jail before they were able to obtain bail or had their case reevaluated.[43]

To post bail, the court required cash or a bank-certified check. Banks were closed from Friday afternoon until Monday morning, so if the defendant or their loved ones did not have cash to pay the bond, they could not go to a bank to retrieve the cash or certify a check.[44] Further, many of the accused struggled to obtain a bond because they had no prior record and were thus unknown to bondsmen. Bondsmen were generally unwilling to write bonds to unknown people, so ironically it was easier to get a bond as a "previous customer" with a prior record than as a first-time offender.[45] Additionally, the phone lines were jammed, so verifying the reliability of the defendant was challenging. Because volunteer lawyers were unfamiliar with their clients, they could not vouch for the "strong community ties" used to establish accountability when writing a bond. Finally, some prisoners and their family members were so confused with bond procedure that they were duped by opportunistic "bondsmen" who falsely claimed they would post bond in exchange for cash sums. In one instance, a group of women chased a man around the court building who had posed as a bondsman and tricked them out of their money.[46]

Making matters worse, few bondsmen were at the courthouse to write bonds despite the great need. Some fled the city in fear while a few quickly met their capacity to fulfill bonds and left the courthouse. Others never arrived because they reportedly thought "the people who were responsible for burning and looting should be put in jail and kept there."[47] Mickey Lewis of the Stuyvesant Insurance Co. was the only Black bondsman in DC and wrote ninety-one out of the 148 bonds in civil disorder cases. Despite the challenges described above, Lewis was willing to work diligently to verify the information of first-time offenders. Only one out of the ninety-one people he wrote bonds for failed to show up in court.[48]

As the judges realized that the disorders were quieting down and many defendants had been in jail for days, they started granting more releases.[49] Judge Greene met with the judges Monday morning, and they decided to "resume full use of the Bail Reform Act."[50] The courts revisited prisoner's bail on Monday, April 8, and many judges granted personal bond upon review.[51]

The policy of restricted release and the challenges of making bail resulted in extended periods of incarceration for many Washingtonians. Of the 604 people assigned monetary bail, only 155 were released from the courthouse by posting cash or a surety bond through a bondsman. The remaining 449 defendants were remanded to jail.[52] On April 10, 172 people were still imprisoned because they could not make bail. By April 25, sixty-seven were still behind bars and on July 26—nearly three months after their arrest—sixteen defendants were still imprisoned. One man was still incarcerated three months later because he could not raise $50; another remained in jail over a $100 bail. Overall, 15.7 percent of those remanded to jail were released the same day they were committed, 19.7 percent spent one day in jail, 15.2 percent spent two days in jail, 11.4 percent spent three days in jail, 24.1 percent spent four to ten days in jail, and 12 percent spent more than ten days in jail.[53]

Criticism and Praise of the Administration of Justice

A few lawyers and organizations challenged the court's actions during the upheaval. The Howard Law Alumni Association of Greater Washington issued a resolution on April 8 in "total disapproval" of the suspension of the Bail Reform Act.[54] The same day, the American Civil Liberties Union filed a lawsuit claiming the administration of justice in DC came to a "virtual standstill" during the disorders. The ACLU alleged that judges suspended the Bail Reform Act and the city wrongfully held curfew violators overnight.[55] The night of April 5, the suit asserted, "curfew violators were transported to Occoquan, Va., in wholesale lots, held overnight, and released the following day with citations." Instead, prisoners should have been "ticketed" at police precincts and immediately released. The ACLU believed this was a "blanket imposition of preventative detention, which at present is wholly unauthorized by law."[56]

The chief judge of the District Court, Edward M. Curran, dismissed the ACLU suit the same day it was filed. General Sessions judges and the DC Bar Association were incensed at the criticism.

At a public courthouse event, General Sessions Chief Judge Harold H. Greene refused to discuss the suit with reporters and stated that the ACLU attorneys who filed the suit were no longer his friends. Greene and other judges and lawyers working the cases believed they took the necessary measures to process the cases as quickly as possible and prevent further violence.[57]

The analysts tasked with evaluating DC's administration of justice during the disorders concluded that the court's actions were justified. The District of Columbia Committee on the Administration of Justice Under Emergency Conditions, a task force established by Mayor Washington to examine the performance of the courts during the uprisings, concluded that restricted release "was neither unreasonable nor unlawful" and the Bail Reform Act was "sufficiently flexible" to justify the judges' policy during the upheaval. While the report noted that some judges set bail regardless of "facts relevant to the charge," the Committee on the Administration of Justice applauded the "imaginative way" judges adjusted the Bail Reform Act and recommended modifying the act to allow consideration of a defendant committing a "serious crime" while waiting for trial.[58]

William Dobrovir, a white attorney and director of the Emergency Justice Project Task Force, wrote a report entitled *Justice in a Time of Crisis* that analyzed the administration of justice during the rebellions. Dobrovir criticized the courts because some defendants were detained too long and were assigned bail "based on considerations other than the likelihood that riot defendants would return to jail," and because some judges used bail as "a form of punishment."[59] Despite these critiques, Dobrovir asserted the courts did a "superb" job and concluded "the pressures and difficulties facing these agencies and the men and women in them would have excused deviations from the ideal of justice far greater than those that may have occurred."[60] Overall, most legal analysts agreed that it was justifiable for judges to "find a way of detaining arsonists and snipers until order is restored, regardless of what the statutes say" because this constituted "self-defense action on the part of a city in great peril."[61]

The District of Columbia judiciary *was* better than other cities during the nationwide April disorders. In Baltimore in 1968, for example, curfew violators were "tried, convicted, and sentenced to terms of up to thirty days in jail within a few hours after their arrest."[62] DC's bail policy was also much more flexible than that of other cities. In Chicago in April 1968, monetary bond was set in nearly every case with a $5,000 minimum for looting and as high as $100,000. In Detroit in 1967, 74 percent of bonds were greater than $5,000. During the Watts rebellion, bond was set at a minimum of $3,000. In DC, however, judges were flexible enough that 43 percent of people were released on nonfinancial bond. Even when financial bond was set, 87 percent of the bonds were $1,000 or less, and many judges allowed defendants to post just a percentage of that sum to be released.[63] Further, a judge was even removed from the bench because he was "gaveling through" defendants without regard to the details of the case.[64]

But the willingness of judges to depart from the Bail Reform Act and ignore the DC Bail Agency's recommendations sacrificed the rights of the accused in the face of a rumored threat to public safety. This decision had major consequences for some Black Washingtonians. They spent days, weeks, and even months incarcerated without being convicted of a crime simply because they were unable to pay their bail.[65]

Additionally, the very process of determining if someone met the qualifications for personal bond was often based on racist assumptions. Judges sometimes decided if someone was a "responsible" person or a flight risk based on racially biased judgments when setting bail. "Some judges believe that they could tell intuitively whether or not a person was dangerous," wrote Dobrovir. "One judge likened the procedure to playing a violin. One judge referred to the 'dark glasses, green pants,' the 'fourteenth street crowd.' Another judge relied on the defendant's attitude, whether he seemed to show remorse."[66] Many Black lawyers felt that some judges "openly display[ed] hostility toward Negro defendants and their attorneys, by setting 'astronomically high bonds.'"[67] Structurally, fifteen of the eighteen judges handling the disorder cases were white. Although Chief Prosecutor Joel D. Blackwell was African American, almost his entire staff was white. Nearly all defendants were Black, and most lawyers representing defendants were white volunteer lawyers. As Black Washingtonians rebelled across the city against white racism and power, those arrested faced a white criminal justice system: "It turned out that most proceedings during the hectic riot period involved black defendants, prosecuted by white men and defended by white men who were appointed by white judges."[68]

7

"Calm and Compassionate Style"
COMMUNITY AID AND RESTORING NORMALCY

THIS WAS A VERY DIFFERENT WEEKEND THAN WHAT THE CITY had planned. Saturday was supposed to be the first day of the annual Cherry Blossom Festival—the peak of DC's annual tourism season that showcased the thousands of beautiful flowering Japanese trees given to DC by the Tokyo mayor in 1912. As many worried about the capital's safety, the city canceled the festival, and many tourists abandoned their reservations. The Washington Senators postponed their season opener baseball game. Journalists noted the contrast between the programed merriment and the reality of a city filled with smoke and fear. "The cherry blossoms were falling. One very long week ago they bloomed around the Tidal Basin and the tourists came to see them, but yesterday the tourists had gone from the still-smoldering city and the blossoms were fading fast," mourned David Holmberg of the *Washington Daily News*.[1] The *Washington Evening Star* observed that "a thin haze still hung over the Capital, suspended like a fog over the cherry blossoms and the parks which today were to have been filled with people celebrating the Cherry Blossom Festival."[2]

Tourists and curious suburbanites instead flocked to observe the damage. The streets were filled with "thousands of white high school and college-age students, knots of Negro youths, young off-duty soldiers and sailors, couples with their children, out in

the car for a bizarre Saturday jaunt."³ On Sunday, "streams of
cars from far Northeast clogged [Benning] road, their occupants
rubber-necking the damage."⁴ Some paid cabdrivers to take them
on tours of the burnt-out "ghetto."⁵ Sightseers snapped photos of
soldiers with machine guns guarding the Capitol.⁶ Business owners also journeyed downtown to check on their stores and were
often devastated by the scene. "I suppose I shouldn't say this, but
it was very hard to stop crying on Saturday," said business owner
Abraham Zevin. Irving Abraham, who owned a store on Seventh
Street NW, remarked, "We were stunned. We just walked back
and forth, back and forth, looking at it. It was just horrible."⁷

Some of the city's residents faced uncertainty about how they
could obtain food to eat and reliable information to help them
understand what was happening. Since many businesses were so
damaged they had to close, nearly five thousand people were displaced from their jobs. Two thousand people were left homeless.⁸
To serve these needs, many Washingtonians united and an ad hoc
organization of community groups and citizens provided vital
services to the city's people. The Department of Public Welfare
searched for housing for those who lost their homes in the flames.
Churches opened their doors so that those who were displaced
could sleep in church pews.⁹ Local organizations also mobilized
to help people whose jobs were destroyed find new employment.
WETA, the local public television station, broadcast an employment services program coordinated by groups including the
Washington Board of Trade and Pride, Inc. The United Planning
Organization and the U.S. Employment Service set up a jobs center on U Street. On Sunday, April 7, over fourteen hundred people
went to a job training center on Bladensburg Road NE.¹⁰

Many living in the most affected neighborhoods faced real difficulties accessing basic necessities in the aftermath of the uprisings.
Food stores in DC relied on deliveries, but many truck drivers did

not want to maneuver into the chaotic and damaged areas. Even if drivers were willing to make deliveries, police barricades made some stores unreachable.[11] Further, since so many grocery stores and pharmacies were closed or destroyed, it was much harder to purchase food and get medicine. The Food and Drug Sanitation Division of the DC Department of Health—which was responsible for inspecting restaurants and other businesses to ensure they met health and safety standards—surveyed 527 grocery stores and drugstores and found that 129 were out of business because they were "either burned out completely, are so badly damaged that they will be out of business until completely renovated and reequipped, or had gone out of business before the disturbance." Thirty-nine were temporarily closed because their stock was too damaged by smoke and tear gas to be sold, eighty-three were closed despite being unharmed, and ninety-seven stores were barricaded so that investigators could not determine the level of damage. With 348 out of 527 grocery stores and drugstores closed, many residents struggled to access food.[12] In Anacostia, some people had to walk over a mile and a half just to purchase a gallon of milk.[13]

The ad hoc assembly of volunteers, community groups, private businesses, and government departments rose up to anticipate and meet the community's need, organizing to feed thousands of hungry Washingtonians. On Saturday alone, two days after the uprisings began, over fifty churches opened their doors to provide food, shelter, and medical treatment. Churches also requested donations of the supplies most needed: bread, milk, and baby food.[14] Many in the surrounding suburbs heeded the call and sent food and other supplies.[15] The U.S. Agriculture Department donated 264,000 pounds of food and distributed seventy thousand pounds of it by Monday.[16] Giant and Safeway grocery stores contributed loaves of bread and half gallons of milk. The Department of Public Welfare worked with the Urban Coalition to set up thirty-five distribution locations to deliver the food to residents.[17] Pride, Inc., the government-funded program co-founded by Marion Barry to provide Black youths with jobs, served food at its headquarters.[18] Howard University students operated a twenty-four-hour emergency relief center from April 5 to 17 and provided food, clothing, and shelter to DC residents. "It shows that black people could organize for the benefit of their brothers and sisters of the community," said Howard volunteer Pearl Stewart.[19] Because it was hard to refrigerate donated food, many centers assembled and distributed nonperishable peanut butter and jelly sandwiches.[20]

Today, we often refer to efforts like this as mutual aid: a voluntary exchange of services and resources for mutual benefit, often with the intent of creating social change. Mutual aid participants typically work collaboratively to figure out ways to meet their community's needs, like food and shelter, while challenging the system that created the need for such aid. Such efforts surged in the spring and summer of 2020 in response to the COVID-19 pandemic and nationwide racial justice protests after a police officer murdered a Black man named George Floyd in Minneapolis, Minnesota.[21]

Hospitals treated the 1,056 people who came through DC emergency rooms with rebellion-related injuries.[22] Few of these injuries were serious, and only eighty-three people were admitted to hospitals from April 5 to 8. Doctors were generally able to handle the considerable number of patients because few people came in for their scheduled appointments due to the chaos and curfew.[23] Medical personnel emphasized treating patients equally even if their injuries were from criminal activity. "District General . . . had calm and compassionate style. . . . Intravenous drips found their way as if by magic into those with shotgun wounds, and the cuts of chronic alcoholics—mostly white and a favorite target of young hoodlums—were efficiently stitched." But even hospitals were not immune from damage. Someone started four small fires in the Children's Building of the DC General Hospital on April 7. All were controlled, and the arsonist was never found.

Medical workers, too, faced signicant obstacles. After bricks shattered ambulance windows, medics broke "the rest of the windows and [kept] on going."[24] Medical workers could not always obtain special passes to be exempted from the curfew, and this occasionally caused personnel shortages. Medical supply deliveries were sometimes delayed because of traffic and the general difficulty of transporting goods amid the tumult.[25] For those treated and in need of medication, it was difficult to fill prescriptions because most pharmacies were damaged or closed.[26]

Volunteers also stepped up to help at the courthouse. Processing the thousands of people arrested in connection to the civil disorders necessitated many attorneys. Judge Harold Greene sent out an unattributed call for volunteer lawyers over the radio and television on Friday, and more than 250 DC attorneys showed up to help.[27] Many of these volunteers were "uptown lawyers" who primarily dealt with corporate or civil law and were inexperienced with criminal cases.[28] To familiarize the attorneys with court proceedings, David McCarthy, dean of the Georgetown University Law Center, organized a briefing course on Saturday morning.[29]

Hundreds of those arrested spent at least one night in jail, so many Washingtonians awoke that weekend to find their loved ones had never returned home. The lack of a central booking system made it difficult to figure out where prisoners were.[30] "Wives visited precinct stations, to be told that there was no record of their husbands' arrests. They would be sent back to the court where, once again, there was no information."[31]

To reduce the confusion, government lawyers created a central information system.[32] Three attorneys set up a central information center in the Court of General Sessions. The center was staffed by over fifty volunteer lawyers, clergy, and Howard University law and divinity students who worked to learn the whereabouts of arrested persons, answer questions about court procedures, and "to expedite the processing of criminal cases by identifying and attempting to overcome delays or obstruction in the administration of justice."[33] From its establishment on April 6 to its end on April 9, the center answered more than a thousand inquires.[34]

Rufus "Catfish" Mayfield, a young Black activist who previously served as the chairman of Pride, Inc., helped identify and secure the release of forty-four detainees who remained in jail the morning of April 7. The individuals had refused to identify themselves after giving false names when arrested. Mayfield agreed to obtain the names of these prisoners after a judge promised to release most of the people into Mayfield's custody on personal bond.[35]

City officials and volunteers also operated hotlines to provide citizens with vital information and calm panic. Set up by the mayor's office, the Urban League and Citizens' Information Service operated a twenty-four-hour hotline staffed by seventy-five to a hundred volunteers who answered the public's questions. Over that weekend, an average of sixteen people per minute called the service. By 2:00 a.m. Saturday morning, the hotlines had received 650 calls; 90 percent rang to offer "personal services, food, clothing, shelter, medical and legal service." Two thousand eight hundred people had called the hotline by late Saturday night, but instead of donating goods and services, 90 percent of callers requested food, shelter, or information.[36] Howard Jones, the project operator, estimated that 60 to 70 percent of calls came from suburbanites who were concerned about their welfare. Many rang to investigate the veracity of swirling rumors which earned the hotline the nickname of "the rumor clinic." "Every Tom, Dick, and Harvey was calling up and wanting to know information about how many fires are we having, what is causing this," noted the fire chief.[37]

Public Safety Director Murphy felt that such rumors were "one of the worst parts of this. We've heard them all from knocking down the [Washington] Monument to diverting the Potomac [River.]"[38]

Some Washingtonians worked to prevent further disorder in the city. The NAACP sent vehicles with speakers attached to Northwest and Northeast DC and begged for calm.[39] On Friday along Fourteenth Street, three Black men drove around and shouted at people to go home.[40] On Seventh Street, an unidentified Black man urged crowds to disperse: "It ain't worth dying for. If you love Martin Luther King and all he stood for, please go back. At least let him get in the ground."[41] Singer James Brown traveled to DC at his own expense and pleaded: "Don't terrorize, organize. Don't burn. Give the kids a chance to learn."[42] "I know how everybody feels," he sympathized. "I feel the same way. But you can't do anything by blowing up, burning up, stealing, and looting. Please go off the streets. From one brother to another, go home."[43] Mayor Walter E. Washington delivered televised addresses detailing how the city was responding to the upheaval every night at eleven so that citizens "could kind of go to sleep and feel that somebody is looking after them. They knew how to assess the situation."[44] Washington handled the crisis with restraint and competence.

News programs adapted their broadcasts to avoid worsening the destruction. Most stations avoided using the word "riot," as the Kerner Commission found some African Americans considered the term inflammatory. Camera operators frequently did not use any additional lighting because the bright lights had often angered protestors in previous uprisings. Radio stations aired frequent "calming statements" encouraging people to stay off the streets during the upheaval. WOL radio station's Dick Lillard refused to broadcast news related to the rebellions. He especially avoided naming "specific locations of trouble. It just encourages people to go there."[45]

By Saturday evening, much of the city was empty as the curfew went into effect at 4:00 p.m.[46] "Eight o'clock at night seemed like four o'clock in the morning because nobody was on the street," said a police officer on duty during the disturbances.[47] By five o'clock, the main streets were "nearly deserted" with only police officers and troops visible.[48] "An eerie atmosphere dominated the well-lit broad streets of downtown Washington, with its modern office buildings, in a silence broken only by the frequent wails of police, fire, and ambulance sirens," described *The Hilltop*.[49] Contrasted with the usual bustle of a Saturday night, "The neon lights never went on. The go-go-girls did not dance."[50] Most of DC stayed home.

Everyday Life Resumes

The capital was tranquil enough on Sunday that many observed their rituals despite the rubble and the troops. Many donned their Sunday best and trekked past debris to go to church that Palm Sunday.[51] "People in Easter finery mince around the rubbish that has spilled from a disemboweled building, the palm fronds in their hands striking a crashing note of dissonance," remarked a *Washington Daily News* reporter. To others, the usual Sunday joy was absent. "It's the most incongruous sight imaginable," observed the *Washington Afro-American*'s Ruth Jenkins,

> A sunny Saturday morning at 14th And U Sts. NW Washington and no Eastertide "business as usual." No bright-eyed children. No cute frilly dresses. No beribboned bonnets. No soft downy bunnies. No colorful jelly beans. No chocolate Easter eggs. But troopers, armed to the teeth, at each street crossing. Drab colored uniforms, rifles and stern looks.[52]

Those who wanted to survey the damage once again created traffic jams as "the city came to look at black Washington spending Palm Sunday at the point of a bayonet."[53] "Sportily dressed golfers" teed off at the Langston Golf Course, close to some of the worst damage in Anacostia.[54] Soldiers who had bivouacked there woke up and left to patrol DC's streets.[55] They smoked cigarettes and drank sodas as they rode in armored trucks to go to their stations, occasionally "lean[ing] over and look[ing] out into the blue skies of Palm Sunday in Washington."[56] The Basilica of the Shrine of the Immaculate Conception in Northeast DC hosted a memorial service for King which over four thousand white and Black Washingtonians attended.[57] "His Palm Sunday was four years ago. . . . His Good Friday three days ago in Memphis," preached the minister. "When will his Easter be?"[58]

The number of fires decreased each hour on Sunday, and firefighters were mostly dispatched to tame the smoke and flames from fires started previously that weekend.[59] The police department considered Sunday to be mostly calm.[60] After the weekend was over, "the key word on the lips of weary city and Federal officials was 'rebuild.'" The Redevelopment Land Agency announced its plans to estimate citywide losses and began knocking down damaged buildings along H Street NE to prevent walls from toppling over unexpectantly. On Monday, April 8, government employees went back to work, although nonessential workers were dismissed an hour and a half early. Schools were in session but also let out early at 1:30 p.m.[61] Teachers encouraged elementary students to discuss and draw their experiences during the upheaval because they had a "great need to talk." "They are using much stronger colors than usual," one teacher noticed. A school principal reported that her school was "much quieter than normal" and attendance was half the usual level."[62] While private businesses were encouraged to open, they closed at 4:00 p.m. to observe the curfew.[63] Some retailers reported increased requests for clothing alterations, possibly for clothing hastily taken from area shops.[64]

Troops continued to aid civilian forces and intermingled with the public. Many helped clean up debris in the streets and in damaged buildings.[65] On Monday, April 9, soldiers performed a concert for students at Spingarn High School in Northeast DC. The forces were armed as they played for the laughing children. Troops stayed at Dunbar, McKinley, Roosevelt, and Spingarn high schools as well as a few junior high schools. Army helicopters took off from school parking lots, military trucks lined school playgrounds, and "in the schools' basement, which is being used as a dormitory, at least a few paratroopers slept through the racket of children, music, and aircraft."[66]

Many schools and organizations in DC were eager to host and entertain the occupying soldiers. By Monday, the troops were "having a ball, they had five or six affairs planned for them around the schools, and one at the Interdepartmental Auditorium, one at the Armory. . . . These guys were being paraded around and feted and partied."[67] The police, meanwhile, were still "battling things out on the front line, doing most of the work, [working] overtime 12 to 14 hours, and getting no entertainment." Mayor Washington perceived this as a "morale problem that was of some substance" and intervened on Monday, April 8, to "have all the parties stopped and all of the activities, except those that involved tickets to the theater, [and] the ball game."[68]

Tuesday, April 9, was the last day that leaders were seriously concerned about additional instances of mass violence. Rumors swirled that Black militants planned a revolt to coincide with King's funeral in Atlanta, Georgia. The FBI received reports that people were storing guns in the Dunbar Hotel in Shaw and would use them that Tuesday.[69] One agent believed radicals planned to "take the lid off" Tuesday night.[70] In the face of such rumors, the mayor and Washington Board of Trade urged businesses to close for King's funeral.[71]

Many stores ran newspaper ads informing people they would be closed on Tuesday. A&P food stores, Giant, Safeway, the Woodward and Lothrop department store, and a Chevrolet dealership ran ads in the *Washington Daily News* and the *Washington Star* announcing they would be closed "in honor" and "In Memoriam" of King.[72] Some businesses did not say they would be closed but simply publicized their "tributes" to King. An ad for the auto supply shop Pep Boys in the *Washington Post*, for example, simply read "IN MEMORIAM The Reverend Dr. Martin Luther King Jr. 1928–1968."[73] While some companies included praise for King, few mentioned any specifics about King's cause or contributions to American society. For example, an ad for the men's clothing store Lewis & Thos. Saltz proclaimed, "We mourn the passing of a great leader / a great American / Dr. Martin Luther King."[74] "Raleighs joins the world in paying tribute to the memory of a great American Dr. Martin Luther King Jr.," read an ad for the clothing store Raleighs.[75] New York Life Insurance reduced King's message to "reason" and "non-violence": "Dr. Martin Luther King Jr. lived and died in the cause of reason. He was a man of non-violence and his cause was just. Dr. King's memory will surely live on in the hearts of men of good will everywhere."[76] Such ads were transparent attempts to appear sympathetic to African Americans' grief to avoid further destruction.

Some businesses only closed downtown stores in potential danger "in honor" of King but opened suburban stores. Despite grocer A&P's ad declaring that it would close "in solemn tribute" to King, the company's stores only closed from 10:30 a.m. to noon in the suburbs. All banks closed in the District, but representatives told reporters they were undecided if they would close in the surrounding suburbs.[77]

The day of King's funeral did not erupt in violence, and by
Wednesday many aspects of normal life returned. The *Eve-*
ning Star's top story on Wednesday covered the war in Vietnam
instead of the uprisings.[78] Cyrus Vance, who was coordinating the
city and federal government's civil disorder response, departed
Washington. The White House resumed giving tours. The Washington Senators baseball team played their twice-postponed season opener, and Vice President Hubert Humphrey threw the first
pitch. The city also relaxed its liquor restrictions on Wednesday,
permitting the 32,000 people attending the baseball game "to sol-
ace themselves with beer as the Senators dropped the year's first
game 2 to 0."[79] The informational hotlines received several hundred phone calls asking "about where one could get a drink."[80]
Residents could stay out until 10:00 p.m. while firearms and flam-
mables were still banned.[81]

Over the next several days, the city gradually further reduced its
restrictions. On Thursday, April 11, the curfew ran from 12:00 a.m.
to 4:00 a.m., and alcohol sales were permitted until 11:00 p.m.
The next day, April 12, Mayor Washington abolished the curfew
and alcohol could be sold until midnight. Washington also asked
President Johnson to gradually remove troops, and Public Safety
Director Patrick Murphy, Police Chief John Layton, and General
Ralph E. Haines coordinated a withdrawal plan. On the same day,
the Maryland suburbs lifted its ban on the sale of firearms and gun
stores were swamped with customers.[82] On April 13, troops began
to depart DC. The next day, officials completely lifted the restrictions on alcohol sales. Finally, on April 15, the city officially ended
the state of emergency and residents could once again purchase
gas, guns, and ammunition. The twelve days of federal military
occupation in DC officially ended on April 16 at 12:00 p.m.[83] With
order restored, DC plunged headfirst into its quest to understand
why the upheaval happened and how to rebuild the city.

8

"A Vacuum and an Opportunity"

CREATING A FRAMEWORK FOR RECONSTRUCTION

"WASHINGTON NOW HAS THE OPPORTUNITY TO REBUILD POLITI-
cally, socially, as well as physically," insisted Rev. Channing E. Phillips, the chairman of the local Kennedy for President campaign
and member of the Black United Front. "The Administration-
shelved Kerner Commission Report on Civil Disorders documented all too painfully that the American consensus, contrary
to American ideals, is racist," Phillips remarked. He further
maintained that "the people in whose neighborhoods it will take
place" should plan and execute the rebuilding efforts in Washington. "The day will not permit back-slapping business-as-usual but
demands creative leadership from a representative D.C. Central
Committee. Senator [Robert F.] Kennedy has called it 'participa-
tory democracy.' We mean to have it in the District of Columbia."[1]

Phillip's statement embodied many Washingtonians' response
to the uprisings. Citizens embraced the task of rebuilding with
hope and seized it as an opportunity to create a more just society
with a politically empowered populace. Residents of the affected
neighborhoods insisted they should have a deciding role in the
planning and physical reconstruction of the city. "Business as
usual" was near-universally denounced by DC officials and citizens alike. While not everyone tied these goals as explicitly to
liberal reports such as the Kerner Commission's or politicians

like Robert F. Kennedy, the blueprint for reconstruction centered on the idea that the government could help create a more equal society.

Others, however, chose to condemn and abandon the capital in the aftermath. While attending a soccer match at the DC Stadium (later named Robert F. Kennedy Memorial Stadium) with his Boy Scout troop, Mary E. Briggs's son was mugged and beaten by a group of African American boys. A resident of suburban Silver Spring, Maryland, Briggs was so angry she refused to return to the city or to care about its future:

> These young hoods that beat up on the good kids of society are nothing more than animals and you have absolutely seen me and mine in Washington for the last time. Washington could burn to the ground, and I'm going to be just like Nero, I'm going to sit back and watch it and think good ridence [sic]. Come "Hell or high water," I have had it with President Johnson's so called fair city and National Capital. . . . If suburban wives and mothers cannot be assured of safety and protection when they bring their families into the city, then perhaps it is time to warn all the suburban areas that the streets of Washington are not safe.[2]

Many Americans shared Briggs's anger at high crime rates, her rejection of President Lyndon Johnson's social programs, and her backlash to Black demands for equal rights. Yet the post-disorder concerns and politics of white, suburban, middle-class Americans like Mary Briggs have received much more analysis than those of urban African Americans like Channing Phillips.[3] These narratives frame the 1968 civil disturbances as the "nail in the coffin" of Johnson's Great Society agenda and the idea that the government should fund widespread programs to combat economic and racial inequality. According to historian Michael Flamm, by 1968 "both conservatives and radicals were united and vocal in their condemnation of the Great Society and the 'false expectations' it had supposedly bred."[4] Richard Nixon used law and order as a key campaign issue, and his election signaled the end of "liberal ascendancy in national politics."[5] This narrative of law and order politics, the death of big government social programs, and the growth of the carceral state is succinctly summarized by journalist and author Clay Risen in the introduction to his book *A Nation on Fire*:

> The 1968 riots provided an entrée for conservatives to finally, fully assert law and order as a national political issue. Something that had been brewing for decades at the local level . . . became the single most important domestic concern in the 1968 presidential race. . . . Whereas politicians beforehand had often portrayed the ghetto as something to integrate into the rest of society, the riots gave impetus to a new domestic militarism that saw the ghetto as an alien territory within American cities, a cancer that had to be isolated from the rest of the body public.[6]

Examining the local response to the 1968 civil disorders in Washington supports much of this account. Suburbanites avoided the city, Washingtonians feared the high crime rates, local groups advocated a "return" to law and order, and President Nixon made DC the focal point of his anticrime agenda.

Yet there is more to the story. Many African American Washingtonians did not abandon the city; they poured themselves into the efforts to rebuild it. If the Johnson administration deemphasized community participation following urban unrest, DC embraced it at an unprecedented level. As the federal government urged "law and order," the DC City Council passed legislation to limit police power and improve community-police relations. Using the ideals, programs, and financing generated by Johnson's Great Society, Washingtonians sought to rebuild the city and address the root causes of the rebellions.

In his book *Neighborhood Rebels: Black Power at the Local Level*, historian Peniel E. Joseph criticizes historical narratives that depict the late 1960s as a "period of decline, white flight, [and] urban alienation." Too often, Joseph argues, Black Power is "seen as triggering the demise of the civil rights era, dooming more promising and effective movements for social justice, and abandoning grassroots community organization in favor of jaw-dropping polemics, galloping sexism, and crude appeals to urban violence and mayhem." Recent scholarship, however, suggests that Black Power advocates often did not abandon community organizing and instead coalesced "around concrete objectives at the neighborhood level." Black Power groups vowed "to take control of the democratic institutions that shaped black life in urban cities and rural town across America." "Civil rights and Black Power, far from being mutually exclusive," Joseph contends, "paralleled and intersected with one another."[7]

The response of the people and government of Washington, DC, to the uprisings adds to the history of liberal-radical cooperation. Moderate civil rights leaders and militant Black Power advocates shared many objectives and often collaborated with each other on efforts to rebuild Washington. African American radicals sought to wield the local government to enact their agendas. In response, the DC City Council often incorporated the demands of Black militants into the government's proposals to rebuild Washington. These ambitious plans were ultimately limited by the federal government's enthusiasm for "law and order" and its waning support for citizen participation programs.

The City Council's Community Hearings

"Washington is a great city, the capital of a great Nation," DC Mayor Walter E. Washington said as he testified to a Senate sub-committee. Although the "recent civil disturbances" accentuated the District's problems, "now, the citizens of Washington . . . have an opportunity to rebuild our community with vision and imagination. . . . The time has arrived to stop looking backward so that we can create the kind of city we all want."[8] Washingtonians, however, did not always agree on what kind of city they wanted, and many activists worried that the rebuilding plans would not meet their demands. Marion Barry articulated this concern at a congressional hearing in May 1968. After describing many of the long-standing social issues in Washington, Barry remarked that "because of the recent rebellions in Washington, much of the area that spawned these problems has been destroyed. This has both created a vacuum and an opportunity." Something would be done to reconstruct damaged neighborhoods, but no one knew "what and how and by whom. More importantly, will what is done correct the basic situation that created . . . the rebellions?"[9]

Many Black Washingtonians supported the uprising and believed it would lead to "social change." According to a report conducted by the U.S. Senate that surveyed Black Washingtonians in the "ghetto," "nearly half its youth residents believed riots served a useful purpose."[10] In an interview, one student said he didn't participate but said he was "glad it happened. Now . . . I feel that Congress will get up off their backs and start reading and listening and start passing some of those bills that have been sent up to them. Congress should get up off some of their money." One

Black woman expressed her hope that after the upheaval Congress would act so "our people can have the type of things that they actually need and want so they won't have to do this type of thing." A middle-class Black woman putting her son through university did not participate because "we middle class Negroes do not express ourselves in the same manner." Nonetheless, she was hopeful: "It took Dr. King's death to bring what had to happen. We've moved ahead—probably 20 years—because of this." "There's a lot of suffering that's taking place and it's unfortunate that good has to come out of violence," said a Black priest. "But this is the only way that is going to bring about change."[11]

To determine how to rebuild Washington and bring about this change, the DC City Council held four public hearings in late April 1968. The council invited "all citizens and organizations in the community to express their views and make recommendations on the rebuilding of the damaged areas."[12] Roughly fifteen hundred people attended the hearings and nearly one hundred testified.[13] The speakers represented a diverse political spectrum of Washingtonians: burned-out business owners who sought compensation, citizens who wanted a more responsive government, established political leaders who called for home rule, and representatives of white citizens associations who demanded "law and order."[14] Of all the perspectives presented in the hearings, "it was felt by the Council that the 'black separatist' voices were the most startling." "The more militant voices spoke up for a 'no-white' policy, suggesting that unless all planning and rebuilding by white people be stopped, another burning would occur," summarized the DC City Council's report on the hearings.[15]

Some advocates of separatist policies at the city council hearings were members of the Black United Front. Stokely Carmichael founded the BUF in January 1968 to create a coalition of moderate and militant Black leaders in hopes of keeping "down political infighting in the black community" and to "let the black community speak with one united voice."[16] The group hoped to take over DC's institutions so they would be Black-led and best serve the community.

The BUF considered the DC City Council hearings a valuable opportunity to shape the city's rebuilding plans. Before the hearings, the BUF announced a special meeting and invited seventy of the individuals scheduled to testify before the council. "The meeting that the Front calls has special significance because it knows that the Black people living in the Black communities want to decide what will happen to, as well as what goes on, in their communities," read a BUF press release. "In order to insure that this will, in fact, be the case with the 'rebuilding,' the Front is requesting that these seventy (70) people meet with our body" so they could collaboratively "come up with one, just one (1), proposal."[17]

Many used the hearings as an opportunity to express frustrations over poor housing, the lack of jobs, and especially the lack of promotions for workers.[18] The DC City Council's report on the hearings concluded, "The lack of housing, employment, and other opportunities for ghetto residents were pointed to as basic factors contributing to the disturbances."[19] Many Black Washingtonians also seized the opportunity to communicate their frustrations with white business owners. "Under severe attack were white suburban owners of inner city businesses, and this criticism applied not only to those whose businesses were destroyed, but also to those still operating," the council concluded in its report. "The charge was repeatedly made that the business profits made in the neighborhood stores supported by neighborhood residents were often taken out of those neighborhoods and often out of the District." [20] Specifically, people were frustrated with "high mark-ups, off-brand of inferior merchandise, high pressure sales tactics coupled with fast closings and incomplete disclosure, and 'easy credit' which is often high interest and contains hidden charges."[21] The council concluded: "It was apparent that many witnesses felt that consumer problems and exploitative practices were a contributing and indirect cause of the recent disturbances."[22]

Washingtonians also criticized the lack of control over their government and communities. "It is no secret that a great number of people in our community have been denied for too long the right of participating in the decisions which determine their destiny and the destiny of neighborhoods throughout the Washington metropolitan area," asserted a Black minister.[23] "In one way or another what came through was the universal demand for the right of self-determination for the neighborhoods that need rebuilding," concluded the DC City Council.[24] Marion Barry echoed this sentiment in a congressional hearing on the uprisings. "Almost without exception, the lower income black communities of this country have been planned and administered from persons coming primarily outside that community," Barry alleged. "Laws, regulations, and law enforcement have moved in the direction of making conditions safer and more secure for the white, non-ghetto residents who are exploiting the lower income black community residents."[25]

To many, the police were the enforcers of such discrimination and operated as an occupying force tinged with corruption. In his statement before the DC City Council, a Washingtonian said many participants in the civil disturbances were angry with the police and courts. Police frequently took their belongings and covered up misconduct.[26] Another argued the police had been a major problem for over fifteen years, especially because the department's leadership was white and the force heavily recruited from Southern states. "These are the things that are on the minds of those people who we find ourselves eventually advising to go home when there is a disturbance," the man warned.[27]

As the BUF had hoped, the DC City Council hearings also provided a forum to communicate how citizens hoped to rebuild and reform DC in the wake of the rebellions. Marion Barry and Reginald Booker were both established DC political figures and members of the BUF's board of conveners—essentially its steering committee.[28] Marion Barry founded the home rule advocacy group Free DC and co-founded Pride, Inc., the federally funded Black youth jobs program. Booker was the outspoken chairman of the Emergency Committee on the Transportation Crisis— the group working to create the Metro rail system and block the planned inner city highway. In their testimonies, Barry and Booker outlined three principles for rebuilding DC: (1) Black citizens should plan their own neighborhoods, (2) the reconstruction should economically empower Black Washingtonians, and (3) reconstruction should reduce economic and racial inequality.

"If you are planning for a black community," Barry insisted, "the planning should be in the hands of black people."[29] Barry contended that low-income Black people wanted "self-sufficiency and self-determination" and would consider "outside control . . . as paternalism on one hand or as colonialism on the other."[30] Second, the Black community should comprise the reconstruction labor force and own the businesses that were rebuilt to produce Black economic power. Barry hoped that as a result of rebuilding, African American Washingtonians would "own at least 51% of the District"[31] and believed burned-out businesses should only be permitted to reopen if the white owners agreed to be less exploitative.[32] Finally, Barry argued that the city's plans for reconstruction should rectify Washington's social ills. "Both the governmental and nongovernmental societal institutions have failed the black residents," Barry asserted. Schools did not adequately teach children, businesses exploited customers, and housing was destroyed by urban renewal. "Housing, education, economic development, public services, etc. are all a part of the fabric that makes up a society and these problems intersect, cross, and overlap at many points," Barry maintained. "Planners must take this into consideration and attack the total state of the problem of the ghetto."[33]

To implement these objectives, Barry suggested that the government and financial institutions should grant Black Washingtonians the time and resources necessary to create a "self-determined" neighborhood. Barry asked the government to deny burned-out business owners the money and bureaucratic approval necessary for them to start reconstruction so Black people could first decide if those business owners would even be allowed to rebuild.[34] To foster Black economic development, Barry recommended that "the city banks, the financing institutions and their officials should move immediately to establish at least a $5 million revolving fund so we will have money to borrow from, because we don't have money."

Next, Barry argued the city should hire African Americans from damaged neighborhoods to tear down the destroyed buildings. Since "black people have not been trained as managers and salesmen and runners of business," Barry advocated that "businesses and [the] government should set up a plan to train black people to be accountants, and how to run a business." Once African Americans learned to be business owners, the white business leaders who taught these skills would be "let . . . go." Barry contended it was reasonable to expect such financial and technical aid because the U.S. government loaned billions of dollars to developing nations in Europe and Asia: "It seems that the same U.S. government that does that for other countries ought to be able to do the same thing [for us]." Finally, to solve the "root causes" of urban violence, Barry suggested the city government investigate exploitative practices by merchants to better protect consumers and to build public housing throughout the entire city instead of concentrating it in the "ghetto."[35] Barry's plan to create a "self-determined" Black community relied heavily on government intervention and white financial institutions.

Like Barry, Booker insisted white people could not understand or plan for African Americans, so Black Washingtonians should create their own reconstruction designs. "Devastated areas where black people are living in hell holes and concentration camps must be rebuilt by black people," he contended. Booker additionally argued that the city must address social issues facing Black Washingtonians such as insufficient public housing, police brutality, unequal employment opportunities, and economic exploitation. If the city failed to address such issues, "not only will it be a long hot summer, but it is going to be a long hot winter and a long hot all year round." Booker recommended policies that resembled Barry's. The city should not permit rebuilding until certain conditions were met: "I think before any money, before one brick, before one spade of mortar is put up, a moratorium should be declared on all rebuilding . . . and there should be an immediate investigation to see why black people have been exploited for so long." To address the deep-seated social inequalities harming low-income African Americans, Booker demanded the DC government research why discriminatory policies persisted. Booker asked the DC City Council to investigate why Black people were "economically exploited," why "all the top jobs in the District of Columbia government are held by white folks who live in suburbia," why the National Capital Housing Authority—the agency responsible for public housing—was "the greatest slum lord," why public housing was concentrated in one area of the city, and why "there is a very small percentage of black people on the police force."[36]

A week after the DC City Council hearings concluded, the BUF held a press conference to outline its proposals for rebuilding

DC. First, like Barry and Booker suggested, the BUF advocated a moratorium on rebuilding until the Black community had time to create a "unified and comprehensive" design. The BUF asked the Small Business Administration (SBA) to freeze disaster relief loans and the Department of Licenses and Inspections to stop issuing rebuilding permits until the Black community created a proposal. The BUF insisted that such a plan be submitted through the BUF itself because it believed "the Black United Front *is* the black community of Washington, D.C." To ensure Black community members led rebuilding, the BUF demanded that work done by white contractors cease and only restart with Black contractors and workers. "This is the first step the District government which is headed by a colored mayor can take to show its good intentions toward the black community," it urged. "Unless such a step is taken now and taken immediately, then the black community must question the sincerity of subsequent steps toward reconstruction."[37] To teach the Black community how to develop and maintain economic power, the BUF recommended that government agencies such as the United Planning Organization and the Department of Housing and Urban Development "serve as technical consultants to the black community." The BUF concluded its statement with a threat: "We wish to emphasize very strongly that black people are going to rebuild this black community. Unless we *do* rebuild it, there will be no stability in the District of Columbia."[38] Barry, Booker, and the BUF's proposals all emphasized Black autonomy and self-determination. Simultaneously, each proposal requested funding and support from "establishment" institutions.

Barry, Booker, and the BUF were recommending explicitly preferential treatment for Black Washingtonians to rectify historical disadvantages, a proposal that echoes those of advocates for reparations. The case for reparations centers on two central historical facts: (1) the labor of enslaved Black Americans generated hundreds of millions of dollars of wealth for their white enslavers and their descendants have never been compensated, and (2) government policies have prevented Black people from accumulating wealth for generations. Human bondage, segregation under Jim Crow, job discrimination, redlining practices that prevented many Black people from homeownership, development policies that displaced Black people who had managed to own property, and unequal education opportunities have all systematically limited the ability of Black Americans to build wealth. Today, the average Black family has ten times less in assets than the average white family in the United States.[39]

Savvy personal finance strategies cannot close this wealth gap created by centuries of unequal opportunity and government-imposed limitations. Government policy created these inequities and government policy is necessary to solve it, according to reparations scholars. Advocates want the federal government to make cash payments to the descendants of enslaved persons and for policies that create wealth-building opportunities for Black Americans that acknowledge and address racial inequality in business ownership, housing, and education. These policies would mimic previous reparations policies, such as the cash payments made to Japanese Americans who were interned by the government during World War II.

As the BUF asked the DC government to offer unique and preferential treatment to Black businesses and individuals, it was advocating for a form of reparations. Government policy had created the historical inequities that made Black people feel so enraged and hopeless that they participated in the rebellions. Now the government could use the opportunity to rebuild to rectify those historical wrongs through policies that specifically addressed the concerns of the Black community.

DC's Coalition

Although the DC City Council was "startled" by these recommendations, it realized many Washingtonians likely supported
these proposals and were more militant than the city council previously had realized. "We recognize that very possibly the ideas
behind those firebrand attitudes are no different from the views
of the vast majority of witnesses," concluded the city council in
its report.[40] The council listened to Black Washingtonians who
spoke at the hearings and understood the depths of their frustrations and their desperation for radical change. Rather than
sidelining or downplaying this radicalism, the council chose to
endorse many of the militants' suggestions. The DC City Council largely endorsed the three themes articulated by Barry and
Booker. First, citizens should have some control over how the city
was reconstructed. "The basic message of the hearings was clear
and it is the dominant theme of this report: all citizens need to be
involved in the economic and social processes of this city," said
the council's chairman, John Hechinger. "There is a need for a
good measure of self-determination for the neighborhoods which
must be rebuilt."[41] Second, the rebuilding efforts should foster,
and even prioritize, Black economic development. The city council found "that special measures are needed now to improve the
economic and social opportunities for Negroes, particularly in
such areas as business and housing."[42] "Policies must be realis-
tic in recognizing the need for economic and political power in
the Negro community," the council stated, "particularly in housing and business development."[43] Finally, the city must alleviate
the systemic causes of the uprisings: "Every avenue of support for
facilities and programs to raise standards of housing, education,
recreation, and health must be explored."[44]

Additionally, the DC City Council directly advocated some of

Barry and Booker's ideas. Barry suggested local financial institutions should create a pool of capital to finance Black-owned enterprises. The city council urged Congress to create "a revolving fund so that Negro entrepreneurs and cooperatives can borrow capital at low interest rates and over long terms in order to start businesses and to finance training in management techniques." Further, the city council encouraged "the local business community, financial institutions, and government agencies take all necessary steps to create a several million dollar loan fund or pool to encourage new business activity, particularly by Negro-owned enterprises." To "compensate for the effects of past discrimination" in lending practices to African Americans, the council believed "banks and other financial institutions" should develop "new lending techniques . . . which go beyond equal treatment to Negro borrowers and to a substantial degree actually compensate for the effects of the past discrimination."[45] This suggestion endorsed the central thesis of reparations.

To economically empower Black Washingtonians, Booker insisted that the neighborhoods be rebuilt by Black people, and Barry encouraged the government to hire local Black workers to demolish damaged buildings. The DC City Council proposed that "the District and Federal governments, where legally possible, restructure their construction and purchasing policies so that contracts are let to businesses and industries which are located in the areas requiring building and which contribute economic support to those areas and their residents." The government should favor businesses "which employ ghetto residents, which are willing to employ the unemployed, which participate in skill and management training programs, and which have compensatory hiring practices."[46] "To the fullest extent possible," Black builders should subcontract the reconstruction and neighborhood residents should "furnish the principal labor pool."[47] To create more job opportunities for young African Americans, the DC City Council encouraged the local and federal government to fund employment programs such as the Barry-led Pride, Inc.[48]

Booker and Barry were critical that public housing was concentrated in Black neighborhoods in DC; the city council suggested the decentralization of public housing.[49] To address the exploitation of Black consumers, the city council requested congressional funding to create an office of consumer affairs that could field complaints and act against businesses with discriminatory and manipulative practices.[50] Finally, the city council advocated insurance reform as a consumer protection measure. When merchants could not obtain insurance, it resulted in "higher prices, lower quality goods, and/or lack of adequate shopping facilities in black communities." The city council endorsed the Fair Access to Insurance Requirements (FAIR) Act to require DC insurance companies to cover businesses and homes in disturbance-affected areas.[51]

While the DC City Council endorsed many proposals made by DC militants, the council firmly rejected the suggestion that white planners and businesses be barred from the rebuilding efforts. The city council denounced "the ideology of two separate societies. . . . The simple fact is that the talents and energies of all races and all economic groups are needed in this city."[52] While the Black United Front urged the Small Business Administration to cease granting loans to damaged businesses, the city council encouraged it to grant long-term loans at low interest rates to merchants who wished to reopen their businesses.[53] "We must recognize and understand the reasons for bitterness of deprived Negro citizens, as we must recognize and understand the bitterness of innocent victims of the destruction, whether they be black or white," the city council emphasized. "All must receive fair treatment as the city moves forward."[54]

Mayor Walter E. Washington also incorporated and moderated

radical demands as he presented his plan to rebuild the city. In his testimony before the Commerce Subcommittee of the Senate District Committee on May 20, 1968, Washington announced a "crash program to rebuild riot-torn areas of the city with planning to be completed in 100 days." Washington recommended that the plan include "citizen participation in planning, additional ownership and operation of businesses by Negroes, [and] more job opportunities for inner-city residents." "Surely," Washington insisted, "this is a time for citizens and public officials to work urgently together. . . . I now call on all citizens, white and black, to join hands in this endeavor."[55] Washington created the Community Development Committee "to oversee rebuilding" and instructed city officials to meet with "community leaders, business groups, private foundations and Federal agencies" throughout the process.[56]

The BUF was one of the groups that consulted with city officials to help formulate the reconstruction designs.[57] In May, members of the BUF met with Julian Dugas, the director of the Department of Licenses and Inspections, and Mayor Washington. After these meetings, the BUF thought the DC government would support its objectives. Charles Jones, a representative of the BUF's press conference delegation, was encouraged that Dugas "committed himself to making sure that if the brothers get their bids in, they will get the contracts" to rebuild the city. To ensure Black contractors received these contracts, the BUF created a Committee on Bidding and Black Contractors. Jones and other BUF members believed Mayor Washington would obtain funding to support the BUF and other community-led planning efforts. "I think the Mayor (Walter E. Washington) understands now that we are a united Black community," said Jones. "He has committed himself to working through the Black United Front as the united Black community."[58]

Nonetheless, the BUF also believed it should continue to pressure and, if necessary, threaten the DC government to fulfill its wishes. "The committee is to make clear to anyone in charge that there will be none other than Black contractors in charge of the rebuilding," the BUF insisted. "The committee should not be afraid to issue warnings of what could occur if the contracts are awarded to white contractors (the possibility of the white contractors' establishments being burned, and so forth)."[59]

Simultaneously, the BUF wanted to prove to the local government that it could lead the community and was a reliable organization. After the BUF created a Task Force on Rebuilding Proposals, it aimed to complete its reconstruction plans within sixty days of the disorders. Finishing the proposal quickly, the BUF believed, would demonstrate to the government that it was self-disciplined and a good-faith partner. If the BUF could shape the rebuilding process, it thought it could "coopt anything the city government may do."[60] Far from abandoning community organizing and local politics, the BUF worked to prove itself as a reliable organization and trusted it could use the political process to create self-determination in Black neighborhoods.

These actions suggest the response to the uprisings was much more complex than calls for "get tough" policing from conservatives and the rejection of government programs. Ultimately, DC's proposal for rebuilding incorporated the concepts, programs, and funding mechanisms that liberal politicians crafted. Community action and "maximum feasible participation" were mandated in many of President Johnson's War on Poverty programs. Even the idea of large-scale planning for a neighborhood drew upon the liberal program of urban renewal. The DC City Council listened to Black radicals and incorporated many of their ideas. In turn, the BUF participated in the District government's planning process. The BUF established a Rebuilding Task Force, met with the government and community, and engaged in the nitty-gritty of city planning. Many Washingtonians believed the DC government could help the city recover from the disorders and were willing to participate in the process. Thus, the mayor, the DC City Council, the BUF and the community groups it represented, and Black citizens loosely agreed on a process that prioritized community participation and Black economic development and would alleviate the inequalities they considered the root causes of unrest.

9

"The Troublemakers . . .
Will Be Dealt With Severely"

THE BACKLASH TO RESTRAINT

TO MANY POLITICAL CONSERVATIVES AND WHITE MODERATES, the uprisings did not indicate the need to restructure society in a more equitable way; rather, they demonstrated the victory of criminals over order. Those who participated in the rebellions were not grief-stricken citizens reacting to Dr. King's death but rather apolitical criminals who seized opportunities to steal. For these people, the government must respond by harshly punishing those who participated in the rebellions, by increasing the power of law enforcement and even by prioritizing private property over human well-being.

White Anger

The idea that "that this was a general Negro uprising in resentment against the assassination of Dr. Martin Luther King . . . is a gross libel on predominantly Negro Washington," a columnist from the *Washington Daily News* opined. "The mobsters couldn't have cared less about Dr. King, alive or dead. They violated every decency for which he stood, seizing upon his death as an excuse to destroy."[1] "There was no grief for [King] in the streets, only greed and mindless plundering," concluded another *Washington Daily News* article.[2] Senator Robert Byrd thought the "carnival spirit" present in the looting had "no logical connection whatsoever with Dr. King's death."[3] Clarence Washington of the Southern Christian Leadership Conference stated that "Dr. King's murder may have triggered this looting yesterday but it's not causing it now. . . . The whole thing had a carnival atmosphere—not solemn, not mournful, not vengeful."[4] "They were in a festive mood," claimed a *Washington Evening Star* editorial, "bent upon grabbing what they could while the grabbing was good."[5] In a letter to the editor of the *Washington Daily News*, a local man clearly articulated the position that the "riots" were a carnivalesque spree of greed unconnected to grief:

> I really don't see how any sensible person could believe that the looters and rioters who have been tearing up the country lately were expressing their deep grief at the death of the Rev. Dr. King. . . . It seems more likely that the revelers were simply carrying out a ritual that is by now well established, an unlovely tradition. The juveniles begin by smashing store windows, then, the kids start grabbing, then the grown-ups move in. . . . [Were looters] really thinking about Martin Luther King, Jr.? . . . The notion is grotesque.[6]

Without fear of arrest, some argued, "criminals" took advantage of the chance to steal consumer goods. "Criminals have used the assassination of Dr. King as an excuse to take the law into their own hands," Senator Strom Thurmond (R-SC) commented about DC in an interview with the *Washington Post*.[7] Senator Russell B. Long described the protestors as "professional robbers, thieves, and arsonists."[8] In a letter to a Washington Board of Trade member, a local businessman wrote that "the recent wholesale looting and burning of business properties by hoodlums, teenage delinquents, black power advocates of violence and criminal elements, should convince the most naïve liberal, that what we have experienced was not a race riot but the willful pillaging of properties under the guise of lamenting the death of Dr. Martin Luther King, Jr."[9] An ad from the DC Retail Liquor Dealers Association, Inc. similarly rejected any political motivation in the upheaval: "This is no revolt of the poor against the wealthy. This is no part of the Civil Rights movement whose real leaders know that Utopia doesn't have to be built on ashes. It is an open attack by a few criminals against a community that lacks firm leadership and the courage to demand that its leaders exercise their authority—or resign."[10]

While some Republicans and Democrats endorsed this understanding of the disorders, the position was "conservative" in that it rejected much of the theory undergirding the policies of President Johnson's Great Society. In this conceptualization, "law and order" had diminished in American society thanks to liberal court rulings and the tactics of civil disobedience employed by Black leaders like King. Already, tough-on-crime advocates believed, the federal government's unwillingness to prohibit or violently curtail protests and civil disobedience resulted in rampant crime in DC. Now "criminals" were so emboldened they were stealing in broad daylight as the police did nothing.

In a speech given on the Senate floor mere days after King's assassination, Senator Byrd alleged that King's assassination was ultimately King's fault for "inviting violence" by "defying the law":

> There is a lesson to be drawn from what happened in Memphis and what has been happening with increasing intensity throughout the nation in recent years. That is, that mass protests, mass demonstrations, and mass marches and the like—whether labeled

nonviolent or otherwise—can only serve to encourage unrest and disorder, and to provoke violence and
bloodshed. And, in the end, those who advocate such
methods often become, themselves, the victims of the
forces they themselves set in motion. This, in a manner, is what happened to Dr. King. He usually spoke
of nonviolence. Yet, violence all too often attended
his actions. And, at the last, he himself met a violent
end. . . . One cannot preach nonviolence, and, at the
same time, advocate defiance of the law, whether it be
a court order, a municipal ordinance. . . . For to defy
the law is to invite violence, especially in a tense atmosphere. . . . Thus we are exhorted to obey the law and
to respect authority, and those who refuse to do this
cause serious risks to themselves and to others. . . .
This, I hope, will be the lesson we will all draw from
the tragic events of recent days in Memphis.[11]

A columnist for the *Evening Star* wrote that Byrd's words were
"singularly prophetic of the disorders and riots during the weekend."[12] In other words, civil rights advocates were to blame for
both King's death and the resulting uprisings because their limited use of civil disobedience spurred many—including King's
assassin—to choose to defy the law writ large.

Many who believed that the rebellions should solely be interpreted as a crime spree were upset at the policy of restraint and
demanded that the police and military use more force. According
to a poll of businesspeople at a national convention in Washington shortly after King's death, 457 out of 551 thought the police
were too lenient.[13] Many of these critics insisted that the police
were ordered to "do nothing" and made no effort to prevent looting. A letter from the Federation of Citizens Associations, the

historically all-white neighborhood groups that often worked to maintain segregation, asserted that "outnumbered police simply stood by—under orders—[and] watched the arson and pillage."[14] Congressman Roy A. Taylor, a Democrat from North Carolina, contended that "police made little effort to stop looters or recover merchandise."[15] In congressional hearings on the disturbances, the head of the House DC Committee, John McMillan, grilled DC Public Safety Director Patrick Murphy about "the reason for not stopping some of the looting that appeared here in the Nation's Capital on these days." McMillan said business owners reported that troops guarding stores "weren't permitted to touch the looters or the people setting fires."[16] Murphy, Layton, and the undersecretary of the army, David E. McGiffert, all agreed that the police and troops never received orders to allow looting or arson.[17] Police records corroborate their claims.

Many white people were highly critical of Murphy and the city's actions because they believed the disorder-suppression methods were not violent enough. Specifically, these commentators argued that the city would have sustained less property damage if people looting and starting fires were shot by police and soldiers. In a letter to Attorney General Ramsey Clark, the Association of the Oldest Inhabitants of Washington—an elite, all-male organization formed in 1865 to protect the interests of white, long-term residents as the population of formerly enslaved Black people quadrupled—stated that in cities where public officials gave orders to shoot to kill "rioters," the disorders were kept under control. "In the good old days—which we remember well since our members must be at least fifty years of age and some are over 90 years of age—looters and arsonists were shot on sight in times of emergencies," they wrote.[18] They demanded "adequate protection not restraint. We want to sleep at night without fear of uncontrolled rioting."[19]

The chairman of the Federation of Citizens Associations asserted that the failure to shoot people lighting fires "clearly indicates
that law and order cannot be restored in Washington under the
direction of the present officials. What will result is more inflammatory actions by the advocates of violence and other opposing
groups."[20] "Tying the hands of our armed forces and law enforcement officials lent encouragement to the philosophy that riot
destruction is the most certain method of enforcing demands,"
claimed the federation.[21] One Washingtonian contended in a letter to the editor of the *Washington Star* that killing arsonists and
maiming looters "had much greater merit than the drivel of the
sob sisters who refuse to separate lawlessness from civil rights
issue. . . . The bleeding hearts about us would have us believe that
restraint and permissiveness toward those who violate our laws
is the only solution to our current wave of racial disturbances."
He concluded that "no citizen, white or black, will be safe on the
streets of Washington until the police show their teeth and noti-
fy the would-be violators in advance that force will be met with
superior force."[22]

Politicians also demanded that the police and troops be authorized to use more violence. Congressman Joel Broyhill called
for legislation to "[make] it mandatory that all police, National
Guardsmen and militiamen shoot to kill each and every looter
or rioter henceforth."[23] Broyhill was additionally frustrated that
officials calling for such measures were "charged by the bleeding
hearts of this nation with being callous and reckless insofar as
human life is concerned."[24] Congressman John Dowdy (D-TX)
praised the individual police officers but criticized the "undue
restraints that were put upon the police in their attempts to enforce
the law and preserve order."[25] "We are trying to untie the hands of
the police," Dowdy asserted, "they have been tied for too long."[26]
Senator Long claimed he "didn't approve of the police being weak

or namby-pamby" and that people looting should be shot if they tried to run from police. "It might cost a few lives to be strong, but I don't see that we are too badly off if a few professional robbers, thieves and arsonists do lose their lives."[27] This appalling suggestion demonstrates how associating Black people with crime was used to dehumanize them and strip them of their rights—even the right to life.[28]

The Rebellions and the Courts

Just as many "law and order" advocates urged the police to use more force to deter crime, some commentators encouraged the courts to prosecute those accused of disorder offenses to the fullest extent of the law. The Washington Board of Trade, for example, contended that "severe penalties should be given for possession of weapons or explosives, and to those caught looting or destroying property."[29] The *Washington Evening Star* and radio station WMAL released a joint statement demanding "justice": "The rioters are arsonists, looters and vandals. These lawbreakers must be punished individually according to the seriousness of their crimes."[30] Senator Byrd stated that he hoped "the troublemakers and looters and other lawbreakers will not be given a mere tap on the wrists and turned loose, but will be dealt with severely."[31]

The DC Court of General Sessions and the U.S. District Court for the District of Columbia were responsible for trying and, if convicted, sentencing the 6,230 adults arrested in connection to the disorders from April 4 to April 15, 1968.[32] The court proceedings were shaped by the 1967 District Antiriot Bill that created harsher punishments for crimes associated with uprisings. The bill set a minimum sentence of two years imprisonment for second-degree burglary, a felony charge used to prosecute those accused of looting.[33]

Cases were initially prosecuted to the "fullest extent of the law" as a felony. During the upheaval, the U.S. Attorney's Office charged defendants accused of looting with the harshest possible crime: burglary in the second degree, a crime punishable by two to fifteen years of imprisonment. The prosecutors believed that the serious charge would give them more flexibility in determining charges when they later reviewed cases with more complete information.[34] But cases tried as misdemeanors were processed faster than felonies and caused fewer problems for the courts. The Court of General Sessions handled misdemeanor criminal cases and was the closest thing to a state lower court in DC. The U.S. District Court for the District of Columbia was a federal court and tried DC's felony cases.

Ninety percent of defendants tried in the Court of General Sessions were sentenced by September 1968, and only fifteen cases remained on December 1, 1968.[35] Prosecuting the felony cases in the U.S. District Court, however, moved slowly and caused significant backlogs. Case backlog in the U.S. District Court increased by 60 percent in the five months following the rebellions.[36] By October 1968, the District Court had only processed thirty-three cases, very few of which resulted in convictions, and still had to try 452 people indicted by a grand jury.[37] By the end of 1968, only 169 cases were completed and 63 percent of defendants charged with burglary in the second degree had not been tried.[38]

The backlog problems were so severe that in October 1968, the prosecuting attorneys decided to try only the "hard core" cases and sent the rest of them back to the Court of General Sessions as misdemeanors.[39] This measure was not only taken because of the significant backlog, however. From the very first felony trial in July, prosecutors expressed misgivings over the weakness of many cases.[40] Their concerns were warranted. In early October, only ten of the forty-seven people tried for rebellion-related felonies had been convicted.[41] First Assistant U.S. Attorney Alfred A. Hantman felt the cases were of "poor quality" and considered offenses "too trivial and [that they] belonged in a lower court." In October 1968, the U.S. Attorney's Office believed that no more than twenty-five of the 452 felony cases still awaiting trial were strong enough to prosecute in the District Court.[42] In total, only 11 percent of felony trials for disorder-related offenses resulted in a conviction.[43] Ultimately, the attempt to prosecute defendants to the fullest extent of the law did not produce firmer punishments, but it did worsen backlog.

The courts also handled another type of case related to the uprisings—lawsuits. Some business owners and politicians were so upset with the city's response they sought to force the DC government to cover the cost of the damage. The House DC Committee held hearings on HR 16948, "a bill to direct the Commissioners of the District of Columbia to remove at the expense of the District of Columbia buildings destroyed or damaged in riots or other civil disorders."[44] In the hearing on the bill, a member of the Washington Board of Realtors asserted that "if the local government had performed its function and duty to maintain law and order during the riots of April, there would be no need now to determine who bears the responsibility of removing the damaged buildings."[45] The executive director of the DC Retail Liquor Dealers Association said that the city "invited" crime so the city should "pick up the check."[46]

As Congressman Basil Whitener (D-NC) pointed out, the bill's proponents often posited white small business owners as the true and most deserving victims of the rebellions. "This is the thing that bothers me, so many having the zeal for the removal of rubble and debris," said Whitener. "I am wondering about those people who have had hospital bills, funeral bills, the loss of earnings . . . the employees in some of the businesses who were innocent of any wrongdoing who have been deprived of their weekly paychecks." He asked why no one was discussing paying for the funeral expenses for a woman who died in the flames or aiding Black business owners who sustained damage. Raymond R. Ruppert, a realtor in the Seventh Street area, made the racist suggestion that welfare payments should be enough for those costs.[47] Such comments led Whitener to wonder if the legislation "put a premium on rubble and lower[ed] it on life and limb."[48]

In May 1968, a local group of merchants, most of whom suffered property damage during the uprisings, created a group called We the People and sued the DC government for allegedly inadequately protecting their businesses. The head of We the People stated that the group aimed to "demand the domestic tranquility guaranteed in the preamble to the Constitution."[49] The insurance companies who covered the businesses also sued DC as they claimed the government should cover the damages. Aetna Insurance Co. asked the DC and federal governments to reimburse it for the $1.2 million it paid in business insurance claims following the upheaval. According to Aetna, the government was responsible because it "deliberately sacrificed property to burners and looters" and thus "'consciously abandoned the rights and interest of property issues,' denying the owners the constitutional rights to equal protection of the law."[50] Another suit filed a year later lodged similar complaints as it claimed that "no action was taken or attempted to restrain . . . agitators and revolutionaries." The plaintiffs contended that the DC anti-disorder plan was insufficient and the city was negligent because it was obvious that "any incident of a significant nature involving the black race would be likely to touch off domestic violence, disorders and rioting which would . . . result in vast damage and destruction to private business and property."[51]

By August 1970, nearly thirty merchants sought compensatory

and punitive damages from the District for negligence during the rebellions.[52] The District, in partnership with the Justice Department, defended its actions, claiming "that 'great care, consideration and detail' went into the response to the riots." In a ruling on October 13, 1970, the U.S. Court of Appeals ruled in favor of the District, absolving its liability for the damage. Because the Court of Appeals refused to establish a "new principle of municipal responsibility," it delegitimized the twenty-six other lawsuits against DC still pending. The judges on the panel believed the government had the right to decide not to use police "at a certain location because of danger to them or the likelihood of increasing or extending the general violence."[53]

Johnson Responds to the Rebellions

Even though this lawsuit was not effective, the backlash to the rebellions influenced the politics and policies of President Lyndon Johnson, Congress, and Mayor Walter E. Washington. Johnson struggled with how to respond to the April upheaval in a way that did not further anger Americans whose top priority was order. This difficulty was apparent as Johnson and his advisers debated what to say in a planned address to Congress following the uprisings. In a meeting of Johnson administration officials on "D.C. Riot and Future Planning," Special Assistant to the President Joseph Califano opened by expressing his "concern about the loss of confidence in the community, in Congress, and in the Press about the ability of the Government to maintain law and order in Washington."[54] Congressman Don Riegle (D-MI) urged Johnson that "the text should be brief and philosophical" and shy away from discussing new programs because the "people are program weary. They won't be moved by more programs." Johnson should "separate out and [condemn] in stark terms at the outset the 1% of

Americans who have given up on America, law and civilization."[55] Johnson must communicate that "the Federal Government *will move immediately*—wherever it has the authority—to suppress rioting and will not tolerate the use of looting and arson as forms of political argument," recommended one aide. He similarly discouraged "new programs for social reform" because white people were "beginning to ask the question: Was it worth it?—meaning the civil rights and poverty legislation of the past few years. They assume that there has been tremendous generosity to the Negro and that this generosity is being repaid with ingratitude."[56] Ultimately, Johnson never gave the speech, in part because he was unsure of how to be the figure of unity that his advisers wanted him to be.[57]

On May 11, while troops still occupied the capital city, Johnson signed into law the Civil Rights Act of 1968. The bill included the Fair Housing Act, which banned discrimination in the sale, rental, and financing of housing. The legislation also further criminalized participation in rebellions. Title X of the bill made it a felony to "travel in interstate commerce . . . with the intent to incite, promote, encourage, participate in and carry on a riot."[58] Black leaders had lobbied against the anti-riot provisions because they worried the provisions limited free speech and could be used to prosecute people for protesting.

In the months following the uprisings, President Johnson also signed legislation that expanded upon the Law Enforcement Assistance Act of 1965 and granted police departments even more money and power. In 1967, Johnson introduced the Safe Streets Act legislation in Congress to distribute federal grants to municipal police departments to be used for "equipment, training, and pilot programs." The House changed the bill so that cities and states would receive the funds with no restrictions or guidelines on how police should use the money. The Senate also altered the legislation so that it limited civil liberties by allowing broader electronic surveillance and expanding what confessions were admissible in court, narrowing the *Mallory* Supreme Court decision. "It epitomized, above all, the conservative contention that the Supreme Court's rulings had handcuffed the police, making it almost impossible to arrest and convict criminals," concluded historian Michael Flamm. Johnson had opposed these amendments to the bill because it gave police departments unchecked resources and power, but after the House and Senate passed the bill following the nationwide uprisings, the president signed the Safe Streets Act into law in July "with considerable reluctance." Nevertheless, it was law.[59]

In the District, Johnson pushed gun control as an anticrime measure, lobbying the Speaker of the House of Representatives, John W. McCormack, to grant the DC City Council more authority so it could pass and enforce stricter gun laws.[60] Johnson also encouraged better police training, higher pay for officers, court modernization efforts, and one thousand additional officers on the DC police force.[61] Behind the scenes, the Johnson administration, in coordination with Mayor Washington, established an expanded intelligence system to infiltrate Black radical groups in DC. In a White House meeting on April 17, 1968, the leaders present decided to create an improved intelligence system in collaboration with the FBI and Secret Service to obtain "better knowledge of the activities of militant groups."[62] While FBI counterintelligence projects such as COINTELPRO already existed, the committee thought a larger program with even better-trained agents was needed. The police would seek information on "what groups are particularly powerful, who are the real leaders, what are the opposing forces and their leadership, who should the police chief deal with, what positions should the department take on particular issues, etc." Officers would collect information that indicated the "potential for civil disorder" such as "speeches and statements of various militants, emergence of new groups within the ghetto, [and] changes in leadership of groups." Successfully analyzing such intelligence would require "special training," "the use of undercover agents to infiltrate and cover various organizations with potential for violence," and officers who had "an understanding of the ghetto and its problems."[63] The U.S. Department of Defense, specifically the Department of the Army, paid the DC government $150,000 to start this counterintelligence program because the army thought "it would be very useful if the Army could receive information . . . which could help indicate the time, place, nature, and possible duration of potential civil disturbances."[64]

The police, military, and many leaders found it convenient to believe that surveilling radicals would solve urban upheaval because infiltrating those groups was much easier than changing the systemic racial and economic inequality that affected millions. Or, as a satirical *New York Times* article joked, "if riots break out, Congress naturally has to investigate the cause and produce solutions. . . . If you can discover that the riots are caused by outside agitators, however, you can let the taxpayer off cheap with a bill to provide prison accommodations for any agitators crossing state lines."[65] Simplifying the cause of the disturbances to a few instigators made it easier to claim that leaders had a solution. Passing anti-riot legislation that further criminalized Black people was easier than creating equal opportunities for them. Weeding out a few radicals was simple, but dealing with the complaints of millions of "average" African Americans was not.[66]

While the Johnson administration had long surveilled the civil rights movement and had passed other measures that strengthened the police force, its agenda had also included ambitious, wide-reaching programs that poured federal resources into reducing structural inequality. Now, however, Johnson's advisers were afraid to talk about more programs or even to acknowledge the Black community's grievances because they worried about alienating white Americans. Johnson used his political capital on measures that focused on combating crime and imposing harsher punishments on those who had participated in rebellions instead of doubling down on solving the underlying issues.

Resurrection City and Strong Policing

Perhaps the clearest example of this shift is the government's response to the Poor People's Campaign. On May 12, 1968, less than a month after the state of emergency ended in Washington, the PPC came to Washington. After King's assassination, the new president of Southern Christian Leadership Conference, Rev. Ralph Abernathy, led the campaign to draw attention to American poverty and lobby Congress to pass legislation to address it. People from all over the country came to Washington and inhabited a village, Resurrection City, near the Lincoln Memorial on the National Mall that consisted of plywood-and-plastic-sheeting huts. At its height, 2,600 hundred people lived in Resurrection City, and it included a dining hall, pharmacy, and city hall. While the PPC was a multicultural coalition, two-thirds of Resurrection City's residents were African American. The PPC's largest event was a demonstration named Solidarity Day that took place on June 19, the Juneteenth holiday celebrating emancipation in Texas. Fifty thousand people attended.[67]

The PPC endured significant challenges. Instead of discussing the issue *of* poverty as PPC organizers had hoped, many members of Congress and the media instead viewed Resurrection City as an example of the problems *with* those in poverty. Any perceived misbehavior or problem within the village was turned into a spectacle and was fuel for public criticism. Second, the people of Resurrection City suffered torrential rains and unseasonably cold weather. For twenty-eight of the forty-two days that people lived in Resurrection City, it rained, creating enormous mud puddles and miserable living conditions.[68]

Following Solidarity Day on June 19, tensions grew between the police and Resurrection City residents. On June 20, officers used tear gas outside the village after Black youths threw rocks at them following an argument. Then a few young African Americans threw missiles over the Resurrection City fence at passing cars and police officers late at night on June 23. The U.S. Park Police, a unit of the National Park Service that patrols federal parks like the National Mall, responded by bombarding Resurrection City with tear gas. Screaming residents evacuated their dwellings, choking and even vomiting from the noxious fumes. Some had to be rescued and received medical attention. The response was shockingly disproportionate. "You don't shoot tear gas into an entire city because two or three hoodlums are throwing rocks," remarked one SCLC official.[69]

The next day, June 24, the parks permit that allowed Resurrection City to exist expired (the date was preestablished). Anticipating trouble, one thousand police officers showed up at the village that morning and 250 Civil Defense Unit officers wearing riot helmets and carrying guns moved into the camp. Next to Resurrection City's city hall, they found 115 people singing freedom songs. They were all arrested.

Early that afternoon, about one hundred people gathered at the SCLC's DC headquarters at Fourteenth and U Streets NW, the same place where the April rebellions began. As the crowd ebbed and flowed throughout the day, police officers maintained a visible presence in the area. Around 5:30 p.m. when there were approximately five hundred people in the crowd, a few youths decided to break windows. In contrast to the policy of restraint used in the April uprisings, DC police responded with immediate force. Two busloads of CDU officers armed with tear gas assembled, arranged themselves into shoulder-to-shoulder formations, and marched into the crowd. When a few people threw rocks at them, the police fired tear gas and then used more of the chemical irritant to break up crowds in the area. Clusters of people would assemble to watch the police's conduct, then officers would launch even more tear gas canisters to disperse those groups.

By 7:00 p.m., the police requested backup from the military, and Mayor Washington, with federal backing, sent in the DC National Guard. As news of the chaos spread across the city over the radio, people began to gather in other Black neighborhoods, most significantly along H Street NE. At 8:45 p.m., radio stations announced that Mayor Washington had imposed a curfew from 9 p.m. to 5:45 a.m. Police arrested 173 people that night and detonated one thousand canisters of tear gas. This aggressive response was disproportionate to what was a minor incident. There were scattered instances of looting, just twenty windows were broken in the entire city, and only three fires were started. In a dramatic departure from April 1968, the police had immediately responded with force and quickly requested federal intervention. This time, conservatives in Congress and the business committee praised the city's response, often by directly comparing it to the April uprisings. Senator Robert Byrd, for example, said, "Had the same firm and prompt action been manifested in the April riot, the city and Washington's business community would have been spared the looting, the arson, and the destruction it suffered."[70]

Police leadership and Mayor Washington had taken the scrutiny from congressional committees and businesses to heart after the rebellions that spring. DC's preparations for urban unrest following the Detroit uprisings had embraced restraint and focused on not provoking participants. In April, the police initially stayed on the fringes and avoided having a visible presence because it risked public outrage and escalation. Many people blamed the magnitude of destruction in the city on these measures. At the slightest sign of unrest in June 1968, police course-corrected and used the aggressive tactics that law-and-order advocates demanded, earning their praise. DC's response to the Poor People's Campaign harmfully reinforced the idea that Black people and protest were a threat to the city that warranted hostile and violent intervention.

Of course, Mayor Washington and President Johnson did not only advocate increased surveillance, more police funding, and tamping down Black protests in the wake of the uprisings. They also pushed for policies that addressed this structural inequality like the Civil Rights Act of 1968 and anti-poverty programs. But the programs of Johnson and other liberals to reduce crime and radicalism through granting law enforcement more authority and money undermined these other programs to address economic and racial inequality. The anticrime policies strengthened the group that forcefully harassed and oppressed Black people: the police. The measures also reinforced a long-standing, racist idea: crime, intentionally associated with Black people, threatened white Americans; limiting civil rights and expanding police power was the solution. The "right" of white people to feel unthreatened outweighed the rights of Black Americans. This increased criminalization and subjugation of African Americans only created further barriers to equal opportunity.[71]

10

"We Want to Rebuild. . . . What Do You Want?"

COMMUNITY CONTROL AND RECONSTRUCTION

WALTER E. WASHINGTON WAS IN HOSTILE TERRITORY. HE HAD come to testify before the House DC Committee on two bills that had been written by conservative politicians in response to the April rebellions. Washington opposed both bills. First, HR 16948 would mandate that the DC government pay for the cleanup of private businesses after the uprisings.[1] Second, a thinly veiled attempt to curtail future civil rights protests, HR 16941, would require monetary bonds from those seeking a parade or protest permit in Washington, DC. In other words, groups that wanted to hold a protest would have to pay a deposit to get a permit to hold the protest legally. Under this system, government officials would be able to demand unattainably high bond prices to effectually ban an undesired protest or demonstration. The bills rebuked Mayor Washington and his government in two ways: one asserted that the District had done such a poor job handling the uprisings that it should be held financially responsible for business owners' cleanup expenses; the other suggested that the federal government had so little faith in the city's ability to manage protests that Congress would effectively prevent demonstrations from occurring in the first place.

The witnesses preceding Mayor Washington depicted the capital as a city held hostage by protesters and criminals with a government that was unwilling and unable to protect its inhabitants. American citizens had lost their "right" to visit the capital and walk its streets.[2] As Washington testified, he challenged the lawmakers' critical appraisal of DC and urged them to encourage, rather than rebuke, the capital and its people in the aftermath of the rebellions:

> I believe the time has come when the Nation's Capital should really be the place that all people of the Nation look to. . . . I think it is necessary to react to some of the statements [by members of Congress], not emotionally, but sincerely, because I believe in this theme, and I believe in the city. I believe in the people. We are going to protect them. And we are going to do this if just given a decent opportunity to do so.[3]

In response to the members of Congress who criticized his ability to govern and chastised his hometown, Washington demanded that the legislators respect the city he led. While the capital was shrouded in smoke just weeks before, the mayor foregrounded a message of hope and determination: "I believe in the city. I believe in the people."

The mayor hoped to transform the capital through the process of reconstruction. In separate testimony before the Commerce Subcommittee of the Senate DC Committee on May 20, 1968, Mayor Washington announced a "crash program to rebuild riot-torn areas of the city with planning to be completed in 100 days." Washington suggested that the plan include citizen participation, more job opportunities for people in the affected communities, and increased business ownership by African Americans.[4] These ideas had been advocated by those who testified in the April DC City Council hearings and were endorsed by the city council.

While the framework and proposals for rebuilding seemed solid, no one yet knew exactly what policies and actions would emerge.

At the conclusion of the one-hundred-day planning period, Mayor Washington announced that he had secured a $600,000 grant from the Ford Foundation to support rebuilding. With the grant, the mayor created the Reconstruction and Development Corporation (RDC) in August 1968 to lead the effort to develop rebuilding plans.[5] Charles Cassell, a member of the Black United Front's steering committee, praised the RDC as a "cross section . . . of knowledgeable and responsible people who would help to guide the reconstruction in the devastated areas, so that what grows from such rebuilding will not be a replacement of what was there before, but will be some kind of community development which will bring to the people living in that community the control of that community." Further, Cassell suggested that there had been "no problems in dealing with any government agency" as the BUF collaborated on rebuilding efforts. While it was "too early to say what the net effect of these relationships will be," Cassell applauded the city government's efforts and believed it wanted to "bring . . . the people . . . control of that community."[6]

While the RDC and other DC agencies created the rebuilding blueprint, the city launched numerous efforts to foster citizen participation. The RDC hired groups to go door-to-door and ask residents, "What would you like to have in this area? This area has been burned out. We want to rebuild it. What do you want?"[7] The Redevelopment Land Agency, the federal agency responsible for urban redevelopment in DC, funded a survey of fifteen hundred businesses in the area to learn their desires as well.[8] The Model Inner City Community Development Organization, the community group coalition created by Walter Fauntroy to advocate for more equitable city planning, surveyed thousands of DC residents to learn how people wanted their neighborhoods to be reconstructed. Planners held many meetings and invited people to learn about the proposals for their community and communicate their input. In total, over half of the Shaw neighborhood's fifty thousand residents were surveyed by various agencies.[9]

As the rebuilding got underway, the city hired Black-owned businesses and workers. The National Capital Planning Commission, another federal agency tasked with guiding urban planning in the broader Washington area, hired Shaw Joint Venture, an all-Black survey team, to assess the damage to five thousand buildings.[10] By 1971, 40 percent of the construction contracts granted by the RLA went to minority contractors. Through a collaboration with the Small Business Administration, the RLA hired Black firms to perform "plumbing, heating, electrical work, carpentry, plastering and rooftop repairs." The RLA also established special provisions for the training and employment of renewal area residents. When building the Lincoln Westmoreland apartment building, the first housing complex completed as part of the rebuilding effort, the RLA contracted Black firms to perform ten out of nineteen subcontracting jobs. By 1972, all but one of the redevelopment projects underway included Black architects, attorneys, planners, housing consultants, or mortgage brokers on the development teams.[11]

Several of the proposals to reduce economic exploitation and increase Black opportunity suggested by Black leaders and the DC City Council were enacted. The Fair Access to Insurance Requirements Act became law in fall 1968 and required "the 200 companies that write property insurance here to provide coverage for businesses or homes that have been denied insurance because they are located in areas where riots have taken place." Previously, insurance companies would not cover businesses or homes in certain areas of the city, especially those with substantial Black populations.[12] The Labor Department gave Pride, Inc. a $3.8 million grant in August 1968 to create jobs for eleven hundred DC teens.[13] Also in August 1968, the SBA created "Project Own" to increase lending to historically disadvantaged communities to increase homeownership rates. Over the next year, the SBA nearly tripled the amount of loans to people who were not white.[14] Through the RDC, the city granted modest loans to minority contractors.[15] In 1969, DC created an office under the Department of Economic Development to investigate bad business practices and protect consumers.[16]

Home rule was the biggest success for Washingtonians after the disorders. Congress granted DC home rule in 1973 at the urging of politically savvy and persistent Washingtonians. Fed up with House DC Committee chair John McMillan's refusal to permit any bill on home rule out of his committee, DC's delegate to the House of Representatives, Walter Fauntroy—who, like Congresswoman Eleanor Holmes Norton (D-DC) today, was not allowed to vote on legislation—organized a campaign to unseat McMillan. The Voting Rights Act of 1965 had dramatically increased Black people's ability to vote in the South, and Fauntroy took advantage of this new power. Washingtonians took buses into McMillan's North Carolina district and canvassed against him. It worked, and with McMillan voted out of office, Democratic Representative Charles Diggs Jr., a Black congressman from Michigan, became the chair of the House DC Committee. Together, Diggs and Fauntroy wrote the Home Rule Act of 1973, and President Richard Nixon signed it into law that December.

Yet Congress still retrained significant power over the District's affairs. To this day, DC is barred from going into debt on any project that is not part of a capital or economic development program, and all budgets must be certified as balanced by an appointed chief financial officer. The House Oversight Committee approves the DC budget, reviews its legislation, and can even overturn its laws. Members of Congress have exploited this power to override the democratic will of Washingtonians and enforce their own ideologies. For example, in 2017 during his tenure as the chairman of the House Oversight Committee, Representative Jason Chaffetz (R-UT) threatened to launch an investigation if DC used its tax dollars to defend undocumented immigrants from deportation. Since DC residents passed a referendum to legalize cannabis in 2014, members of Congress have used their control over DC's budget and affairs to block the legalization of marijuana sales. For decades, the Dornan Amendment has barred DC from using tax dollars to cover abortion care for Washingtonians enrolled in Medicaid. The continued power of Congress over the District's affairs is rooted in the long history of white fear of Black political power and the racist belief that a majority-nonwhite populace is incapable of independently governing itself. Even this limited system of home rule could be rolled back at any time. In 2022, senior Republicans in Congress, including the House minority leader, Kevin McCarthy (R-CA), were considering ramping up congressional oversight of the District if Republicans regained the House majority. Georgia Congressman Andrew Clyde, a Republican, even claimed he is writing legislation that would repeal home rule.[17]

Despite these limitations, DC used home rule to enshrine the importance of citizen participation into its new government. In a referendum vote on May 7, 1974, DC citizens voted to create Advisory Neighborhood Commissions (ANCs), community-based bodies of the capital's local government that are still in place today. The DC City Council divided the city into thirty-six ANCs each with its own elected representatives, creating a "remarkable space for neighborhood autonomy."[18] The "sunshine" provision of the Home Rule Act "provided machinery to give the people notice of proposed governmental actions affecting their well-being" to assure "the much-needed two-way communication between the people and their government which had been identified as a prime need at the time of the riots."[19] In the first elections after home rule, nine out of eleven African Americans and both white members elected to the DC City Council were veterans of the civil rights movement, reflecting "a remarkable shift from protest to politics." The newly elected city council passed provisions to protect and aid historically discriminated groups. Among other initiatives, DC passed rent control measures, incentives for government contracts for minorities, strong affirmative action and anti-gender-discrimination laws, and consumer protection laws.[20]

The RLA, MICCO, and Citizen Participation

But as the District of Columbia rebuilt physically and socially, it often ran into opposition from the federal government. The effort to rebuild Northwest #1—an urban renewal area that included Shaw, the long-standing center of Black DC and one of the neighborhoods most damaged in the uprisings—reveals the promise and limits of Washingtonians' responses to the rebellions. Rather than abandoning the capital, many Washingtonians were optimistic that the city could design and build neighborhoods that were affordable and beautiful, and that met the needs of the Black community. The limitations of these projects demonstrate the power the federal government held over the capital. With little autonomy, DC reformers struggled to implement proposals that ran counter to the agenda of President Nixon and federal agencies.

While most of the city's redevelopment was orchestrated through a complicated process involving the DC government, the Department of Housing and Urban Development, and the National Capital Planning Commission, the process in the Shaw neighborhood was controlled by the Redevelopment Land Agency, a federal office that had the power to buy land, condemn buildings, and purchase property in urban renewal areas. The RLA established Northwest #1—the area bounded by Fifteenth Street NW, Florida Avenue NW, North Capitol Street, and M Street NW— and designated it for urban renewal in the early 1960s.[21]

Civil rights leader and DC City Council member Walter Fauntroy had worked for years to ensure that urban renewal in Shaw would take place "with, by, and for" its residents.[22] Fauntroy created the Model Inner City Community Development Organization in 1966 to seize the RLA's provision for citizen input in planning and to demand that redevelopment occur on the terms of the community. MICCO's membership was composed of nearly 150 citizen groups that included local churches, school parent-teacher associations, and service organizations.[23] In March 1967, the RLA hired MICCO to "involve the community in urban renewal planning" and help citizens draft their own proposals for renewal.[24] Although MICCO advised the RLA, the RLA had sole authority over what developers it selected and plans it adopted.[25]

After much of the Shaw neighborhood was damaged in the uprisings, the RLA and MICCO crafted a plan to rebuild. This proposal would be implemented under the Neighborhood Development Plan (NDP) program recently created by Congress as part of the Housing Act of 1968. Through the NDP, neighborhoods created a long-term plan for the entire redevelopment of the community to guide future planning. The specific funding and year-to-year development projects were determined each year in different "action programs." Every year, the community and public agencies would create and approve the next year's plan. Over time, the yearly incremental changes would "achieve the objectives set forth in the urban renewal plan for the whole area."[26]

To formulate the long-term, overarching plan, MICCO surveyed community residents by going door-to-door and holding

community meetings. MICCO found that the community wanted a housing plan that would "not force residents to move out of
Shaw," "provide new and rehabilitated housing at rents they can
afford," "reduce overcrowding," and provide maximum opportunity for homeownership. Ninety-seven percent of Shaw residents
wanted to limit traffic to a few main streets. Another 97 percent
of those surveyed desired a subway station in their neighborhood
and agreed that major business centers should be constructed
around the stations. One hundred percent agreed with MICCO's
proposal to put "major public agencies like welfare, a health clinic,
social security and local government offices in one central location in or near one of the major shopping areas."[27]

The resulting plan, approved by city and federal agencies in
January 1969, reflected the desires of Shaw residents.[28] The plan
would redevelop the neighborhood in stages, rehabilitating some
existing buildings instead of razing whole blocks and putting up
new structures like the RLA had done in Southwest DC the previous decade. It would create "new and rehabilitated, low and moderate income housing, shopping malls, new schools, a job training
center, a civic center and a clinic."[29] As requested by the community, the plan developed "social services and community facilities within the Shaw area" and would locate "major social services
(such as health, welfare, and employment) at a centralized point,
with other services (such as recreation spaces and day care facilities) being located throughout the area for convenience."[30] The
design further proposed new schools, a library, and parks. Traffic
flowing through the community would be limited to specific areas.
Shopping centers would be located around the proposed subway
stop. Finally, the plan would create "new employment, job training, ownership and business opportunities for Shaw residents."[31]

The plan used nonprofit community groups to rebuild instead
of private developers. The DC government would buy land from

the current property owners in damaged areas and then sell it to "non-profit sponsors," primarily churches and community organizations, who were willing to improve the property in accordance with the city-approved redevelopment plan. The federal government, specifically the Department of Housing and Urban Development, would provide 75 percent of the money and DC the other 25 percent to buy the property. Churches and other nonprofits would have the ability to buy the property at its fair market value from the government. The money paid by the nonprofit groups could then be loaned back to them in the form of a Federal Housing Administration loan to help pay for construction costs.[32]

For NDP 1, the redevelopment plan for 1969–70, the RLA would create four sites for renewal by purchasing property, including rebellion-damaged buildings along Seventh Street NW and vacant lots. Further, the RLA would rehabilitate row houses through a new initiative called the Turnkey III program, named so because it aimed to fix up houses so that all new residents had to do was turn the key to the home. This initiative contracted outside organizations to fix up existing housing. Tenants could then pay an affordable rent that went toward eventual homeownership.[33] The biggest success of NDP 1 came when the RLA broke ground on the Lincoln Westmoreland apartment complex. Sponsored by two churches and designed by a firm of Black architects, the project was the "first nonprofit, low- and moderate-income housing development built anywhere in the country under the provisions of the 1968 Housing Act."[34] NDP 2 aimed to build new housing for large families, replace the rest of the buildings on blocks where redevelopment started in the first year, tear down the worst housing in Shaw, and build a shopping center along Seventh Street.[35] "The MICCO process really works," proclaimed a pamphlet outlining the second-year action plan.[36]

The RLA's support for citizen participation and "the MICCO

process," however, was quickly eroding as projects faced worsening delays. By the summer of 1970, the Lincoln Westmoreland remained the only new building under construction. Rebuilding delays primarily resulted from two issues: relocating displaced people and funding. The RLA was required by law to provide relocation housing for residents who needed to move so their buildings could be reconstructed. It was increasingly difficult, however, to find adequate housing for relocating people because public housing and funding were already in short supply. In June 1970, for example, a joint report by the RLA and the NCPC found that the plan for the National Capital Housing Authority to provide one thousand units of low-income housing was in serious trouble because the NCHA was "bankrupt." The RLA's projects had counted on using those one thousand units to house the families that would be displaced by rebuilding in Shaw.[37] "One of the major factors affecting our ability to accelerate the development process and meet these schedules is the availability of adequate relocation resources," wrote DC RLA head Melvin Mister.[38] "The recent expansion of the District's urban renewal activities under the Neighborhood Development Program, and the extensive acquisition of occupied properties as part of the NDP, has resulted in a tremendous increase in the Agency relocation workload."[39] By 1971, the issue of insufficient relocation housing was so severe that Mister insisted that the RLA could not undertake any new rebuilding projects.[40]

Additionally, the NDP process required RLA funding, but securing that money became more difficult. To build low-income housing, developers relied upon federal mortgage subsidies from the FHA that reduced the cost of building. These cost reductions allowed developers to charge a lower rent so that more people could afford the housing. The financing specialist for DC's RLA branch believed that "it's impossible to construct housing that anyone can afford any other way." Yet, aligning with President Nixon's promise to slash funding to "big government" federal programs, Congress appropriated only $25 million dollars for the nationwide NDP. Additionally, projects worth $129.9 million were already backlogged awaiting money. While low-income housing and urban renewal was planned and even approved in DC, the funding did not exist.[41] In 1970, President Nixon put a moratorium on new construction of subsidized housing, worsening the funding crunch.[42] With little available money, the RLA's director struggled to fund projects that the RLA had already begun, and the RLA greatly limited its proposals for new undertakings.[43]

In response to the very real obstacles to redevelopment and the resulting delays, the federal government and project consultants challenged the community, nonprofit-driven approach and sought the involvement of large private companies instead. In December 1970, RLA advisers recommended that the city "build housing for moderate to high-income families first in the redevelopment of the Shaw area, in order to stabilize the primarily low-income section." These projects would attract private developers eager for the lucrative opportunity to construct buildings that catered to wealthy buyers. The developers and new affluent residents would "improve" the neighborhood. MICCO criticized the recommendations and instead encouraged first building first low-income housing for those living "in some of the worst housing of the area." Walter Fauntroy contended that most of the wealthier families in the area already owned their homes and could acquire rehabilitation grants to improve their preexisting housing instead. "We are determined to build the beloved community . . . by providing for the needs of the poorest of Shaw first," Fauntroy insisted.[44]

Then, in July 1971, the RLA proposed "a new housing plan for the Shaw area, designed to attract large, experienced developers to build in the riot-scarred area." Instead of waiting for developers to come up with a proposal that could be negotiated and approved by the city and community, the RLA would combine properties slated for renewal into larger parcels and select a developer through competitive bidding. The RLA contended that competitive bidding on parceled properties would speed up rebuilding, reduce costs, and improve the quality of housing: "The mere fact of competing made the prospective developers sharpen their pencils on costs, and sharpen their wits to produce the best possible benefits for the community."[45] Some in Shaw worried that if the RLA used a competitive bidding process, the nonprofit sponsors slated to develop projects would not have the capital to win over private businesses.[46] "It seems that the community senses the danger of losing meaningful and fruitful community participation if competitive bidding is your choice," said Rev. Earnest R. Gibson. "We have had competition within the negotiation process, but the arbiter of the competition has been not a relatively disinterested bureaucracy, but concerned citizen groups."[47]

Despite the RLA's efforts to lobby MICCO to support competitive bidding, MICCO preferred a different approach. The organization had spent the last year negotiating a proposal with the Development Corporation of America (DCA), a building company based in Boston, to develop the set of lots referred to as "Parcel A." Fauntroy and MICCO believed the firm "offered the community the best deal: Eventual ownership of land by two co-sponsoring Shaw churches; a development team selected with MICCO's advice; employment of Blacks in all stages, and 150 relocation units assured for displaced Shaw residents in DCA's Edgewood Terrace Apartments."[48] The DCA could start work before the RLA would be able to select a developer through competitive bidding.[49] Nevertheless, in November 1971, the RLA rejected MICCO's proposal to develop Parcel A with the DCA and instead opened competitive bidding on the land. The RLA had turned against community-led development and felt that competitive bidding was essential to attracting more substantial national investors.[50]

Subsequently, the relationship between the RLA and MICCO quickly deteriorated. In February 1972, the RLA made Walter Fauntroy's resignation a precondition to renewing MICCO's contract as a community developer. Although the RLA had previously concluded that Fauntroy could remain MICCO president after he was elected as DC's nonvoting delegate to Congress, the RLA now insisted Fauntroy's position was too much of a conflict of interest. Fauntroy did resign, and the RLA renewed MICCO's contract, but the partnership did not last long. In January 1973, the RLA ended MICCO's contract and, later that year, it recommended heavily curtailing community participation and consolidating city planning power.[51] "The present diffused responsibilities for urban renewal planning as well as related community development programming should be eliminated," the RLA insisted. "The authority and responsibility for approving plans should be clearly lodged in the Mayor and the City Council."[52]

The RLA's erosion of support for community participation mirrored President Nixon's opposition to the process. After Nixon toured the damaged areas during his first month in office in 1969, he made it clear that he wanted "action" fast. Specifically, Nixon insisted construction begin on Seventh Street NW by September 1969.[53] On April 9, 1969, Nixon again called for faster rebuilding and promised DC $29.7 million to do so. "No wonder our citizens are beginning to question Government's ability to perform," Nixon said. "There could be no more searing symbol of governmental inability to act than those rubble-strewn lots and desolate, decaying buildings, once a vital part of a community's life and now left to rot."[54] Nixon blamed the slow progress on community participation. "Nixon Administration sources have said that citizen involvement in planning delays decision-making to a point at which urban renewal has become intolerably slow," reported the *Washington Post*.[55] The president showed "little enthusiasm for 'citizen participation'" and "sought to return most of the power to city halls."[56] But Nixon's push to speed up rebuilding by bypassing citizen participation upset many groups, ironically slowing down the rebuilding process on H Street NE.[57]

Despite the repudiation of citizen participation and the insistence that private corporations would speed up rebuilding, the renewal process did not accelerate nor did the funding and relocation issues disappear after private companies got involved. "The biggest problem in rebuilding has been this: the housing planned for all three riot corridors [Fourteenth Street NW, Seventh Street NW, and H Street NE] was mostly for moderate-income families earning between $6,000 and $13,000 a year, while most of those facing displacement were the poor," reported the *Washington Post*. "Without housing to accommodate the displaced, the program could only proceed so far."[58] Private firms could not proceed since they also could not find anywhere to place the current residents. The dire lack of housing for displaced families was only made worse in 1973 when Nixon announced federal cuts to many urban programs including low- and moderate-income housing programs and urban renewal. Nixon further imposed a moratorium on subsidized housing construction, affecting private developers who also relied on federal loans and grants to build the housing.[59] Reginald Greene of the DC Department of Housing and Community Development Center commented that "there's just not enough money to do the kinds of things that need to be done. There was no real eagerness on the part of private investors to invest in the city after the riots and civil disturbances."[60]

Ten years after the rebellions, all completed housing was nonprofit sponsored and designed in consultation with the surrounding community. In Shaw, the Lincoln Westmoreland apartment complex and housing, built by the First Rising Mt. Zion Baptist Church, the New Bethel Baptist Church, the Deliverance Church of God in Christ, the Immaculate Conception Church, and the United House of Prayer, was complete.[61] On H Street NE, the Horning Brothers/Group Ministry Community Housing Corporation built housing in several different locations. On Fourteenth Street, the completed Columbia Heights Village project was created by the CHANGE—All Souls Housing Corporation, a shared undertaking between the All Souls Church and a Great Society–created anti-poverty community group.[62] "During the past few years, some of the largest housing developments in the City have come through the cooperation and sponsorship of church and community coalitions working with the city government," summarized a report on the city's progress ten years later. "These groups have done tremendous amounts of work to plan with the city for housing to meet the needs of the community."[63]

In the ten years following the uprisings, the DC government constructed many of the public resources that Black residents requested. It built two libraries, ten schools, four recreation centers, and six parks. On Fourteenth Street, the city built a large health facility that made it easier for Shaw residents to access medical care.[64] The newly built Martin Luther King Jr. Memorial Library in downtown DC became a vibrant community center. With a multiracial, citywide coalition including attorneys and the often-radical Emergency Committee on the Transportation Crisis, Congress at long last killed the DC highway program and funded the DC Metro. The public subway system opened in 1976. "These major programs of public works stemmed from a policy of replacing inadequate and outmoded facilities to meet the needs of neglected areas," reflected the tenth anniversary report.

In the same report, the section labeled "Private Sector Activities" only listed projects "underway or planned." Despite the

RLA's insistence that private bidding would speed up reconstruction, the only completed projects originated from the original, community-driven blueprints.[65] The process, however, destroyed the public's confidence in urban renewal after the second attempt failed to produce the results the community had demanded. Urban renewal in the capital "totally lost credibility among all elements of the community," a citizens' commission appointed by the DC City Council found. The panel concluded the urban renewal had "lost the confidence of the people of our neighborhoods, our businessmen, our professionals, and, in fact, most of those public officials who are charged with its responsibility."[66] In the wake of the rebellions, DC embarked on an ambitious plan to reconstruct its damaged neighborhoods based on citizen input and by using community organizations. These initiatives embraced the legislative mandates and federal initiatives created by President Johnson's Great Society such as the Neighborhood Development Plan and "maximum feasible participation." DC officials and activists alike hoped that the process would generate jobs for African Americans, provide quality housing for low-income Washingtonians, and create a beautiful community out of the ruins. DC completed many of these goals as it built public facilities, hired Black people and businesses, and enshrined citizen participation into its new home rule government.

But much of DC's rebuilding efforts were controlled by the federal government instead of the District. Federal support of community participation and nonprofit sponsors quickly dissipated as Nixon and the RLA did not obtain the quick results they unrealistically expected. Nixon slashed federal spending on urban development programs, imposed a moratorium on federal housing projects, and explicitly offered financial incentives to disincentivize community involvement in DC reconstruction efforts. The RLA followed suit, cutting nonprofit community groups out of rebuilding and instead welcoming large corporations to develop the area. Private developers, however, did not rapidly rebuild rebellion-damaged neighborhoods as Nixon and the RLA hoped. In fact, ten years after April 1968, every completed housing project in the capital was built by nonprofit community groups.

These efforts to reconstruct Shaw demonstrated the power of the federal government to impose its priorities in the capital, even when it went against the will of Washingtonians. Even though MICCO's success was limited, its efforts broaden our understanding of how cities reacted to urban unrest. More than 50 percent of the area's residents were consulted about what they wanted in their community. The government listened and actually built many of those projects, often hiring businesses and workers based in that neighborhood. The process also trusted community groups to create housing that benefited low-income residents instead of just turning a profit. This history provides an inspiring, alternative model of urban policy and development.

11

"A Great Deal of Public Interest and Debate"

CRIME AND POLICING AFTER THE REBELLIONS

IN JUNE 1968, A FLORIDA MAN WROTE A LETTER TO PRESIDENT Lyndon Johnson asking if it was "safe this summer" to bring his grandchildren to Washington, DC. While the man had previously visited the capital with his children and grandchildren, "now, we are apprehensive. What is happening when patriotic Americans are concerned for the safety of their grandchildren touring the Nation's capital?"[1] "We have received a number of inquiries such as yours," DC Police Chief John Layton responded. He encouraged the man to visit and assured him that "the areas in which practically all of the [riot] damage occurred, are in sections of the city not in proximity to the usual points of tourists' interest."[2] The Washington Convention and Visitors Bureau instructed local travel agents to inform tourists that they would not stay close to the damaged sections while visiting Washington.[3] Both Layton and travel agents distinguished between two versions of the capital; one featured the monuments and was clean and safe, the other was a dangerous inner city.

Efforts to attract visitors were undermined by some members of Congress who urged their constituents to avoid the capital. "I would not be sensitive to my responsibility as a Member of the Congress if I failed to warn my constituents that they should not plan to visit the Nation's Capital this summer," said Republican

Congressman Joe Waggoner of Louisiana. "It is not safe on the streets at any hour of the day or evening, singly or in groups." Waggoner warned that "lawlessness threatens everyone who enters the city" and predicted it would be "a miracle if the streets are not covered with blood before the summer is over." "Perhaps sometime in the future it may be safe to walk the streets here in the Capital, but there is no indication that the extremists and liberal cranks now in control intend for it be anytime soon."[4] The same day Waggoner delivered this speech on the House floor, the chairman of the House DC Committee, John McMillan, entered a statement into the *Congressional Record* asserting that on a recent trip back to North Carolina, "The chief topic of discussion with practically every person I talked to was the lack of law enforcement in Washington."[5] McMillan lamented that "it is a sad day when we have experienced the receiving of messages from people back home, from groups of students, high school graduates, who normally look forward to a pleasant visit to the Nation's Capital" but now were afraid to come. "These youngsters, I guess, will have to forego their rights as American citizens to come and enjoy the Nation's Capital because of the threats," he concluded.[6]

Crime in Washington was indeed high and rising in 1968. The murder rate in DC tripled between 1960 and 1969, and by 1969 the DC crime rate was nearly three times the national rate.[7] In 1968, instances of rape were 50 percent higher than in 1967 and there were on average thirteen robberies a day.[8] In the months following the uprisings, four merchants were murdered by thieves and newspapers reported multiple "pay or burn" incidents—groups threatening to burn businesses down if they did not give them money.[9] Ben's Chili Bowl co-owner Virginia Ali recalled that patrons' cars were broken into outside of the restaurant: "It was just kind of these horror stories."[10] As scholar James Forman wrote about the complex issue of spiking crime, "whatever the reason, the stark fact remains: D.C. had become a much more dangerous place in the 1960s, as residents witnessed the largest decade-long crime wave ever recorded, then or since."[11]

Since desegregation, concern over crime was such a dominant force in American politics that citizens and politicians demanded anticrime measures such as strengthened police departments even when crime rates were low. Calls for law and order grew as urban crime rates rose in the late 1960s. They reached a fever pitch after uprisings erupted in more than one hundred cities after Martin Luther King's assassination. In Washington, some people were so scared of urban crime that they swore off cities and receded to the suburbs. Others lobbied the federal government to install troops to guard the capital against criminals.

The local and federal governments desponded very differently to DC crime in the wake of the uprisings. Richard Nixon successfully channeled fears of urban crime, especially crime in the capital, to win the White House. As president, he turned the capital into an anticrime policy laboratory over the objections of DC leaders and residents. Despite the ineffectiveness of these measures, they were modeled across the country, disproportionately harming communities of color. The DC City Council, on the other hand, passed legislation to limit the police's use of firearms in the months following the rebellions. Amid rising crime rates and public panic, the city council ignored calls to expand police authority and instead launched initiatives to grant citizens more control over law enforcement.

Growing Concerns over Crime in Washington

As Washington recovered from the disorders, dealt with increasing crime, and braced for the upcoming Poor People's Campaign, national politicians and local advocates often argued that tougher law enforcement would prevent crime and future disorders. The Federation of Citizens Associations of the District of Columbia criticized the DC government for placing "unreasonable curbs and restraints" on the troops and police officers,[12] endorsed a bill that would make it impossible to hold office if one was convicted of a riot crime,[13] demanded Public Safety Director Patrick Murphy be fired since they did not trust him to maintain law and order,[14] and adopted a resolution that requested troops patrol the Poor People's March.[15] In a statement before the DC City Council, the president of the federation, John Immer, emphasized that "first and foremost, we are concerned about the physical safety of the people of the District and their protection from acts of violence on the streets or in their homes. Personal security is basic to an orderly society."[16] Similarly, the Washington Board of Trade called for more police officers on the streets and condemned the Poor People's Campaign.[17]

Some who called for "law and order" in Washington demanded federal intervention, military occupation, and even dictatorship. Senator Robert Byrd encouraged federal troops to "stay indefinitely" because "if Washington is to be subjected to a summer campaign of demonstrations, as has long been planned, the presence of Federal troops will be reassuring."[18] In May, broadcast company WMAL "reluctantly" supported Byrd's proposal "to station troops throughout the crime-ridden areas of the city until order is restored."[19] The BOT's president, William Calomiris, also advocated prolonged troop occupation in DC to contain crime.[20] One month later, a WMAL editorial again asked that "troops be brought into the city to help restore order." "Semi-martial law is not a pleasant idea," the editorial claimed, "but there seems little choice."[21] "Many say dictatorship is not the answer," said a self-proclaimed "slum landlord" testifying in House DC Committee

he city's response to the rebellions. "Well,
now. They certainly would never put up
in Washington, D.C. and the nation."[22]
d cities altogether after the disorders.
...os, the Fairfax School District placed an
.. on school trips to DC following the unrest. "We
...nt to keep the field trips away from all city slums until the
atmosphere is less tense," reported school officials.[23] Hotel and
restaurant business in Washington was 25 percent lower in April
1968 than an average year and 21.5 percent lower in May.[24] Eight
hundred thousand fewer people visited the major Washington
tourist spots in April 1968 than did in April 1967.[25]

As white suburbanites were reluctant to enter the District, some
establishments took measures to assuage their concerns over
crime. Reuben Jackson, a Black Washingtonian who was a teenager in 1968, used to arrive early to the DC Stadium to watch bat-
ting practice before the uprisings. Previously, people who came to
see players take their warm-up swings could go to the lower seats
to watch and then return to their "nosebleed" seats once the game
began. After April 1968,

> There was clearly a concerted effort to protect the
> people from the suburbs who "dared" quote come
> into D.C. And there were cops sort of ringing the sta-
> dium. Literally, if you left your seat to go to the bath-
> room, you had to have your ticket stub with you. And
> I mean they may have stopped the white kids, but they
> stopped us every chance they got. When we'd try to
> go down to watch batting practice, because a lot of the
> kids from the suburbs, I think, parents had those, we
> called them the "good seats," we weren't allowed to do
> it. They'd look at your ticket stub and go, "Uh, uh. You

don't sit here. Go back upstairs." So, there was a mu[ch]
more palpable tension. . . . It was like some little, I don't
know, it's like the stadium became this little South
Africa where you had your little area. I kind of said
to my parents, you know, "I don't remember having to
carry a ticket just to go to the bathroom to prove that
you were in there." And it stopped me from going. I
didn't go. That was '68.

Jackson was so dismayed at the Senators' new policy, he did not
go to another baseball game even up until the Senators left Washington in 1971.[26]

It was not just tourists and suburbanites who were concerned
over crime and safety in the District, however. "Due to the serious crime situation, we can no longer expect our members to
attend evening meetings," remarked the citizen association for
the Brookland neighborhood in Northeast DC. The association
suspended its membership in the larger Federation of Citizens
Associations "until such a time as the streets of our great city will
once more be safe for the average citizen in his pursuit of serving
his community."[27] The DC Central Library, located near some of
the worst damage on Seventh Street, had fewer visitors after the
upheaval. "On fall and winter evenings when we normally would
expect to have quite a number of students and other young people asking for help on assignments or for magazines . . . we had
instead an almost empty division after about 6:30 or 7:00 PM,"
wrote librarian Eleanor Bartlett. Many patrons called the library
and "told us on the telephone that they would not come to Central
nor would they allow their children to come."[28] Even though the
number of visitors to the Central Library declined, there was a
"resurgence of interest in black history" at libraries throughout
the city. After DC libraries were unable to meet the demand for

material on Black culture and civil rights, the library created a collection of books that stayed at specific locations so more people could access the literature.[29]

Ben's Chili Bowl co-owner Virginia Ali also recollected that people were scared to come into the damaged U Street area: "The riots had a very profound effect, and people were actually afraid to come into the neighborhood." Some of her white and Black acquaintances were frightened to eat at the restaurant. Instead, some called and asked, "Could you get someone to fix me six chili dogs and just run them right into the car?"[30] The *Washington Afro-American* reported that "crime has become a major preoccupation of Washington residents. The danger of being robbed, raped, mugged, or murdered now surpasses sex—and even politics—as a topic of conversation."[31]

Solutions to Crime in DC

But there was simultaneously another problem regarding public safety: police brutality and lack of accountability. When tensions surrounding the police spiked in the summer and fall of 1968, the capital considered several measures to limit police authority. Some believed granting neighborhoods more power over police precincts would reduce longstanding tension and reduce the likelihood of further uprisings.

Like today, deaths of Black people at the hands of police officers were a major problem and a rallying cry for accountability and change. DC police shot and killed seventeen people between January 1967 and October 1968.[32] Led by the Black United Front, Black Washingtonians demanded oversight of the police force after officers killed two Black men in the summer and fall of 1968.[33] First, on July 14, 1968, a police officer killed Theodore Lawson, a Black man, at the corner of Fourteenth and U Streets.[34] In response, the DC City Council created the DC City Council Public Safety Committee on Police-Community Relations, which the city council chairman, John Hechinger, directed to "prepare a report for action." "What is needed now in this city," he emphasized, "is to develop and implement the specific, concrete steps to an effective policy community relations program, not additional hearings."[35] In creating the report, the committee consulted with the local ACLU, the BUF, and members of the community, whose written and spoken feedback the committee solicited.[36]

The resulting report concluded that improved police-community relations were a prerequisite to an effective police force and "safe streets": "The present situation creates a climate where a minor incident can escalate into one of major proportions. Unless relationships between the police and major elements of the community improve, it is difficult to see how the current high rates of crime which threaten the well-being of the city can be substantially reduced." The report encouraged community influence and input, noted the need to better handle citizens' complaints about the police, and urged the department to hire more Black police officers.[37] On August 20, 1968, the DC City Council adopted the report as a statement of policy.[38]

The urgency for action increased after October 8, when a white police officer killed another Black man, Elijah Bennett, allegedly for jaywalking. At a rally held at the New School for Afro-American Thought, the same place Stokely Carmichael held his press conference after King's assassination, Black leaders associated with the BUF condemned unchecked police power. "How many times are you going to watch your brothers being shot down in the streets?" asked militant activist Julius Hobson. "How many rallies are we going to have? How many marches?" Chuck Stone, a member of the BUF, issued an ultimatum: "Either Mayor Washington comes out for black control of this police force in 7 days or step down." The crowd cheered. In a moment indicative of the extreme frustration of the community, Carmichael's assertion that "We must legitimate the killing of honkey [white] cops in our communities" was met with "wild" cheers.[39]

By the end of that month, Mayor Washington announced a strategy to address the issues of police violence and overreach. First, he created an ad hoc committee on public safety. The committee suggested "radical changes" to how DC handled cases when officers killed citizens. These included ending the power of the coroner, the person who conducted autopsies, to declare a homicide "justifiable." It also recommended ending the U.S. Attorney's power to present police homicide cases to a grand jury since the committee believed the U.S. Attorneys, who regularly worked with the police department, were too close to the officers they were supposed to hold accountable. Instead, the committee proposed, a civil rights attorney from the Justice Department should prosecute such cases. Finally, the mayor's committee suggested that citizens should have a larger say in determining policies regarding police discipline and use of firearms.[40]

In November, the DC City Council also proposed several specific measures to better police-community relations. To improve the grievance mechanism for citizens regarding the police, the city council recommended creating a board composed of two citizens and a police officer to hear complaints, determine "the facts" of the situation, and set a punishment if necessary. Previously, a special trial board of one civilian attorney and two police officers evaluated citizen complaints.[41] The city council also suggested a precinct advisory board system. Each precinct board would have nine members—seven citizens and two police officers. The board would interview any new officers coming into the precinct and those up for promotions, develop "comprehensive community relations and crime prevention programs," and "advise the

Captain, the Chief, the Public Safety Director . . . Mayor [and] Council regarding personnel and police matters." The board would meet with the precinct captain at least once a month and the captain would "give reasonable adherence to the advice of the board."

If its recommendations were not followed, the board could ask the police chief and public safety director to review the captain's decision to ignore the board's recommendation. As the city council noted, the plan was "an attempt to structure a significant bargaining process on the part of the police captain and the community." It was "not citizen control as the phrase is often used. But the powers are sufficient so that policies of the Department can be carefully scrutinized by citizens."[42] Citizens would not have direct control over the police; their role would be to advise rather than to decide. Still, the proposal was grounded in the idea that citizens should have some control over policing in their neighborhoods.

This proposal was an early attempt at creating a civilian review board of police forces. In 1968 and today, many departments deal with misconduct internally. If a police officer is accused of wrongdoing, it is other officers that investigate and determine the appropriate response to the allegation. This process is embedded with significant bias that creates a lack of accountability. Civilian review boards grant oversight capabilities to people who are not part of the police, although many boards are limited by a lack of enforcement power. DC was not the first to consider a civilian review board. New York City's Civilian Complaint Review Board, for example, was established in 1953, and Philadelphia created its Police Review Board in 1958. Today, the Department of Justice's Office of Community Oriented Policing Services estimates that there are more than two hundred police review boards across the country.[43]

The DC City Council also considered legislation that would

change the circumstances under which police officers could discharge their guns. "The regulations would require that an officer
use only the minimum amount of force necessary to subdue a suspect," said the chairman of the DC Public Safety Committee. "In
all cases an officer would be required to exhaust all reasonable
means of apprehending a person before he could resort to deadly
force." Additionally, the measure would ban warning shots, firing
weapons from a moving vehicle, and firing when attempting to
apprehend a fleeing person for a misdemeanor or felony (except
in very specific circumstances). The DC City Council believed
that under their new guidelines, six out of the seventeen recent
instances of police shootings of civilians would have been prohibited and six more "would have been subject to investigation to
determine whether the officer had been justified." Two lives would
have been saved.[44] The *Washington Afro-American* described the
legislation as "stiff gun rules."[45]

The DC City Council's consideration of these regulations "generated a great deal of public interest and debate."[46] Police Chief
Layton opposed the proposed guidelines, although he agreed
there was a "need for strict control and supervision of police officers in the use of their service revolvers."[47] Many white Washingtonians were concerned that the legislation would limit the ability
of police officers to do their job and worsen crime rates. "We were
disappointed that we did not find any words in the report regarding the responsibilities of the individual citizen in maintenance
of law and order," read a statement passed by the Federation of
Civic Associations. "One might almost say that the emphasis in
the report on the demand for changes in police actions and attitudes would lead one to think that lawlessness is the fault of the
police." It suggested that the "vast majority" of Washingtonians
supported the police and urged the city council to "give full support to the police from the top of the Government down . . . [and]

give short shrift to those who attempt to downgrade the police to satisfy their own political aims."[48]

Eventually, the DC City Council passed the police regulations on December 17, and the bill went to the mayor the following day.[49] Mayor Washington vetoed it. While he agreed "in principle" with the regulation, the mayor explained, it presented "enforcement problems from an administrative point of view and, in my opinion, must be clarified and strengthened, particularly with respect of the meaning of 'deadly force' and the provision relating to moving vehicles." The mayor suggested that the city council substitute the term "physical force" for "deadly force," allow warning shots in more circumstances, and expand the allowances for shooting at a vehicle.[50] This created a substantially broader interpretation of when police weapons could be discharged.

John Hechinger, the chair of the city council, refused to accept the mayor's proposed amendments because he believed it gave too many allowances. "I say again—as I have said repeatedly before—that these guidelines in no way disarm or handicap our police force!" he declared in response. "This police force at any strength cannot do its job without the support of its citizens."[51] The city council fell one vote short of overriding Washington's veto and later altered the legislation to incorporate the mayor's revisions. Mayor Washington signed it into law on January 21, 1969.[52] While the DC City Council passed the provision on community review boards and precinct boards, Mayor Washington did not act upon it as he considered them "recommendations" instead of a requirement to implement.[53]

There is no clear documentation of why Mayor Washington did not approve the community review and precinct boards. The city council passed the provisions slightly more than a month before President Nixon was inaugurated. Under the 1967 reorganization of the DC government, the president appointed DC's mayor-commissioner. Washington was likely wary of passing legislation that ceded some police control to the community right before the staunchly pro-police Republican president determined if he would reappoint Washington as mayor. While Washington personally opposed many of Nixon's suggestions to decrease DC crime, Nixon's presidency likely influenced his position on police reform.

Even though most of these attempts to curb police authority failed, the efforts of the majority-Black city deserve consideration, especially as Americans continue to grapple with the crises of racial inequality and police brutality. While most are more familiar with white suburbanites and conservative politicians' responses to the 1968 rebellions, studying the people who opposed those ideas and proposals shifts our historical understanding away from the dominant, white narrative. Citizens and the DC City Council challenged the widespread understanding of American crime and policing and demanded different urban policing policies. They prioritized Black people's frustrations with police overreach over demands to reduce crime. Instead of criminalizing Black people, some DC leaders were willing to address their grievances.

Richard Nixon and DC's Model Crime Bill

Richard Nixon weaponized the panic over high crime rates to win a presidential election and to pass policies that have deeply damaged communities of color for decades. In the 1968 presidential election, Nixon made the recent uprisings and crime rates in Washington, DC, a central campaign issue. Nixon famously pronounced himself the "law and order" candidate and argued that the national crime rates proved that President Johnson's liberal agenda had failed. "It is not a Great Society when millions of women refuse to walk in their neighborhoods or visit their parks after dusk—out of fear. It is not a Great Society when millions of men buy locks for their doors and watchdogs for their homes and rifles and pistols for themselves—out of fear," Nixon proclaimed at a meeting of the Republican Platform Committee.[54] Nixon criticized Johnson's vice president and the Democratic presidential nominee, Hubert Humphrey, as he directly connected the rebellions to the failure of Johnson and Humphrey: "The great majority are fed up with the policies of my opponent. They have seen the visible ruins of Watts and Harlem and Detroit and Washington, D.C."[55] Nixon released a position paper on crime which asserted that "the role of poverty as a cause of crime in America has been grossly exaggerated" and advocated that the police must have more power to solve crime.[56]

Nixon gave special attention to DC, alleging Johnson bore direct responsibility for crime and the uprisings in the capital. "Washington, D.C., is the one city in this country where the Federal Government is the agency responsible for law enforcement," Nixon asserted at a campaign rally in Chattanooga, Tennessee. "It is the one city in America where crime statistics give a precise reading of a national Administration's concern over the national crime crisis."[57] After Hubert Humphrey said he was "proud" of the Kennedy and Johnson administrations, Nixon responded: "Is he proud of the fact that under this Administration a violent mob burned down a great section of America's Capital—something that hasn't been done to Washington, D.C., since British troops left 155 years ago? No mob tried to burn down Washington, D.C., when Dwight D. Eisenhower was in the White House."[58] On the campaign trail, Nixon repeatedly called Washington the "crime capital of the world"[59] and used it as the prime example of why "get tough" policies were needed: "Crimes are committed almost routinely. . . . When I see a Congressional or Senate secretary cannot work at night unless she is escorted home, I say we need new leadership which can sweep the Nation's capital streets clear." "I pledge that a Nixon Administration will make it a first order of business to sweep the streets of Washington free of these prowlers and muggers and marauders, and restore freedom from fear to the Nation's capital," Nixon proclaimed.[60]

Further, Nixon framed DC as a testing ground for his "law and order" initiatives that would shape national policy. Washington, DC, "should be a model city as far as law enforcement is concerned—a national laboratory in which the latest in crime prevention and detection can be tested and the results reported to a waiting nation."[61] Nixon pushed for a larger police force, more arrests, speedier trials, and a less "permissive system." These steps would help make DC "a model for the cities of this Nation, and an example to the world." "D.C. should not stand for Disorder and Crime," he argued. "A Nixon administration will sweep the streets of Washington clean of these marauders and criminals and remove from this city the atmosphere of aggression that hangs over it."[62]

Many Washingtonians did not take kindly to Nixon's characterization of their city as the "crime capital of the world" and insisted the claim was inaccurate. "One supposes that [Nixon] singles out the District of Columbia because he has written off the District's three electoral votes to his Democratic opponent," wrote Washington Post columnist William Raspberry, "or because the city has no elected officials and, therefore, no power to punish him for his gratuitous insults."[63] Mayor Washington issued a "strong rebuttal" to Nixon's "constant campaign reference to the District as the 'crime capital of the world,'" citing statistics that showed that DC did not have the worst crime rates in the country. Solutions to urban crime were "not found in slogans such as 'Get tough,' 'Sweep the streets of prowlers and criminals,' 'Make the people work.'" The city, the mayor asserted, was faced with "human problems . . . chronic and inherited poverty, unemployment, bad and insufficient housing, defective education, intergroup prejudice and discrimination and the continued denial of justice." Resolving these structural issues was a prerequisite to reducing crime.[64] The *Washington Post* editorial board also chastised Nixon for this repeated false claim.[65]

In November 1968, Americans narrowly elected Nixon to the presidency and he quickly made DC the cornerstone of his "law and order" policies.[66] Less than a week after his inauguration in January 1969, Nixon announced a "War on Crime" in the District that proposed measures he described as a "model anti-crime package."[67] Nixon's proposed twelve-point plan included no-knock police warrants and altering the 1966 Bail Reform Act to permit "preventative detention" that allowed allegedly dangerous criminals to be held without bail while awaiting trial. Nixon suggested ten additional judges for the DC courts, forty more assistant U.S. Attorneys, and one thousand more police officers. Nixon would also give funds to DC through "Large City Special Grants" via the Safe Streets Act.[68] The National Law Enforcement Council considered the plan a "golden opportunity" to experiment with different methods that could eventually be used nationally.[69] Ironically, despite his criticism of Johnson's alleged lack of interest and ineffectiveness on crime, Nixon's strategy relied heavily on provisions of the Safe Streets Act and funding from the Law Enforcement Assistance Administration (LEAA)—both created by Johnson.

Many of Nixon's proposals were included in the District of Columbia Court Reform and Criminal Procedure Act of 1970, better known as the 1970 DC Crime Bill. The bill incorporated much of the long-standing agenda of conservatives to reduce the rights of the accused after liberal Supreme Court decisions such as *Mallory* had expanded those rights. For example, the law "pioneered" techniques such as preventative detention (detaining people who had not been found guilty of a crime without bail for as long as two months), enhanced the police's power to surveil citizens through wiretaps, and legalized "no knock" raids so the police could enter homes without a warrant or announcing their purpose.[70] Further, the legislation required mandatory minimum sentences for armed offenses and created harsher standardized punishments for other crimes. The bill also restructured DC's courts, allowing Nixon to appoint thirteen new judges. DC courts had been primarily composed of liberal judges; now the courts were infused with conservatives. By a vote of 54–33 in the Senate and 332–64 in the House, the District of Columbia Court Reorganization Act of 1970 became law on July 29, 1970.[71]

Walter Fauntroy characterized the DC Crime Bill as "the cutting edge of fascism and oppression in the United States."[72] The *Washington Afro-American* opined that while it knew the crime situation was bad, "officials are grabbing at straws. . . . Holding people because they 'probably' will commit a crime is 'probably' unconstitutional."[73] The NAACP's Roy Wilkins wrote that "in Washington, no matter how it is lorded over with statistics, the District Crime law, with its preventative detention and no-knock provisions is a crackdown measure that can bring unfair detention and persecution as well as the wholesale branding of a race."[74] After Congress initially failed to act on the legislation, Nixon invited House and Senate leaders to a briefing on crime in the District and his legislation. He did not give city officials notice of the meeting or invite them and scheduled the meeting when Mayor Washington was out of town.[75] By purposely excluding DC officials from this briefing, Nixon sidestepped and silenced their opposition.

Nixon wielded his power over the capital and worked to make DC a "model city" for crime prevention in additional ways. In January 1970, the president summoned Deputy Mayor Graham

Watt to the White House and "bluntly informed" him that the "immediate objectives of the Nixon Administration were (1) to achieve a reduction of street crime by May 1, 1970, and (2) to develop a community climate of confidence in public safety." If the DC government and police could not meet those goals, Nixon would use his power to replace the city government and appoint a new DC City Council and mayor. The following Tuesday, Mayor Washington announced a project to strengthen "the criminal justice system."[76]

The Nixon administration subsequently directed considerable amounts of LEAA money to the police. During Nixon's tenure, almost one-eighth of LEAA's funding went to DC, resulting in the highest rate of police to citizens in the world. President Nixon also met with police in October 1970 and wrote letters to the police officers commending their achievements in an attempt to reduce crime by improving police morale.[77] Police Chief Jerry Wilson, at the president's request, toured the country to discuss the methods used by DC police and the success Nixon believed they had achieved. "Basically, I was to emphasize three points: contemporary polls showed that Americans viewed crime as the worst urban problem; President Nixon shared this concern and was personally committed to keeping crime reduction as a high national priority; and achieving significant crime reduction required a commitment by state and local government and strong interest and leadership at all levels of government," Wilson reflected. In his 1972 reelection campaign, Nixon touted his "law and order" program in Washington, DC.[78]

Despite Nixon's claims that "law and order" worked in Washington, crime rates remained high and devastated the Black community. In 1974, the number of murders in DC reached a new high and gun violence became the leading cause of death for men under the age of forty in DC. In 1975, a commission created by

Mayor Washington "found that 20 percent of men in D.C. and an astonishing 45 percent of women said they never went out alone at night."[79] The increase in the police department's size, funds, and permitted investigative tactics did not "sweep the streets of Washington clean of these marauders and criminals" as Nixon promised in the 1968 presidential election.

Nonetheless, the DC Crime Bill set a precedent, and other governments used it to create a "more punitive approach to patrol, arrest, and sentencing and the wider adoption of mandatory minimums and preventative detention."[80] No-knock raids increased along the East Coast, and New York State modeled its own mandatory minimum sentences on DC's in 1973. In 1978, the state of Michigan also established minimum sentences for certain drug offenses.[81] In the 1970s, DC did, indeed, become a model for the rest of the nation. These measures, first tested in the capital, have played a significant role in the proliferation of mass incarceration: the large-scale imprisonment of Americans who are disproportionately people of color. Since 1970, the number of Americans incarcerated has increased by 500 percent.[82]

This history is somber. Nixon used his political and financial control over the capital to create a false narrative of successful crime prevention. Against the opposition of many Black Washingtonians, Nixon imposed tough-on-crime policies on DC that disproportionately harmed its Black residents. Nixon funneled federal funds to the DC police and sent the police chief on a national tour with prescribed talking points. Even though crime rates did not go down in Washington, Nixon based national anticrime legislation on DC's crime bill. The damage inflicted by these policies is still unfolding.

Time and time again, however, Black Washingtonians fought against Nixon's plans and, when they were defeated, they decried the loss of civil liberties. As Nixon labeled DC the "crime capital of the world" during the 1968 presidential election, Mayor Washington and others challenged this characterization through statistical analysis and op-eds. As Nixon proposed growing police forces to "sweep the streets of Washington clean," the DC City Council passed legislation to limit the police's use of firearms and launched initiatives to grant citizens more control over law enforcement. After the 1970 DC Crime Bill passed, Washingtonians fiercely criticized its harsh measures. Remembering this dissent is a reminder that the legacy of the 1968 uprisings goes beyond white backlash and tough-on-crime legislation. It includes those who rebuked police power and Richard Nixon's anticrime agenda.

Epilogue

"FIFTY YEARS AFTER BURNING IN THE RIOTS, 14TH STREET IS A glittering stretch of gentrified DC," proclaimed journalist Marisa Kashino in *Washingtonian* magazine on the fiftieth anniversary of Martin Luther King Jr.'s assassination in 2018. Although the "14ᵗʰ Street corridor lay in ruin" in 1968,

> Fifty years later, it's all hard to picture. On the corner of 14th and R, studio apartments start at $2,100 a month in a building that once was a homeless shelter; on the ground floor, a [luxury goods] Shinola store hawks $800 watches. A block away, Teslas and Range Rovers queue at the valet stand outside the French restaurant Le Diplomate, once the crumbling shell of a dry cleaner. Up at T Street, an old auto showroom used for decades as a black Pentecostal church now houses [upscale furniture store] Room & Board.[1]

Ten years earlier, writing to commemorate the fortieth anniversary of the civil disturbances, journalists Paul Schwartzman and Robert Pierre of the *Washington Post* similarly contrasted DC's past and present. "The intersection where it all began that catastrophic night, the once-ragged corner of 14th and U streets, is now a crossroads at the center of Washington affluence." The other two "riot-corridors" were also transformed from "beyond desperate" to thriving neighborhoods: Seventh Street became "a neon-lit pathway lined with boutiques, taverns, restaurants serving fusion cuisine and a world-class convention center"; H Street boasted $1 million condos and nightclubs "throb[ing] with the young and hip." DC, Schwartzman and Pierre proclaimed, had transitioned from "ruin to rebirth."[2]

This narrative of the "revitalization," "rebirth," "renewal, or "renaissance" of Washington and other American cities credits private businesses and real estate investors for the changes in urban neighborhoods.[3] Schwartzman and Pierre attributed Shaw's transformation to developers who "rediscovered cities": "Boarded-up husks and rubble-strewn lots were reborn as faux-loft apartments, luring white professionals to predominantly black neighborhoods."[4] A 1993 *Washington Post* article suggested private business had succeeded where the government failed:

> At a time when cities nationally are scavenging for ways to salvage blighted areas, the U Street corridor is emerging as an illustration of urban renewal occurring largely without city subsidies, federal financing or the blueprints of urban planners. Instead, the revival is being led by an eclectic group of young entrepreneurs . . . and other investors who have been closely watching the area's demographic shifts for years. Their efforts could make U Street . . . the first commercial area in the city to recover from the torching and looting that followed Martin Luther King Jr.'s assassination 25 years ago this month.[5]

To Luci Blackburn, a senior manager in the DC Housing and Development Department, the arrival of restaurant chains such as Pizza Hut, McDonald's, and Dunkin' Donuts in the 1990s was "'confirmation' of the rebirth of U Street."[6] Gay Jervey, writing for the *New York Times* real estate section, posited that skyrocketing real estate values demonstrated that DC had recovered from the urban uprisings. After describing the property destruction of 1968, Jervey contended that "the U Street Corridor has since had a rebirth. 'In the last six years, real estate values have nearly quadrupled.'"[7] The wealth of the neighborhood and the businesses within it were considered barometers of a community's health.

Gentrification, or the process in which "affluent residents replace those of more modest means, especially as housing markets heat up,"[8] has certainly transformed Washington, DC. While African Americans comprised 90 percent of the U Street/Shaw neighborhood's population in 1970, by 2010, 53 percent of its residents were white.[9] Black Washingtonians comprised more than 70 percent of DC's population in 1970; in 2011, DC's Black population dipped below 50 percent.[10] After an influx of (often white) young professionals, DC has one of the highest median incomes in the nation. Simultaneously, one in five Washingtonians live in poverty.[11] The rapid rise in real estate prices and changing demographics have displaced many long-term African American Washingtonians both residentially and culturally.[12] To Kenneth Tolliver, an African American who grew up in Shaw, gentrification felt like losing his home and history:

> Man, I walk my block [I grew up on] on occasion for
> a nostalgia trip, and on a couple of occasions I've got-
> ten looks, like, you know, because I walk slow and I
> may have stopped in front of the house I used to live

in, like. . . . What am I doing here? That's an eerie feeling. I walk through the back yard and the bricks that I
helped the guy up the street lay are still there—we put
a patio down with dirt, a brick patio—and think about
the cookouts they used to have, you know, how nice it
used to be to sit out back and stuff. Now it's like I'm a
stranger in my own home.[13]

When asked if Shaw today was "more friendly" or "better off economically" than it used to be, Black Washingtonian Elizabeth Williams Frazier replied, "Economically, yes. More friendly? . . . No."[14]

An entire literature has emerged examining gentrification and
its impact on DC. Scholars often focus on the former "riot corridors," especially Fourteenth Street, in their studies.[15] Scholars
like Derek Hyra, Sabiyha Prince, and Brandi Thompson Summers
take a critical approach to gentrification to explore "the formation of hierarchies and how diverse populations have been dif-
ferentially impacted during these decades of marked change."[16]
By exploring "the tension between growth and inequality," DC
gentrification literature challenges the triumphant narrative of
privatized "rebirth" and documents the inequality and displacement that often accompanies "revitalization" in the areas damaged in 1968.

Washingtonians worked to rebuild DC long before private businesses considered urban areas a "hot market." While many groups
who fled urban centers in the wake of desegregation, uprisings,
and high crime rates are now "rediscovering" the city, hundreds of
thousands of Washingtonians never left. DC did not lie in hopeless
ruins, waiting passively for loft apartments, luxury boutiques, and
chic coffee shops to save it. Determined leaders proclaimed that
they "believed in the city" and generated partnerships between

the government, community organizations, and citizens with the goal of creating a racially and economically just capital.

This builds upon the work of other scholars to complicate several narratives of the late 1960s. I highlight the political aspects of the disturbances and connect the events to the demands of decades of prior activism. The civil disorders challenged the same powerful institutions that generations of activists had previously picketed, boycotted, and sued. The participants most commonly attacked the most accessible representations of white people's power over Black communities: white-owned and/or -operated stores, white commuter highways, "occupying" police forces, and (rarely) individual white people. Black Washingtonians had targeted these manifestations of the "power structure" as they demanded freedom, economic opportunities, good education, accountable policing, voting rights, and political power for over a century. Pauli Murray, the Coordinating Committee for the Enforcement of the DC Anti-Discrimination Laws, Julius Hobson, the Congress on Racial Equality, and the Associated Community Teams all mobilized Black Washingtonians against white businesses to oppose segregation and gain employment opportunities. Free DC instructed Washingtonians to boycott small white-owned businesses in Shaw and along H Street who refused to back home rule. Organizations like the Emergency Committee on the Transportation Crisis and the Model Inner City Community Development Organization criticized city planning that displaced Black residents for the benefit of white Washingtonians. Prior to 1968, the city nearly erupted in uprisings several times as citizens protested police brutality and abuse of power. Thus, the 1968 upheaval was not a radical break from previous civil rights activism, as it predominantly affected the institutions that both moderates and militants had long worked to change.

This, of course, does not mean that all participants were politically motivated or that all damage carried a revolutionary message. Rebellions are complex events that cannot be compressed into a single, coherent narrative. The human element of the upheaval must be preserved. This book carefully incorporates oral histories and first-person accounts to bolster our understanding of the complexities of the historical moment. People within the Black community interpreted the uprisings differently and participated for different reasons.

Leaders across the political spectrum used the disorders to push their preexisting agendas. This point is not a criticism of those who harnessed the upheaval to demand racial and economic equality, but rather an examination of how urban uprisings translated into political advocacy and change. In the aftermath, government officials and citizens alike agreed that DC must "rebuild politically, socially, as well as physically."[17] The mayor, the DC City Council, community organizations, and citizens loosely agreed on process that prioritized community participation and Black economic development and would alleviate the economic and racial inequalities they considered the root causes of unrest. This framework utilized, or at least reclaimed, the preexisting principles and programs of the Great Society such as "maximum feasible participation" and piecemeal urban renewal. Black Power leaders and organizations often worked with DC's government to advocate for Black autonomy and economic development. Radical organizations often believed that to realistically achieve self-determination and political power, it would take the financing and support of the government.

DC did embark on a massive project to reconstruct damaged neighborhoods, especially Shaw, in ways that reflected the desires of neighborhood residents and created opportunities for Black people that could compensate for the long history of racial discrimination. After surveying more than 50 percent of Shaw residents to ask what they wanted in their communities, DC built new schools, libraries, parks, medical centers, and other public facilities that served Black people. The city often contracted these jobs to Black-owned businesses and hired workers from the historically Black neighborhood. Churches and other nonprofit community groups built housing for low-income residents. To address long-standing grievances with the police force, the DC City Council passed legislation to limit when officers could utilize firearms and to install civilian review boards to provide oversight of the police department.

Ultimately, many of these proposals and projects failed. The mayor would only sign a more conservative bill regarding use of force by the police, and he killed the proposal for a civilian review board. President Nixon cut funding to the rebuilding project in Shaw, and the Redevelopment Land Agency switched to using private developers to build moderate- and high-income housing complexes. DC was ultimately under the control of the federal government. Still, the history of these Black-led efforts in a city with a nearly 70 percent Black population are an important part of the history of the 1968 rebellions. The uprisings did not just spur white suburbanites to vote for Richard Nixon and eschew the civil rights movement; they also inspired many to double down on efforts to alleviate structural inequality and to engage in the nitty-gritty details of public policy.

While this work broadens the narrative of 1968 beyond reactionary calls for "law and order," it simultaneously contributes to the study of the "long backlash" to the Black freedom movement. Leaders used crime statistics to oppose Black freedom long before Richard Nixon's 1968 presidential campaign.[18] Even when the crime rate in DC was lower or comparable to that of other urban areas, politicians claimed criminal activity in the capital demonstrated that desegregation was a failure and that Black people could not govern. After the uprisings, Nixon made crime in DC a central campaign issue. Once in office, he defunded many of Johnson's Great Society programs and replaced them with a "War on Crime" in the capital that culminated in the passage of the 1970 DC Crime Bill. Today, we understand that decades of such policies have devastated urban neighborhoods and families while discrediting solutions to urban problems that reformers had tried to enact, leaving those problems festering a half-century later.

Americans were forced to reckon with this fact in June 2020 as hundreds of thousands of people joined nationwide demonstrations against police brutality and racism after the murder of George Floyd, a Black man, by a police officer. The protests in DC grabbed international headlines, especially after federal officers deployed tear gas and used physical force to clear peaceful protesters from Lafayette Square near the White House. The curfew imposed by DC Mayor Muriel Bowser from June 1 to June 4, 2020, faced criticism after law enforcement officers used tear gas, low-flying helicopters, and violent tactics to enforce it. More than seventy demonstrators took refuge in a home in Dupont Circle after police officers boxed them in on Swann Street NW.[19] Low-flying helicopters hovered near protesters in DC's Chinatown neighborhood in an attempt to disperse crowds.[20] The events of 1968 and 2020 were not comparable in terms of magnitude—fewer than five hundred people were arrested in connection to the protests in 2020, while more than six thousand were arrested in 1968.[21] Nonetheless, it was hard to not feel a sense of déjà vu.

That summer, many conservatives immediately decried the protests and chastised participants as criminals.[22] Much like Nixon, President Donald Trump seized on this characterization of the demonstrations to push a tough-on-crime, pro-police agenda. That summer, the Trump administration launched Operation Legend, a federal law enforcement program that dedicated hundreds of agents to "fight violent crime" in several cities. "The words 'law and order' are words that Democrats don't like to use," the president told a Minnesota crowd. "They don't think they're politically good. There's nothing wrong with law and order. . . . You shouldn't be ashamed of it."[23]

At the same time, some local governments have launched ambitious plans to change the role of the police and to center the concerns of people of color. For example, Minneapolis and other cities promised to reduce or end the presence of police officers in schools. San Francisco launched crisis response teams to replace police when responding to behavioral health calls. Many states changed their standards for use of force, often to specify that deadly force was permissible only after exhausting all nonviolent options.[24] It remains to be seen if these reforms will snowball to truly transformational policies that deconstruct systemic inequality, or if they will be a minor exception to policies that disproportionately target and incarcerate people of color.

As civil rights activist and future DC mayor Marion Barry declared at a DC City Council hearing in May 1968, the rebellions "created a vacuum and an opportunity." "Will what is done correct the basic situation that created the need for . . . the rebellions?" he asked.[25] More than fifty years later, that work is far from complete and the systemic racism and inequality that prompted the uprisings remains intact. This book tells the stories of the Washingtonians who ambitiously seized an "opportunity" to rebuild the capital in a way that challenged this "basic situation" by protecting and fostering Black political and economic power. "I believe in the city," they asserted. "I believe in the people."[26]

Acknowledgments

THIS BOOK IS ONE OF MANY THAT BEGAN AS A TERM PAPER IN DR. Leo Ribuffo's graduate course on twentieth-century American history. Throughout my graduate studies at the George Washington University, Leo provided invaluable insight, encouragement, and wit. I am indebted to many others at GWU. Dr. Eric Arnesen, my PhD adviser, meticulously edited my dissertation, ensuring it contained sound scholarship and clear prose. Thank you for your continued help and keen eye as I adapted my dissertation into this book. Dr. Katrin Schulteiss, thank you for your mentorship and kindness during my time as the editor of the History News Network. I am also grateful for Dr. Erin Chapman, Dr. Chris Klemek, and Dr. Angela Zimmerman, who each challenged me and motivated me to produce the best history I could. Dr. Chris Tudda fostered my love of history in undergrad and first encouraged me to pursue a PhD. Tom Blanton, executive director of the National Security Archive at GWU, offered guidance at many points during this process. Paul Hayes—my college debate coach, mentor, and friend—honed the professional and communication skills that have molded my career.

I am grateful to everyone at The New Press for believing in this project and for publishing it. Thank you to my excellent editor zakia henderson-brown for her invaluable edits, insights, and support. Your work sharpened and clarified my scholarship.

Thank you to my friends and colleagues at American Oversight. I couldn't ask for a better place to work.

Thank you to my dear friends who fill my life with joy and meaning. Whether we're watching the Nationals in 401, grabbing a drink at the Dew Drop Inn, exploring the Shenandoah, or singing along to "The Wreck of the Edmund Fitzgerald," you all make DC home.

To my family—Brian, Melody, Kari, Keith, and Kaleb Sommers—thank you for the overwhelming love, care, and silliness that you give me. I would go to the ends of the earth for each of you. Mom, Dad, Durl, and Wendy, thank you for giving me a refuge where I could write during many phases of this process. Grandma (Marilyn Sommers), thank you for making my undergraduate degree possible. Your lifelong love of learning is an inspiration to me. Erin Wasik, thank you for a lifetime of reminders to seek out adventure and go a little easier on myself. I owe so much of who I am to you.

To my husband, Nate Jones, thank you for your edits, your encouragement, and your support at every stage of this project. Simply put, I could not have done it without you. I love you and our life together in our bright blue house.

Notes

Introduction

1. *Rehabilitation of District of Columbia Areas Damaged by Civil Disorders: Hearings Before the Subcommittee on Business and Commerce of the Committee on the District of Columbia United States Senate*, Ninetieth Cong. 149–150 (1968) (statement of Carroll Harvey, executive director of Pride, Inc.). I use the terms "rebellions" and "uprisings" to refer to the events following Dr. King's assassination in Washington, DC. This term centers the political dissent that motivated many who participated. Others use the word "riot," but that term can link the events to criminality, futileness, and violence. See Michael Katz, *Why Don't American Cities Burn?* (Philadelphia: University of Pennsylvania Press, 2012); Elizabeth Hinton, *America on Fire: The Untold History of Police Violence and Black Rebellion Since the 1960s* (New York: Liveright Publishing, 2021).

2. Keith L. Alexander and Meryl Kornfield, "Among More Than 400 Arrested During Protests in the District, Most Cases Involve Curfew Violations and Burglary," *Washington Post*, June 16, 2020.

3. Clay Risen, *A Nation on Fire: America in the Wake of the King Assassination* (Hoboken, NJ: John Wiley & Sons, Inc., 2009), 247. Samuel J. Walker, *Most of 14th Street Is Gone: The Washington, DC Riots of 1968* (New York: Oxford University Press, 2018), 118.

4. Nick Kirkpatrick and Katie Mettler, "A City Destroyed by Riots, Then and Now," *Washington Post*, April 5, 2018.

5. Jack Moore, "'Everything Was on Fire'—Remembering the DC Riots 50 Years Later," WTOP, April 2, 2018.

6. For an excellent overview of recent scholarship and different

interpretations of civil unrest, please read the roundtable on the issue in *Labor: Studies in Working-Class History* 14, no. 4 (December 2017): 31.

7. Moore, "'Everything Was on Fire.'" Explore Marya McQuirter's excellent digital history project at https://www.dc1968project.com.

1

"We Want to Free DC from Our Enemies": Black Activism in the Capital

1. Chris Meyers Asch and George Derek Musgrove, *Chocolate City: A History of Race and Democracy in the Nation's Capital* (Chapel Hill: University of North Carolina Press, 2017), 34–38.

2. Constance McLaughlin Green, *Washington: Capital City, 1879–1950* (Princeton, New Jersey: Princeton University Press, 1963), 18, 32–48; Tom Lewis, *Washington: A History of Our National City* (New York: Basic Books, 2015), 83–84; Kate Masur, *An Example for All the Land: Emancipation and the Struggle over Equality in Washington, D.C.* (Chapel Hill: University of North Carolina Press, 2010), 19–21.

3. Constance McLaughlin Green, *The Secret City: A History of Race Relations in the Nation's Capital* (Princeton, NJ: Princeton University Press, 1967), 32–48; Jefferson Morley, *Snow-Storm in August: Washington City, Francis Scott Key, and the Forgotten Race Riot of 1835* (New York: Nan A. Talese/Doubleday, 2012).

4. Many Black people who were formerly enslaved freed themselves through manumission: the buying of oneself from their enslaver. The free population in DC also grew because Virginia forced African Americans to leave the state within six months of being freed. Many crossed the border into DC and made it their home. Green, *The Secret City*, 16, 38–39; Blaire Ruble, *Washington's U Street: A Biography* (Washington, DC: Woodrow Wilson Center Press, 2010), 20; Howard Gillette Jr., *Between Justice and Beauty: Race, Planning, and the Failure of Urban Policy in Washington, D.C.* (Philadelphia: University of Pennsylvania Press, 1995), 27; Carl Abbott, *Political Terrain: Washington, D.C. from Tidewater Town to Global Metropolis* (Chapel Hill: University of North Carolina Press, 1999), 49. No city had a larger free black population by percentage of total population. Green, *The Secret City*, 16, 38–39; Ruble, *Washington's U Street,* 20; Gillette, *Between Justice and Beauty*, 27.

5. Gillette, *Between Justice and Beauty*, 28–39; Masur, *An Example for All the Land*, 22–27; Abbott, *Political Terrain*, 61–64; James Oakes, *Freedom National: The Destruction of Slavery in the United States, 1861–1865* (New York: W.W. Norton & Company, 2013), 272–277. Additionally, Radical Republicans increased Black rights in DC during the civil war as they prohibited racial discrimination on street cars, overturned the Fugitive Slave Law, and reorganized the District's judiciary system.

6. Masur, *An Example for All the Land*, 22–27; Abbott, *Political Terrain*, 61–64; Gillette, *Between Justice and Beauty*, 28–32, 50–56; Blaire, *Washington's U Street*, 28–29. For an in-depth examination of civil rights during Reconstruction in Washington, see Masur, *An Example for All the Land*.

7. Green, *Washington*, 325; John Kelly, "Remembering the 'Lost Laws' in Washington," *Washington Post*, February 11, 2018; Gillette, *Between Justice and Beauty*, 39–42; Masur, *An Example for All the Land*, 26–33; Oakes, *Freedom National*, 189–191, 416–421.

8. Ruble, *Washington's U Street*, 23–26.

9. Gillette, *Between Justice and Beauty*, 57–68; Masur, *An Example for All the Land*, 214–256; Lewis, *Washington*, 194–207; Asch and Musgrove, *Chocolate City*, 152–184.

10. Eric S. Yellin, *Racism in the Nation's Service: Government Workers and the Color Line in Woodrow Wilson's America* (Chapel Hill: University of North Carolina Press, 2013), 22–32; Eric S. Yellin, "'It Was Still No South to Us': African American Civil Servants at the Fin De Siècle," *Washington History* 21 (2009): 22–47.

11. Green, *The Secret City*, 137; Donald Roe, "The Dual School System in the District of Columbia, 1862–1954: Origins, Problems, Protests," *Washington History* 16, no. 2 (Fall/Winter 2004/2005): 26–43; Asch and Musgrove, *Chocolate City*, 168–173. The students attended M Street High School, later renamed Dunbar High School.

12. Green, *The Secret City*, 132, 151; Asch and Musgrove, *Chocolate City*, 169.

13. Green, *The Secret City*, 137; Asch and Musgrove, *Chocolate City*, 168–173.

14. Michael Andrew Fitzpatrick, "'A Great Agitation for Business': Black Economic Development in Shaw," *Washington History* 2, no. 2 (Fall/Winter 1990/1991): 48–73; Ruble, *Washington's U Street*, 61–62; Asch and Meyers, *Chocolate City*, 210–213.

15. In 1870, for example, 75 percent of the DC population were unskilled laborers or domestic workers. Asch and Musgrove, *Chocolate City*, 178. For more on domestic laborers in DC, see Elizabeth Clark-Lewis, *Living In, Living Out: African American Domestics in Washington, D.C. 1910–1940* (Washington, DC: Smithsonian Books, 1994).

16. Asch and Musgrove, *Chocolate City*, 179–182; Ruble, *Washington's U Street*, 23–26. For an in-depth look at the history of alley dwellings in Washington, see James Borchert, *Alley Life in Washington: Family, Community, Religion, and Folklife in the City, 1850–1970* (Urbana, IL: University of Illinois Press, 1980).

17. Yellin, "It Was Still No South to Us," 32; Yellin, *Racism in the Nation's Service*, 62–67, 94–104, 110–111, 170–172; Green, *The Secret City*, 156–157.

18. Gillette, *Between Justice and Beauty*, 82–83; Green, *The Secret City*, 197–208.

19. Green, *The Secret City*, 163–176, 201; Asch and Musgrove, *Chocolate City*, 193–196, 219–226; Treva B. Lindsey, *Colored No More: Reinventing Black Womanhood in Washington, D.C.* (Urbana, IL: University of Illinois Press, 2017), 8–24.

20. David F. Krugler, "A Mob in Uniform: Soldiers and Civilians in Washington's Red Summer, 1919," *Washington History* 21 (2009): 48–77; David F. Krugler, *1919, the Year of Racial Violence: How African Americans Fought Back* (New York: Cambridge University Press, 2015), 2–8, 15–34, 66–98; Asch and Meyers, *Chocolate City*, 231–236.

21. Krugler, "A Mob in Uniform," 48–77; Krugler, *1919, the Year of Racial Violence*, 66–98; Green, *The Secret City*, 190–193, 197–208.

22. Asch and Musgrove, *Chocolate City*, 226.

23. Green, *Washington*, 459.

24. Gillette, *Between Justice and Beauty*, 138–144; Green, *Washington*, 413; Green, *The Secret City*, 233–237.

25. Gillette, *Between Justice and Beauty*, 144–150; Asch and Meyers, *Chocolate City*, 277–284; Geneva Valentine testimony, June 10, 1944, cited in William Robert Barnes, "Origins of Urban Renewal: The Public Housing Controversy and the Emergence of a Redevelopment Program in the District of Columbia" (PhD diss., Syracuse University, 1977), 144.

26. Asch and Meyers, *Chocolate City*, 288–290; Kenesaw M. Landis, *Segregation in Washington* (Chicago: National Committee on Segregation in the Nation's Capital, 1948), 88.

27. Gregory Borchardt, "Making D.C. Democracy's Capital: Local Activism, the 'Federal State,' and the Struggle for Civil Rights in Washington, D.C." (PhD diss., George Washington University, 2013), 110–111.

28. Peniel E. Joseph, "The Black Power Movement: A State of the Field," *Journal of American History* 96, no. 3 (December 2009): 751–776.

29. Lauren Pearlman, "Democracy's Capital: Local Protest, National Politics, and the Struggle for Civil Rights in Washington, D.C., 1933–1978" (PhD diss., Yale University, 2013), 45.

30. Pauli Murray, *Song in a Weary Throat: Memoir of an American Pilgrimage* (New York: Liveright Publishing Corporation, 1987), 298.

31. Pearlman, "Democracy's Capital," 45–46; Kelly, "Remembering the 'Lost Laws' in Washington." Thompson's Cafeteria was at 725 Fourteenth Street NW, the corner of Fourteenth and New York Avenue. Today there is a Wells Fargo bank at that location.

32. Affidavit of Mary Church Terrell, January 1950, container 1, folder 7, "Coordinating Committee for the Enforcement of the D.C. Anti-Discrimination Laws Records, 1949–1954," DC History Center, Washington, DC; Asch and Meyers, *Chocolate City*, 297–304.

33. Phillip B. Perlman, "Memorandum for the United States Amicus Curiae," container 1, folder 11, "Coordinating Committee for the Enforcement of the D.C. Anti-Discrimination Laws Records, 1949–1954," DC History Center, Washington, DC.

34. "Petition for Leave to File Brief Amicus Curiae and Brief Amicus Curiae," container 1, folder 10, "Coordinating Committee for the Enforcement of the DC Anti-Discrimination Laws Records, 1949–1954," DC History Center, Washington, DC; Phineas Indritz, "Great Washington Area Council of American Veterans Committee, Inc. (AVC) and American Veterans Committee (Chapter One) Amicus Curiae," June 30, 1951, container 1, folder 11, "Coordinating Committee for the Enforcement of the DC Anti-Discrimination Laws Records," DC History Center, Washington, DC; Perlman, "Memorandum for the United States Amicus Curiae."

35. President's Committee on Civil Rights, *To Secure These Rights: The Report of Harry S Truman's Committee on Civil Rights* (New York: Simon & Schuster, 1947), 88–89.

36. Joan Quigley, *Just Another Southern Town: Mary Church Terrell and the Struggle for Racial Justice in the Nation's Capital* (New York: Oxford University Press, 2016), 143–163; Greg Borchardt, "Making DC

Democracy's Capital" (PhD diss., George Washington University, 2013), 29–46.

37. Lauren Pearlman, *Democracy's Capital: Black Political Power in Washington, D.C. 1960s–1970s* (Chapel Hill: University of North Carolina Press, 2019), 22–24; Asch and Meyers, *Chocolate City*, 333–335.

38. Borchardt, "Making D.C. Democracy's Capital," 128–139; Asch and Meyers, *Chocolate City*, 337–339.

39. Borchardt, "Making D.C. Democracy's Capital," 126–150; Anne M. Valk, *Radical Sisters: Second-Wave Feminism and Black Liberation in Washington, D.C.* (Urbana, IL: University of Illinois Press, 2008), 21–23.

40. Julius W. Hobson, letter to the editor, *Washington Post*, November 30, 1964; quoted from Borchardt, "Making D.C. Democracy's Capital," 150.

41. Valk, *Radical Sisters*, 22–23, 26–34; Borchardt, "Making D.C. Democracy's Capital," 149–154; David Fergus, *Liberalism, Black Power, and the Making of American Politics* (Athens, GA: University of Georgia Press, 2009), 14.

42. For example, in 1965–1966, the "median percentage of capacity for the predominantly Negro elementary schools was 115%" while for predominantly white elementary schools they were at 77 percent capacity. While every student who applied for kindergarten in mostly white elementary schools got a spot, there was a waiting list of 6,236 children for predominantly Black elementary schools. The median amount of funds spent per student was over $100 higher at white schools than black schools. See "Civil Liberties Fund: An Evaluation of the Decision in *Hobson vs. Hansen*," February 1968, box 13, folder: "An Evaluation of *Hobson v. Hansen* National Capital Area Civil Liberties Defense and Educational Fund, 1968," Julius Hobson Papers, 1960–1977, DC Community Archives, Washingtoniana Collection, Martin Luther King Jr. Memorial Library, Washington, DC, 11–13.

43. "Civil Liberties Fund: An Evaluation of the Decision in *Hobson vs. Hansen*," Julius Hobson Papers, 1–7.

44. "Get in Step for Freedom Now!" box 13, folder: "Announcements, News Releases, New Letters, Etc.," Julius Hobson Papers, 1960–1977, DC Community Archives, Washingtoniana Collection, Martin Luther King Jr. Memorial Library, Washington, DC.

45. "Why We Boycott for Quality Education," box 13, folder: "Announcements, News Releases, New Letters, Etc.," Julius Hobson Papers,

1960–1977, DC Community Archives, Washingtoniana Collection, Martin Luther King Jr. Memorial Library, Washington, DC.

46. "District of Columbia Citizens for a Better Education," November 2, 1967, box 13, folder: "Announcements, News Releases, New Letters, Etc.," Papers of Julius Hobson, 1960–1977, DC Community Archives, Washingtoniana Collection, Martin Luther King Jr. Memorial Library, Washington, DC.

47. *Home Rule and Reorganization for the District of Columbia: Hearings Before the Subcommittee on Home Rule and Reorganization of the Committee on the District of Columbia United States Senate*, Eighty-First Cong. 196–198 (1951) (statement of Clifford H. Newell of the Arkansas Avenue Community Association). In the nearly all-Black Cardozo neighborhood, not one of the 2,793 people voting were against home rule. These numbers are according to plebiscite held by suffrage organizations in 1938 and 1946. See Borchardt, "Making D.C. Democracy's Capital," 239.

48. *Home Rule and Reorganization for the District of Columbia: Hearings Before the Subcommittee on Home Rule and Reorganization of the Committee on the District of Columbia United States Senate*, Eighty-First Cong. 70 (1951) (statement of Kenneth Adams, president of the Young Republicans Club of the District of Columbia); *Home Rule and Reorganization for the District of Columbia*, statement of Clifford H. Newell, 196–198; one Congressman reported that more than twelve people told him "in private and not in confidence that they are opposed to this bill because of their fear it would give the Negro domination over the District of Columbia," *Home Rule and Reorganization for the District of Columbia: Hearings Before the Subcommittee on Home Rule and Reorganization of the Committee on the District of Columbia United States Senate*, Eighty-First Cong. 221 (1951) (statement of Marshall L. Shepard of the Recorder of Deeds of the District of Columbia).

49. "Area Residents Support Home Rule, But They Don't Get Excited About It," *Washington Post*, October 4, 1966.

50. Borchardt, "Making D.C. Democracy's Capital," 243–260; Robert L. Asher, "GOP in House Strongly Urge D.C. Home Rule," *Washington Post*, September 4, 1966.

51. Paul W. Valentine, "Suit by Hobson Asks Election of D.C. Heads," *Washington Post*, April 26, 1966; "U.S. Sees No D.C. Right to Local Vote," *Washington Post*, January 28, 1967.

52. Borchardt, "Making D.C. Democracy's Capital," 232, 259–272.

53. Borchardt, "Making D.C. Democracy's Capital," 259–261; Valk, *Radical Sisters*, 19–21.

54. Borchardt, "Making D.C. Democracy's Capital," 259–261; Valk, *Radical Sisters*, 19–21.

55. The man in sunglasses in the image on the cover is Rufus "Catfish" Mayfield, then the chairman of the board of Pride, Inc. In the photo, Mayfield is with boys and young men who work with Pride, Inc. on projects to clean up their neighborhood. Marya McQuirter, "14 august 1968 & black youth union prepares to march to district building," DC Project 1968; Jack Moore, "DC Uprising: After the riots, an activist on trial," WTOP, April 4, 2018.

56. Borchardt, "Making D.C. Democracy's Capital," 260–270; Catherine Maddison, "'In Chains 400 Years . . . And Still in Chains in D.C.!' The 1966 Free D.C. Movement and the Challenges of Organizing in the City," *Journal of American Studies* 41, no. 1 (April 2007): 169–192.

57. "Trade Board Seen as Enemy in District's Poverty War," *Washington Afro-American*, March 9, 1965.

58. Borchardt, "Making D.C. Democracy's Capital," 261.

59. "Red Sympathizers Support Home Rule, McMillan Asserts," *Washington Post*, January 5, 1966; Harry S. Jaffe and Tom Sherwood, *Dream City: Race, Power, and the Decline of Washington, D.C.* (New York: Simon & Schuster, 1994), 62.

60. *Civil Disturbances in Washington: Hearings Before the Committee on the District of Columbia House of Representatives*, Ninetieth Cong. 153 (1968) (statement of DC Mayor Walter Washington).

61. Harland Bartholomew and Associates City Planners, "Redevelopment Plans for the Southwest Survey Area, District of Columbia," 2, P1102, Kiplinger Research Library Archives, Washington, DC.

62. Asch and Meyers, *Chocolate City*, 320–325; Gillette, *Between Justice and Beauty*, 151–162.

63. "Federal City Council Report," 13, P470, Kiplinger Research Library Archives, Washington, DC.

64. Gillette, *Between Justice and Beauty*, 163.

65. "District of Columbia Redevelopment Land Agency Annual Report 1967," P746, Kiplinger Research Library Archives, Washington, DC.

66. "Southwest Guide 1956–1956, A Joint Publication of the Southwest

Community Council, Inc. and the Southwest Neighborhood Assembly," 56–57, P1104, Kiplinger Library, Washington, DC.

67. Borchardt, "Making D.C. Democracy's Capital," 173–175.

68. Gillette, *Between Justice and Beauty*, 163–166; Blaire Ruble, *Washington's U Street*, 183–185.

69. Gillette, *Between Justice and Beauty*, 163–166; Ruble, *Washington's U Street*, 183–185.

70. *Hearings Before the United States Commission on Civil Rights: Housing in Washington*, 13 (1962) (testimony of Eunice Grier).

71. *Hearings Before the United States Commission on Civil Rights: Housing in Washington*, 81 (1962) (testimony of David A. Sawyer, executive director of the Commissioners' Council on Human Relations).

72. *Hearings Before the United States Commission on Civil Rights: Housing in Washington*, testimony of David A. Sawyer, 81.

73. The FHA officially abolished this practice in 1960, but it still set a pattern for private lenders. *Hearings Before the United States Commission on Civil Rights: Housing in Washington*, 223 (1962) (testimony of Thomas C. Barringer, director of the FHA District of Columbia Insuring Office); *Hearings Before the United States Commission on Civil Rights: Housing in Washington* 223–229 (1962) (testimony of Rev. Charles M. Mason Jr., past chairman of the social action committee of the Silver Spring Ministerial Association).

74. Kenesaw M. Landis, *Segregation in Washington: A Report of the National Committee on Segregation in the Nation's Capital* (Chicago: National Committee on Segregation in the Nation's Capital, 1948), 34.

75. *Hearings Before the United States Commission on Civil Rights: Housing in Washington*, 315–19 (1962) (testimony of Marjorie McKenzie Lawson).

76. *Hearings Before the United States Commission on Civil Rights: Housing in Washington*, 228–229 (1962) (testimony of Paul P. Cooke, national vice chairman of the American Veterans Committee); *Hearings Before the United States Commission on Civil Rights: Housing in Washington*, 228–229 (testimony of Rev. Charles M. Mason Jr; *Hearings Before the United States Commission on Civil Rights: Housing in Washington*, 189 (testimony of Eugene Davidson, realtor ["realtist" in original] and former president of the Washington Real Estate Brokers Association).

77. Borchardt, "Making D.C. Democracy's Capital," 180–209.

78. Originally quoted in *Shaw Power*, October 1969, cited in Gillette, *Between Justice and Beauty*, 174.

79. Gillette, *Between Justice and Beauty*, 173–180: Asch and Meyers, *Chocolate City*, 349–351.

80. Asch and Meyers, *Chocolate City*, 364.

81. Borchardt, "Making D.C. Democracy's Capital," 211–231. Gillette, *Between Justice and Beauty*, 165–169. For an in-depth look at the anti-highway movement, see Zachary M. Schrag, *The Great Society Subway: A History of the Washington Metro* (Baltimore: Johns Hopkins University Press, 2006).

2

"The Nation's Capital Is in a Sweat":
Crime, Policing, and Rising Tensions

1. Gregory Borchardt, "Making D.C. Democracy's Capital: Local Activism, the 'Federal State,' and the Struggle for Civil Rights in Washington, D.C." (PhD diss., George Washington University, 2013), 75. Mary L. Dudziak, *Cold War Civil Rights: Race and the Image of American Democracy* (Princeton, NJ: Princeton University Press, 2000), 99.

2. "Congressman James C. Davis Speaks to the States' Rights Council," November 28, 1956, M393, box 3, folder 6, McCain (William D.) Pamphlet Collection, University of Southern Mississippi Digital Collections.

3. *Hearings Before the Subcommittee to Investigate Public School Standards and Conditions and Juvenile Delinquency in the District of Columbia of the Committee on the District of Columbia House of Representatives*, Eighty-Fourth Cong. 264, 266 (1956) (statements of Miriam Beall, teacher at Roosevelt High School, and Marjory W. Nelson, teacher at McFarland Junior High School). Gerber asked nearly every witness about "sex problems." For example, see *Hearings Before the Subcommittee to Investigate Public School Standards and Conditions and Juvenile Delinquency*, 24, 36, 43, 61, 66–67, 76, 80, 126, 139, 159, 189, 196, 264–265, 267, 269, 272, 291, 294, 300, 303–304, 367.

4. *Hearings Before the Subcommittee to Investigate Public School Standards and Conditions and Juvenile Delinquency*, 61, 108, 216, 238, 276.

5. Clarence Mitchell, "From the Workbench: An Unhooded Klan Meet-

ing," *Baltimore Afro-American*, October 6, 1956, cited in Borchardt, "Making D.C. Democracy's Capital, 99–100; "Hatchet Job," *Washington Post*, September 20, 1956, cited in Borchardt, "Making D.C. Democracy's Capital," 97.

6. "Congressman James C. Davis Speaks to the States' Rights Council."

7. "I Was Mugged," *Washington Evening Star*, January 21, 1958; Jerry V. Wilson, *The War on Crime in the District of Columbia 1955–1975* (Washington, DC: National Institute of Law Enforcement and Criminal Justice, Law Enforcement Administration, United States Department of Justice, 1978), 4–5.

8. "Tougher Crime Laws Sought," *Washington Post*, January 25, 1958; "D.C. Crime Curb Is Urged in Senate," *Washington Post*, August 18, 1959, originally cited in Wilson, *The War on Crime in the District of Columbia*, 5.

9. Wilson, *The War on Crime in the District of Columbia*, 1–8.

10. *Crime in the District of Columbia: Joint Hearing Before the District of Columbia Committees of the Senate and the House of Representatives on the Increasingly Serious Crime Situation in the District of Columbia*, Eighty-Eighth Cong. 12 (1963).

11. Wilson, *The War on Crime in the District of Columbia*, 12.

12. There is a growing and influential body of work on "law and order" as a strategy to curtail civil rights gains. See Michael Flamm, *Law and Order: Street Crime, Civil Unrest, and the Crisis of Liberalism in the 1960s* (New York: Columbia University Press, 2005); Elizabeth Hinton, *From the War on Poverty to the War on Crime: The Making of Mass Incarceration in America* (Cambridge, MA: Harvard University Press, 2016); Michelle Alexander, *The New Jim Crow: Mass Incarceration in the Age of Colorblindness* (New York: The New Press, 2012).

13. "Congressman James C. Davis Speaks to the States' Rights Council."

14. "Johnston Calls Press Lax on Integration," *Washington Post*, September 3, 1959. Johnston further argued, "Police cannot solve evils caused by forced integration." In another speech, he claimed that DC and New York had high crime rates because they were "two places where forced integration has been experimented with more than any other places in the United States."

15. "Ellender Calls District a 'Cesspool of Crime,'" *Washington Post*, June 17, 1963. He had recently been barred entry by three African nations

for making similar comments. After listing figures of how much of DC was controlled by black people he argued, "You have the worst conditions in Washington where they are at the head than of any big city in the country. . . . To me, that just shows their inability to govern."

16. J.W. Anderson, "Anxiety of a City at Night Enters Politics," *Washington Post*, July 26, 1964.

17. *Crime in the District of Columbia: Joint Hearing Before the District of Columbia Committees of the Senate and the House of Representatives on the Increasingly Serious Crime Situation in the District of Columbia*, Eighty-Eighth Cong. 7 (1963) (statement of Robert V. Murray, chief of the Metropolitan Police Department of the District of Columbia); Wilson, *The War on Crime in the District of Columbia*, 5–11; J.W. Anderson, "Anxiety of a City at Night Enters Politics," *Washington Post*, July 26, 1964.

18. *Crime in the District of Columbia: Joint Hearing Before the District of Columbia Committees of the Senate and the House of Representatives on the Increasingly Serious Crime Situation in the District of Columbia*, statement of Robert V. Murray, 7, 34.

19. *Crime in the District of Columbia: Joint Hearing Before the District of Columbia Committees of the Senate and the House of Representatives on the Increasingly Serious Crime Situation in the District of Columbia*, statement of Robert V. Murray, 5, 52–55.

20. *Crime in the District of Columbia: Joint Hearing Before the District of Columbia Committees of the Senate and the House of Representatives on the Increasingly Serious Crime Situation in the District of Columbia*, 3–4.

21. "Remarks by B. M. McKelway, Citizen's Crime Commission Dinner. Shoreham Hotel, Washington, D.C., December 10, 1962," printed in *Crime in the District of Columbia*, 21–22.

22. *Crime in the District of Columbia: Joint Hearing Before the District of Columbia Committees of the Senate and the House of Representatives on the Increasingly Serious Crime Situation in the District of Columbia*, Eighty-Eighth Cong. 115 (1963) (statement of John E. Winters, deputy chief of the Metropolitan Police Department of the District of Columbia).

23. *Crime in the District of Columbia: Joint Hearing Before the District of Columbia Committees of the Senate and the House of Representatives on the Increasingly Serious Crime Situation in the District of Columbia*, Eighty-Eighth Cong. 86 (1963) (statement of Oliver T. Gasch, former U.S. Attorney).

24. *Crime in the District of Columbia: Joint Hearing Before the District of*

Columbia Committees of the Senate and the House of Representatives on the Increasingly Serious Crime Situation in the District of Columbia, statement of Oliver T. Gasch, 88–90; "Tougher Crime Laws Sought," January 25, 1958, *Washington Post*, January 25, 1958; "Hill Demands Crackdown on D.C. Crime," *Washington Post*, August 26, 1959; *Crime in the District of Columbia: Joint Hearing Before the District of Columbia Committees of the Senate and the House of Representatives on the Increasingly Serious Crime Situation in the District of Columbia*, 58; *Crime in the District of Columbia: Joint Hearing Before the District of Columbia Committees of the Senate and the House of Representatives on the Increasingly Serious Crime Situation in the District of Columbia*, statement of Robert V. Murray, 50; *Crime in the District of Columbia: Joint Hearing Before the District of Columbia Committees of the Senate and the House of Representatives on the Increasingly Serious Crime Situation in the District of Columbia*, statement of John E. Winters, 119.

25. Carroll Kilpatrick, "Goldwater Sees U.S. Becoming a 'Jungle,'" *Washington Post*, September 25, 1964.

26. "A Word to McClellan," *Washington Afro-American*, September 8, 1959.

27. "Poor Students of History," *Washington Afro-American*, August 23, 1966.

28. Borchardt, "Making D.C. Democracy's Capital," 129–130.

29. "Hobson Resigns from Police Advisory Post, Hits Units," *Washington Afro-American*, September 14, 1965.

30. "Hobson Resigns from Police Advisory Post, Hits Units," *Washington Afro-American*.

31. Behind Park Road in between Thirteenth and Fourteenth Streets NW.

32. "Act Threatens to March on Police Stations: Charges Officers with Misconduct," *Washington Afro-American*, September 18, 1965; "Near Riot Still Causing Comment," *Washington Afro-American*, September 14, 1965; Paul Valentine, "An Alley Game That Became a Near-Riot," *Washington Post*, September 25, 1965.

33. Alfred E. Lewis, "W. Virginia Senator Probing Police Role in Melee Following Football Game," *Washington Post*, November 17, 1965.

34. "Memo to Capt. Gooding," *Washington Afro-American*, September 14, 1965.

35. "Act Threatens to March on Police Stations: Charges Officers with Misconduct," *Washington Afro-American*. "Hobson Resigns from Police Advisory Post, Hits Units," *Washington Afro-American*, September 14, 1965.

36. Claude Koprowski and Jesse W. Lewis Jr., "Police Curb Outbreak in Northwest," *Washington Post*, August 24, 1966; Harrison Young, "Layton Now Will Talk to Anacostia Probers," *Washington Post*, September 3, 1966.

37. Young, "Layton Now Will Talk to Anacostia Probers," *Washington Post*.

38. "Troops Use Here Urged in Senate," *Washington Post*, September 23, 1966.

39. "Playing With Dynamite," *Washington Post*, September 3, 1966.

40. "Support Your Police," *Washington Post*, October 10, 1966.

41. "Police Morale," *Washington Post*, July 4, 1967.

42. John Carmody, "Detectives' Charges Disturb Colleagues," *Washington Post*, April 24, 1966.

43. William Raspberry, "D.C. May Lose What Little Voice It Has on Police," *Washington Post*, December 24, 1967; "Police Lack Support, Byrd Report Charges," *Washington Post*, August 8, 1967.

44. "Byrd, Broyhill Denounce Booker Death Probe," *Washington Post*, May 12, 1967.

45. "News Media Not Presenting Police Side, 70 Wives Charge," *Washington Post*, September 9, 1968.

46. William Raspberry, "D.C. May Lose What Little Voice It Has on Police," *Washington Post*, December 24, 1967.

47. "Support Your Police," *Washington Post*.

48. "Hobson Resigns from Police Advisory Post, Hits Units," *Washington Afro-American*.

49. John W. Hechinger Sr. and Gavin Taylor, "Black and Blue: The DC City Council vs. Police Brutality, 1967–1969," *Washington History* 11, no. 2 (Fall/Winter 1999/2000): 10.

50. Betty James, "D.C. Leaders Hail Riot Report, But Hill Reaction Is Mixed," *Washington Star*, Vertical Files, "Riots, 1968 (April)," Washingtoniana Collection, Martin Luther King Jr. Library, Washington, DC.

51. James, "D.C. Leaders Hail Riot Report, But Hill Reaction Is Mixed," *Washington Star*.

52. For more on the Detroit disorders, see Sidney Fine, *Violence in the Model City: The Cavanaugh Administration, Race Relations, and the Detroit Riot of 1967* (Ann Arbor, MI: University of Michigan Press, 1989).

53. Barrye La Troye Price, "King to King: A Study of Civil Unrest and Federal Intervention 1968–1992" (PhD diss., Texas A&M University, 1997), 58.

54. All National Guard units were required to participate in thirty-two hours of training on riot operation techniques, an eight-hour exercise, and sixteen hours of command and staff training.

55. Ben Gilbert, *Ten Blocks from the White House: Anatomy of the Washington Riots of 1968* (New York: Frederick A. Praeger, 1968), 90; Price, *King to King*, 85.

56. *Civil Disturbances in Washington: Hearings Before the Committee on the District of Columbia House of Representatives*, Ninetieth Cong. 2 (1968) (statement of Patrick V. Murphy, director of the Office of Public Safety of the District of Columbia).

57. Original quote from Patrick V. Murphy and Thomas Plate, *Commissioner: A View from the Top of American Law Enforcement* (New York: Simon & Schuster, 1977), 99, cited in Clay Risen, *A Nation on Fire: American in the Wake of the King Assassination* (Hoboken, NJ: John Wiley and Sons, 2009), 77.

58. Original quote from Murphy and Plate, *Commissioner*, 102; cited in Risen, *America on Fire*, 77.

59. "Force Ready for Summer, Murphy Says," March 26, 1968, Vertical Files, "Riots: April 4–15, 1968," Washingtoniana Collection, Martin Luther King Jr. Library, Washington, DC.

60. "Give a Little to Avert Riot, Says Layton," *Washington Post*, February 20, 1968.

61. Gilbert Y. Steiner, "The Brookings Institution Seminar on the District of Columbia Riot," May 20, 1968, Brookings Institution, Washington, DC.

62. Elizabeth Hinton, *From the War on Poverty to the War on Crime: The Making of Mass Incarceration in America* (Cambridge, MA: Harvard University Press, 2016), 56–57.

63. Hinton, *From the War on Poverty to the War on Crime*, 87–89.

64. Hinton, *From the War on Poverty to the War on Crime*, 91–92.

65. Nicholas Horrock, "D.C. Police: No Faith in Mace," *Washington Evening Star*, April 11, 1968.

66. William Raspberry, "Punish, Don't Destroy Looters," *Washington Post*, April 15, 2015. It also created a maximum sentence of ninety days imprisonment for "rioting," defined as engaging in "a public disturbance involving an assemblage of five or more persons which by tumultuous and violent conduct" damages people or property. Rioting could be tacked on to felony charges of looting or could be a stand-alone misdemeanor charge. William Shumann, "Looting Suspects Held for Grand Jury as Court Tackles Riot Cases," *Washington Post*, April 18, 1968.

67. William Raspberry, "Washington Lays Antiriot Plans Wisely," *Washington Post*, March 4, 1968.

68. For an excellent biography of Carmichael, see Peniel E. Joseph, *Stokely: A Life* (New York: Basic Civitas, 2014).

69. Minutes of the Black United Front, February 13, 1968, box 16, folder 14 "Black Empowerment, Black United Front, April–May 1968," MS 2070, Walter Fauntroy Papers, Gelman Library Special Collections at the George Washington University, Washington, DC.

70. Peniel E. Joseph, *Stokely: A Life* (New York: Basic Civitas, 2014), 235; "Minutes of the Black United Front."

71. For more on Carmichael's interest in unifying the black community, see Joseph, *Stokely: A Life*, 231–236.

72. Robert L. Asher, "Stay Calm in Protests, City Urged," *Washington Post*, March 3, 1968.

73. "Calm in the Capital," *Wall Street Journal*, June 23, 1967.

74. Russell, Marsh, and Kennedy, Inc., "Riot," March 25, 1968, box 284a, folder 34 "Special TF: Civil Disturbances—correspondence," Greater Washington Board of Trade Records, Special Collections Research Center, George Washington University, Washington, DC.

75. "Paying for the Damage," March 31, 1968, box 284a, folder 36 "Special TF: Civil Disturbances—clippings," Greater Washington Board of Trade Records, Special Collections Research Center, George Washington University, Washington, DC.

76. Robert L. Asher, "Stay Calm in Protests, City Urged," *Washington Post*, March 3, 1968.

77. G.C. Moore, "Memo to Mr. C.W. Sullivan: Re: COUNTERINTELLIGENCE PROGRAM," March, 21, 1968, "FBI COINTELPRO Black Extrem-

ists Surveillance Files for April–July 1968 with Documentation on Stokely Carmichael, Martin Luther King Jr., Eldridge Cleaver, Elijah Muhammad, LeRoi Jones, SCLC, and the Nation of Islam," FBI Files on Black Extremist Organizations, Part 1: COINTELPRO Files on Black Hate Groups and Investigation of the Deacons for Defense and Justice, 6–7, ProQuest History Vault: Black Freedom Struggle.

78. "Memorandum to the Director of the FBI," April 4, 1968, "FBI Surveillance Records from the COINTELPRO Black Extremist Program from August 1967–April 1968, Including Memo on the Establishment of Counterintelligence Program Targeting 'Black Nationalist-Hate Type Organizations' and Goals of the Program," FBI Files on Black Extremist Organizations, Part 1: COINTELPRO Files on Black Hate Groups and Investigation of the Deacons for Defense and Justice, 1968—April 4 report, ProQuest History Vault: Black Freedom Struggle.

79. Memo to FBI Director J. Edgar Hoover, April 2, 1968; memorandum to FBI Director J. Edgar Hoover, April 4, 1968, "FBI Surveillance Records from the COINTELPRO Black Extremist Program from August 1967–April 1968, Including Memo on the Establishment of Counterintelligence Program Targeting 'Black Nationalist-Hate Type Organizations' and Goals of the Program," "Counterintelligence Program Black Nationalist-Hate Groups Racial Intelligence (Washington Spring Project)," memo to W.C. Sullivan to G.C. Moore, March 26, 1968; Memo to W.C. Sullivan to G.C. Moore, March 29, 1968, "FBI COINTELPRO Black Extremists Surveillance Files for April–July 1968 with Documentation on Stokely Carmichael, Martin Luther King Jr., Eldridge Cleaver, Elijah Muhammad, LeRoi Jones, SCLC, and the Nation of Islam." All documents found in "FBI Files on Black Extremist Organizations, Part 1: COINTELPRO Files on Black Hate Groups and Investigation of the Deacons for Defense and Justice," ProQuest History Vault: Black Freedom Struggle.

80. Federal Bureau of Investigation, "Outlook for Racial Violence in Washington, D.C.," March 11, 1968, reproduced in *Declassified Documents Reference System* (Farmington Hills, MI.: Gale, 2015).

3
"They Take This Nonviolent Man and Kill Him Violently":
April 4, 1968

1. *South of U Oral History Project—Life, Riots and Renewal in Shaw,* Yvonne Baskerville interview transcript, May 2012, Dig DC archives, https://digdc.dclibrary.org/islandora/object/dcplislandora%3A68566/pages.

2. *South of U Oral History Project—Life, Riots and Renewal in Shaw,* Elizabeth Williams Frazier interview transcript, April 2012, Dig DC archives, https://dcplislandora.wrlc.org/islandora/object/dcplislandora%3A68545/pages.

3. Bonnie Perry Interview, October 22, 2002, box 1, folder 4, MS 0769, 1968 Riots Oral History Collection, Kiplinger Research Library Archives, Washington, DC.

4. Virginia Ali Interview, February 23, 2003, box 1, folder 1, MS 0769, 1968 Riots Oral History Collection, Kiplinger Research Library Archives, Washington, DC.

5. Ben Gilbert, *Ten Blocks from the White House: Anatomy of the Washington Riots of 1968* (New York: Frederick A. Praeger, 1968), 14. Unless specified otherwise, all times are in Eastern Standard Time.

6. Gilbert, *Ten Blocks from the White House,* 13.

7. Gilbert, *Ten Blocks from the White House,* 14.

8. "Preliminary Action and Status Reports Relating to the Mayor, Director of Public Safety and the Police Department Relative to April 1968 Civil Disorders in the District of Columbia," *Report on Civil Disturbances in Washington, D.C., April 1968,* Gelman Library Special Collections, George Washington University, Washington, DC. Documents from this report are indicated by their title within the report as the document does not use page numbers. The Office of Emergency Preparedness characterized the initial mood at Fourteenth and U as one of "shock and sadness." "Operation Bandaid One," 1968, box 1, folder "April 4–8," RG 23, Office of Emergency Preparedness Records, District of Columbia Archives, Washington, DC. Gilbert's *Ten Blocks from the White House* also describes the initial mood of people on the street as one of shock; see Gilbert, *Ten Blocks from the White House,* 15.

9. Gilbert, *Ten Blocks from the White House,* 13–14; "Operation Bandaid

One," Office of Emergency Preparedness Records, 1; "Stokely Helps Quell Row," *Washington Daily News*, April 3, 1968; Peniel E. Joseph, *Stokely: A Life* (New York: Basic Civitas, 2014), 250–251.

10. Gilbert, *Ten Blocks from the White House*, 14.

11. Gilbert's *Ten Blocks from the White House* records the announcement at 8:19 p.m., while police accounts place it at 8:20 p.m. Gilbert, *Ten Blocks from the White House*, 4; "Preliminary Action and Status Reports Relating to the Mayor, Director of Public Safety and the Police Department Relative to April 1968 Disorders in the District of Columbia," 1, *Report on Civil Disturbances in Washington, D.C., April 1968*.

12. "Death Puts Gloom on Dinner Party," *Washington Star*, April 5, 1968; Gilbert, *Ten Blocks from the White House*, 36. Ramsey Clark's oral history confirms that Vice President Humphrey was speaking that night. See "Attorney General Ramsey Clark oral history interview on race riots during the Johnson administration," March 21, 1969, 22, found in "Civil Rights During the Johnson Administration, 1963–1969, Part III: Oral Histories," ProQuest History Vault: Black Freedom Struggle.

13. "King Death: A Turning Point?" *Washington Star*, April 7, 1968.

14. "Death Puts Gloom on Dinner Party," *Washington Star*. For more on Johnson's decision-making in the crisis, see Risen, *A Nation on Fire*.

15. Virginia Ali Interview, February 23, 2003.

16. Gilbert, *Ten Blocks from the White House*, 17. Also see "The City's Turmoil: The Night It Began: Chronology of a Night of Turmoil," *Washington Post*, April 14, 1968.

17. "The Shaw Community: The Impact of the Civil Rights Movement, as told by Mrs. Virginia Ali, owner of Ben's Chili Bowl," 26–27, box 1, folder 9: "Interview with Virginia Ali," MS 2285, Ben's Chili Bowl Papers, Gelman Library Special Collections, George Washington University, Washington, DC.

18. *South of U Oral History Project—Life, Riots and Renewal in Shaw*, Betty May Brooks-Cole interview transcript, Dig DC archives, https://dcplislandora.wrlc.org/islandora/object/dcplislandora%3A68592/pages.

19. This is a reference to King's famous "I Have a Dream" speech, delivered on August 23, 1963, at the Washington March for Jobs and Freedom. King said the Declaration of Independence and Constitution promised all people equal rights, but America had never lived up to his promise—it wrote

African Americans a "bad check, a check which has come back marked 'insufficient funds.'" King said the people at the march had come to "cash this check, a check that will give us upon demand the riches of freedom and the security of justice."

20. Reuben M. Jackson Interview, box 1, folder 2, MS 0769, 1968 Riots Oral History Collection, Kiplinger Research Library Archives, Washington, DC.

21. William Raspberry, "Dr. King and His Killer Became Symbols," *Washington Post*, April 7, 1968.

22. Multiple accounts document this shift. See Gilbert, *Ten Blocks from the White House*, 15; "The City's Turmoil," *Washington Post*; "Operation Bandaid One," Office of Emergency Preparedness Records, 2; "Preliminary Action and Status Reports Relating to the Mayor, Director of Public Safety and the Police Department Relative to April 1968 Civil Disorders in the District of Columbia," *Report on Civil Disturbances in Washington, D.C., April 1968*.

23. "Operation Bandaid One," Office of Emergency Preparedness Records, 2.

24. "The City's Turmoil," *Washington Post*. This article places the call at 8:26 p.m., six minutes after King's death was announced.

25. Gilbert, *Ten Blocks from the White House*, 17; see also "The City's Turmoil," *Washington Post*.

26. "The City's Turmoil," *Washington Post*. The account of Carmichael leading a crowd to ask stores to close is also supported by police accounts. See "Preliminary Action and Status Reports Relating to the Mayor, Director of Public Safety and the Police Department Relative to April 1968 Civil Disorders in the District of Columbia," *Report on Civil Disturbances in Washington, D.C., April 1968*.

27. Gilbert, *Ten Blocks from the White House*, 15; "Statement by the President on the Assassination of Dr. Martin Luther King, Jr.," April 4, 1968, *The American Presidency Project*, https://www.presidency.ucsb.edu/node/238016. The presidential diary also indicates Johnson gave the speech between 9:05 and 9:10 p.m. "President's Daily Diary, April 4, 1968," Lyndon B. Johnson Presidential Library, Austin, TX.

28. Gilbert, *Ten Blocks from the White House*, 18, 20–21; "The City's Turmoil," *Washington Post*.

29. Operation Bandaid One," Office of Emergency Preparedness Records, 3–4. The report specifically indicates a crowd of three hundred people at 2324 Fourteenth Street, which is at the intersection of Fourteenth and Belmont NW. Reports from the Office of Emergency Preparedness, described by Bill Branch of the DC Archives as "the Department of Homeland Security for Washington," indicated that the crowd at Fourteenth and U grew especially large after 9:00 p.m., and between 9:25 and 9:40 p.m. people gathered at Fourteenth and T and Fourteenth and Belmont.

30. Gilbert, *Ten Blocks from the White House*, 21; "The City's Turmoil," *Washington Post*. It is likely these accounts were drawn from the plainclothes police officers in the crowd. The report from the Office of Emergency Preparedness also mentions that Carmichael was "in Northwest Washington trying to stop looting." See "Operation Bandaid One," Office of Emergency Preparedness Records, 8.

31. Gilbert, *Ten Blocks from the White House*, 22; "The City's Turmoil," *Washington Post*.

32. Gilbert, *Ten Blocks from the White House*, 22–23; "The City's Turmoil," *Washington Post*. The Office of Emergency Preparedness also received reports that Carmichael was attempting to stop looting. "Operation Bandaid One," Office of Emergency Preparedness Records, 8.

33. "District: New Wave of Violence Erupts in Northwest," *Washington Evening Star*, April 5, 1968.

34. Gilbert, *Ten Blocks from the White House*, 20; "The City's Turmoil," *Washington Post*.

35. "Preliminary Action and Status Reports Relating to the Mayor, Director of Public Safety and the Police Department Relative to April 1968 Civil Disorders in the District of Columbia," *Report on Civil Disturbances in Washington, D.C., April 1968*. The Office of Emergency Preparedness received the first information of window-breaking at 10:10 p.m. and the first report of breaking and entering at 1930 Fourteenth Street at 10:15 p.m. The preface to its report put the start of the disturbance at just before 10:00 p.m. Operation Bandaid One," Office of Emergency Preparedness Records, preface, 4–5.

36. Virginia Ali Interview, February 23, 2003.

37. Gilbert, *Ten Blocks from the White House*, 21; "The City's Turmoil," *Washington Post*.

38. Lillian Wiggins, "Stores Looted, Rocks Thrown at D.C. Police,"

Washington Afro-American, April 9, 1968. Due to what appears to be a scanning error, this article (part of the newspaper published on April 9 and 13) is included in the online collection with the April 16 edition of the *Afro-American* (https://news.google.com/newspapers/p/afro?nid=BeIT3YV 5QzEC&dat=19680416&printsec=frontpage&hl=en). As a bit of DC history trivia, Lillian Wiggins is the same reporter who years later coined the term "the Plan," referring to the conspiracy theory that white Washingtonians were working to take the city away from the control of Black Washingtonians.

39. Gilbert, *Ten Blocks from the White House*, 27. The cars were from a used car dealer called Barry-Pate and Addison.

40. Gilbert, *Ten Blocks from the White House*, 23–34; "The City's Turmoil," *Washington Post.*

41. Wiggins, "Stores Looted, Rocks Thrown at D.C. Police," *Washington Afro-American.*

42. Operation Bandaid One," Office of Emergency Preparedness Records, 1–4; "Chronological Sequence of Events- April 4–5 1968 (within the Army Operations Center)," 1–2, "Situation Room Information Memos, Troop Movements and Riots 1968, Martin Luther King Jr. Assassination, Selected Civil Rights Files—James Gaither, 1968" found in "Civil Rights During the Johnson Administration, 1963–1969, Part I: The White House Central Files," ProQuest History Vault: Black Freedom Struggle; Gilbert, *Ten Blocks from the White House*, 35–36.

43. Christopher Howland Pyle, "Military Surveillance of Civilian Politicians 1967–1970" (PhD diss., Columbia University, 1974), 97–98.

44. "Chronological Sequence of Events April 4–5 1968 (Within the Army Operations Center)," 1–2, "Situation Room Information Memos, Troop Movements and Riots 1968, Martin Luther King Jr. Assassination, Selected Civil Rights Files—James Gaither, 1968."

45. "Preliminary Action and Status Reports Relating to the Mayor, Director of Public Safety and the Police Department relative to April 1968 Disorders in the District of Columbia," 1, *Report on Civil Disturbances in Washington, D.C., April 1968.*

46. "The City's Turmoil," *Washington Post.* The authors of the article interviewed Patrick Murphy for this article, so it is likely this is from his own account.

47. "Operation Bandaid One," Office of Emergency Preparedness Records, 4; "The City's Turmoil," *Washington Post.*

48. Gilbert, *Ten Blocks from the White House*, 36; "The City's Turmoil," *Washington Post*. The Office of Emergency Preparedness recorded Murphy at 9:31 p.m. at Fourteenth and T Streets, which would make sense if he was walking back to the area from a meeting with the other officer. "Operation Bandaid One," Office of Emergency Preparedness, 4.

49. *Civil Disturbances in Washington: Hearings Before the Committee on the District of Columbia House of Representatives*, Ninetieth Cong. 4–6, 13, 41–21 (1968).

50. "Preliminary Action and Status Reports Relating to the Mayor, Director of Public Safety and the Police Department relative to April 1968 Disorders in the District of Columbia," *Report on Civil Disturbances in Washington, D.C., April 1968*.

51. Gilbert, *Ten Blocks from the White House*, 19; "The City's Turmoil," *Washington Post*. The authors of the article interviewed Walter Fauntroy, so it is likely this is from his own account.

52. Gilbert, *Ten Blocks from the White House*, 22–23; "Operation Bandaid One," Operation of Emergency Preparedness Records, 5–6.

53. "Operation Bandaid One," Office of Emergency Preparedness Records, 4.

54. "Preliminary Action and Status Reports Relating to the Mayor, Director of Public Safety and the Police Department relative to April 1968 Disorders in the District of Columbia," 2–3, *Report on Civil Disturbances in Washington, D.C., April 1968*; Gilbert, *Ten Blocks from the White House*, 37–38.

55. "Operation Bandaid One," Office of Emergency Preparedness Records, 5–6; Gilbert, *Ten Blocks from the White House*, 25, 36–39.

56. Gilbert, *Ten Blocks from the White House*, 40. This is supported by the Office of Emergency Preparedness report that officers received a radio command that for "any violence, take all proper police action." "Operation Bandaid One," Office of Emergency Preparedness Records, 7.

57. "The District Fire Department's Role in the Civil Disturbances of April 4, 5, 6, 7, and 8, 1968," *Report on Civil Disturbances in Washington, D.C., April 1968*.

58. Gilbert, *Ten Blocks from the White House*, 27.

59. "Operation Bandaid One," Office of Emergency Preparedness Records, 7; Wiggins, "Stores Looted, Rocks Thrown at D.C. Police,"

Washington Afro-American; "Preliminary Action and Status Reports Relating to the Mayor, Director of Public Safety and the Police Department relative to April 1968 Disorders in the District of Columbia," 3, *Report on Civil Disturbances in Washington, D.C., April 1968.*

60. Gilbert, *Ten Blocks from the White House*, 29; "Operation Bandaid One," Office of Emergency Preparedness Records, 9; "Army Guards D.C. Streets," *The Hilltop*, April 26, 1968, 1. *The Hilltop* is Howard University's student newspaper.

61. "Preliminary Action and Status Reports Relating to the Mayor, Director of Public Safety and the Police Department relative to April 1968 Disorders in the District of Columbia," 3, *Report on Civil Disturbances in Washington, D.C., April 1968*; Gilbert, *Ten Blocks from the White House*, 40.

62. Gilbert, *Ten Blocks from the White House*, 41–42; "Chronological Sequence of Events April 4–5 1968 (Within the Army Operations Center)," 4, "Situation Room Information Memos, Troop Movements and Riots 1968," "Martin Luther King Jr. Assassination, Selected Civil Rights Files—James Gaither, 1968." The belief that riots only occurred at night was generally accepted: a study of twenty-four disorders determined that major incidents in each case happened at night.

63. Gilbert, *Ten Blocks from the White House*, 41–42, 44, 90; "Preliminary Action and Status Reports Relating to the Mayor, Director of Public Safety and the Police Department relative to April 1968 Disorders in the District of Columbia," 3–4, *Report on Civil Disturbances in Washington, D.C., April 1968*; "Operation Bandaid One," Office of Emergency Preparedness Records, 6.

4

"You Just Can't Expect People Not to Act This Way": Understanding the Rebellions

1. Gilbert, *Ten Blocks from the White House: Anatomy of the Washington Riots of 1968* (New York: Frederick A. Praeger, 1968), 10.

2. "Operation Bandaid One," 1968, box 1, folder "April 4–8," 13, RG 23, Office of Emergency Preparedness Records, District of Columbia Archives, Washington, DC; Memorandum from Director of the Department of Corrections Kenneth L. Hardy to Deputy Mayor Thomas W. Fletcher, "Corrections' Participation in Disturbance Commencing April 4, 1968,

April 16, 1968," *Report on Civil Disturbances in Washington, D.C., April 1968,* Gelman Library Special Collections at George Washington University, Washington, DC. Documents from this report are indicated by their title within the report as the document does not use page numbers.

3. "Dr. King Is Slain in Memphis," *Washington Post,* April 5. 1968.

4. "A Cruel and Wonton Act," *Washington Post,* April 5, 1968.

5. "The King Assassination," *Washington Daily News,* April 5, 1968.

6. Lillian Wiggins, "Stores Looted, Rocks Thrown at D.C. Police," *Washington Afro-American,* April 9, 1968; Gilbert, *Ten Blocks from the White House,* 45.

7. "Operation Bandaid One," Office of Emergency Preparedness Records, 14.

8. Julius Duscha, "Postscript to the Story of Seventh Street," *New York Times,* June 2, 1968.

9. Duscha, "Postscript to the Story of Seventh Street," *New York Times Magazine; South of U Oral History Project—Life, Riots and Renewal in Shaw,* Yvonne Baskerville interview transcript, May 2012, Dig DC archives, https://digdc.dclibrary.org/islandora/object/dcplislandora%3A68566/pages.

10. William Dobrovir, *Justice in Time of Crisis: A Staff Report to the District of Columbia Committee on the Administration of Justice Under Emergency Conditions* (Washington: U.S. Government Printing Office, 1969), 16.

11. "Operation Bandaid One," Office of Emergency Preparedness Records, 15.

12. Hardy, "Corrections' Participation in Disturbance Commencing April 4, 1968, April 16, 1968," *Report on Civil Disturbances in Washington, D.C., April 1968.*

13. "Preliminary Action and Status Reports Relating to the Mayor, Director of Public Safety and the Police Department Relative to April 1968 Civil Disorders in the District of Columbia," *Report on Civil Disturbances in Washington, D.C., April 1968.*

14. Hardy, "Corrections' Participation in Disturbance Commencing April 4, 1968, April 16, 1968," *Report on Civil Disturbances in Washington, D.C., April 1968.*

15. "Operation Bandaid One," Office of Emergency Preparedness Records, 16; Gilbert, *Ten Blocks from the White House,* 51; "The District Fire

Department's Role in the Civil Disturbances of April 4, 5, 6, 7, and 8, 1968," 1–2, *Report on Civil Disturbances in Washington, D.C., April 1968.*

16. Duscha, "Postscript to the Story of Seventh Street," *New York Times Magazine; South of U Oral History Project—Life, Riots and Renewal in Shaw,* Yvonne Baskerville interview transcript.

17. Gilbert, *Ten Blocks from the White House,* 46–48.

18. Phil Casey, "Carmichael Warns of 'Retaliation,'" *Washington Post,* April 6, 1968; "Fauntroy, Carmichael Reactions to Slaying," *Washington Star,* April 5, 1968.

19. "We're Not Afraid . . . We're Gonna Die for Our People," *Washington Post,* April 6, 1968. The time of 11:00 a.m. is corroborated by Gilbert and the Office of Emergency Preparedness, Gilbert, *Ten Blocks from the White House,* 65; "Operation Bandaid One," Office of Emergency Preparedness Records, 15.

20. "We're Not Afraid . . . We're Gonna Die for Our People," *Washington Post.* To watch the video of this press conference, see "Stokely Carmichael, 5th April 1968 After Death of Martin Luther King," Huntley Film Archives, YouTube video, 1:45, https://www.youtube.com/watch?v=dwYYvOjsxjE.

21. Lester McKinnie, leader of the DC chapter of SNCC, also spoke at the press conference and emphasized this same point. "This is a lesson which white America has taught us many times before," he said as he described the deaths of Larry Payne in Memphis and four men in Orangeburg. "This lesson was clear in the day-to-day torture of black people by white people in America and throughout the world. It was to end this torture that Dr. King bravely faced death many times—nonviolent. Dr. King was a brother who dedicated his life to liberating his people through nonviolence. Dr. King was a symbol of nonviolence and white Americans shot him down." See "We're Not Afraid . . . We're Gonna Die for Our People," *Washington Post.*

22. All quotes are from the transcript of the press conference given by the *Washington Post* in "We're Not Afraid . . . We're Gonna Die for Our People." The Office of Emergency Preparedness report said Carmichael told "Negroes to arm themselves and take to the streets." Operation Bandaid One," Office of Emergency Preparedness, 15.

23. George Fletcher, a white man from Woodbridge, Virginia, died the night of April 4, 1968. Fletcher's friends claimed they were driving around DC after getting drinks when they stopped for gas and got into an argument with eight Black men who then stabbed Fletcher. The account is uncorrobo-

rated, and it is impossible to know if this incident was in any way related to King's death or revenge against "whitey." See Gilbert, *Ten Blocks from the White House*, 26–27.

24. Peniel E. Joseph, *Stokely: A Life* (New York: Basic Civitas, 2014), 253–254.

25. "District: New Wave of Violence Erupts in Northwest," *Washington Evening Star*, April 5, 1968.

26. "Architecture and Society Fall Midterm 1996," box 5, folder 5: "School Papers Written About Ben's Chili Bowl," MS 2285, Ben's Chili Bowl Papers, Gelman Library Special Collections at the George Washington University, Washington, DC; "Press Conference," box 1, folder 5: "40th Anniversary Materials," Ben's Chili Bowl Papers; "The Shaw Community: The Impact of the Civil Rights Movement, as Told by Mrs. Virginia Ali, Owner of Ben's Chili Bowl," box 1, folder 9: "Interview with Virginia Ali," Ben's Chili Bowl Papers.

27. Joseph, *Stokely*, 258–259.

28. Michael Adams, "D.C. Leaders Show Grief, Ire," *Washington Star*, April 5, 1968.

29. "Operation Bandaid One," Office of Emergency Preparedness, 4.

30. "Operation Bandaid One," Office of Emergency Preparedness, 2.

31. Adams, "D.C. Leaders Show Grief, Ire," *Washington Star*.

32. "Fauntroy, Carmichael Reactions to Slaying," *Washington Star*, April 5, 1968.

33. "Black Banner Replaces U.S. Flag on Bitter Howard Campus," *Washington Evening Star*, April 6, 1968; Gilbert, *Ten Blocks from the White House*, 63; Adrienne Manns and Robert Nesnick, "Was It Riot or Insurrection?" *The Hilltop*, April 26, 1968.

34. Gilbert, *Ten Blocks from the White House*, 63.

35. Howard was less than a fifteen-minute walk from the office where his press conference occurred.

36. Memorandum from J. Edgar Hoover to President Lyndon Johnson, "Selected Racial Developments and Disturbances," 4:56 a.m., April 6, 1968, DDRS-26392, reproduced in *Declassified Documents Reference System* (Farmington Hills, MI: Gale, 2015).

37. Gilbert, *Ten Blocks from the White House*, 64–67.

38. Gilbert, *Ten Blocks from the White House*, 85.

39. "Synopsis of Service Rendered to the District of Columbia by Communities of Adjacent Jurisdictions," *Report on Civil Disturbances in Washington, D.C., April 1968*; "The District Fire Department's Role in the Civil Disturbances of April 4, 5, 6, 7, and 8, 1968," *Report on Civil Disturbances in Washington, D.C., April 1968*.

40. "Operation Bandaid One," Office of Emergency Preparedness Records, 2.

41. "Situation Room Information Memorandum," April 6, 1968, 12:00 a.m., "Situation Room Information Memos, Troop Movements and Riots 1968, Martin Luther King Jr. Assassination, Selected Civil Rights Files—James Gaither, 1968," in "Civil Rights During the Johnson Administration, 1963–1969, Part I: The White House Central Files," ProQuest History Vault: Black Freedom Struggle.

42. B.B. Colen, "Washington Riot Report: H Street—Like a Combat Zone," *The Hatchet*, April 23, 1968.

43. Gilbert, *Ten Blocks from the White House*, 50–51, 53, 70, 72, 80–81; Gilbert Y. Steiner, "The Brookings Institution Seminar on the District of Columbia Riot," May 20, 1968, 74, Brookings Institution, Washington, DC.

44. "Operation Bandaid," Office of Emergency Preparedness Records, 6; Gilbert, *Ten Blocks from the White House*, 90.

45. The District Fire Department's Role in the Civil Disturbances of April 4, 5, 6, 7, and 8, 1968," *Report on Civil Disturbances in Washington, D.C., April 1968*. Some high-end stores in downtown DC were exceptions to this pattern. Here, a specific store, instead of entire blocks, would be looted and sometimes burned. Some stores on Thursday night were damaged after people left Fourteenth Street and drove to specific retailers. On Friday, some stores were damaged downtown, but since these were more isolated incidents instead of entire crowded blocks, police quickly gained control of the area.

46. Gilbert, *Ten Blocks from the White House*, 81–82.

47. Ronald Sarro, "Panel to Begin D.C. Riot Probe," *Washington Star*, May 26, 1968.

48. Gilbert, *Ten Blocks from the White House*, 95; Colen, "Washington Riot Report," *The Hatchet*.

49. Colen, "Washington Riot Report," *The Hatchet*.

50. Gilbert, *Ten Blocks from the White House*, 85.

51. Gilbert, *Ten Blocks from the White House*, 76–77.

52. Duscha, "Postscript to the Story of Seventh Street," *New York Times Magazine*.

53. *South of U Oral History Project—Life, Riots and Renewal in Shaw*, Jaqueline Rogers Hart interview transcript, April 2012, Dig DC archives: https://dcplislandora.wrlc.org/islandora/object/dcplislandora%3A68520/pages.

54. Faith Davis Ruffins Interview, box 1, folder 5, MS 0769, 1968 Riots Oral History Collection, Kiplinger Research Library Archives, Washington, DC. In her interview, Ruffins believed this happened on the day King was assassinated. As word that King was assassinated did not spread until after 8 p.m. that Thursday, it is more likely this was on Friday, April 5.

55. Ruth Jenkins, "No Busting Easter Shopping Just 'Soul' Signs, Troopers," *Washington-Afro American*, April 9, 1968.

56. Faith Davis Ruffins Interview, 18.

57. Robert Allen, "April's Black Rebellions: A Political Analysis," *The Hilltop*, April 26, 1968. Also see Bobby Isaac, "King's Dream Deferred?" *The Hilltop*, May 3, 1968.

58. *South of U Oral History Project—Life, Riots and Renewal in Shaw*, Betty May Brooks-Cole interview transcript, Dig DC archives, https://dcplislandora.wrlc.org/islandora/object/dcplislandora%3A68592/pages.

59. Duscha, "Postscript to the Story of Seventh Street," *New York Times Magazine*.

60. *South of U Oral History Project—Life, Riots and Renewal in Shaw*, Kenneth Tolliver interview transcript, Dig DC archives, https://dcplislandora.wrlc.org/islandora/object/dcplislandora%3A68528/pages.

61. Gilbert, *Ten Blocks from the White House*, 70, 77.

62. Steiner, "The Brookings Institution Seminar on the District of Columbia Riot." Julian Dugas was the DC official.

63. Marian Burros, "City Faces Food Crisis," *Washington Daily News*, April 8, 1968. Anyone who has ever been in DC during a snowstorm knows exactly how strong of a statement this is.

64. "Transportation—Traffic," *Report on Civil Disturbances in Washington, D.C., April 1968*; "Growing Doubt: Why the Delay," *Washington Daily*

News, April 6, 1968; Richard Starnes, "D.C. Loses Its Innocence," *Washington Daily News*, April 8, 1968.

65. "Operation Bandaid," Office of Emergency Preparedness Records, 19.

66. "Guard Call Late? Mayor Is Satisfied, but Questions Asked," *Washington Daily News*, April 6, 1968. For a personal account of this, see *South of U Oral History Project—Life, Riots and Renewal in Shaw*, Kenneth Tolliver interview. See also "Memorandum to the President of the United States," from Walter Washington, Patrick Murphy, and John Layton to President Lyndon Johnson, April 5, 1968, "Washington, D.C. Civil Rights Issues Including Riot Prevention, Poor People's Campaign, and Urban Renewal, 1968–1969," found in "Civil Rights During the Johnson Administration, 1963–1969, Part I: The White House Central Files," ProQuest History Vault: Black Freedom Struggle.

67. "Transportation—Traffic," *Report on Civil Disturbances in Washington, D.C., April 1968*; "Growing Doubt: Why the Delay," *Washington Daily News*.

68. "Guard Call Late?" *Washington Daily News*; Gilbert, *Ten Blocks from the White House*, 72.

69. "Transportation—Traffic," *Report on Civil Disturbances in Washington, D.C., April 1968*. For example, Gerard Ivanhoe Sawyer, a government engineer, abandoned his bus and walked home after it took him over two hours to go less than two miles. Gerard Ivanhoe Sawyer, diary entry, April 5, 1968, box 2 1962–1977, MS 0789, Gerard Ivanhoe and Margaretha Nicol Sawyer Dairies, Kiplinger Library, Washington, DC; "Transportation—Traffic," *Report on Civil Disturbances in Washington, D.C., April 1968*.

70. "Guard Call Late?" *Washington Daily News*, April 6, 1968.

71. Mary E. Stratford, "District Rioting Unleashed Ugly Emotions," *Washington Afro-American*, April 9, 1968. Due to an assumed scanning error, the second half of the article appears with the April 16 edition of the paper (https://news.google.com/newspapers/p/afro?nid=BeIT3YV5Q zEC&dat=19680409&printsec=frontpage&hl=en). See "Stark Fear Overcame the Lone Man," *Washington Afro-American*, April 16, 1968.

72. Gilbert, *Ten Blocks from the White House*, 48–49.

73. "Transportation—Traffic," *Report on Civil Disturbances in Washington, D.C., April 1968*; "Operation Bandaid One," Office of Emergency Preparedness Records, 19.

74. Jenkins, "No Busting Easter Shopping Just 'Soul' Signs, Troopers," *Washington Afro American.*

75. "Drivers Use Lights in Memorial Gesture," *Washington Star*, April 6, 1968; Stratford, "District Rioting Unleashed Ugly Emotions," *Washington Afro-American.*

76. Stratford, "District Rioting Unleashed Ugly Emotions," *Washington Afro-American.*

77. David Lawrence, "Tragedy of Riots Deep-Rooted," *Washington Evening Star*, April 9, 1968.

78. Gilbert, *Ten Blocks from the White House*, 147..

79. William Raspberry, "Potomac Watch: Punish, Don't Destroy Looters," *Washington Post*, April 15, 1968.

80. "John Smith Oral History," 22–26, box 1, folder 4, MS 0769, 1968 Riots Oral History Collection, Kiplinger Research Library Archives, Washington, D.C.; Gilbert, *Ten Blocks from the White House*, 159–161.

81. "John Smith Oral History," 22–25; Gilbert, *Ten Blocks from the White House*, 163, 169–170.

82. "John Smith Oral History," 23.

83. Gilbert, *Ten Blocks from the White House*, 173. When asked if they thought the uprising was a plot, the men responded: "I don't think that's relevant. We took advantage of an incident. If it was planned, you see, there would be nothing left of the city. There would be very few white people around here, also." Gilbert, *Ten Blocks from the White House*, 164–168.

84. Allen, "April's Black Rebellions: A Political Analysis," *The Hilltop*, April 26, 1968.

85. Gilbert, *Ten Blocks from the White House*, 179.

86. Ward Just, "Generation Gap in the Ghetto," *Washington Post*, April 7, 1968.

87. *South of U Oral History Project—Life, Riots and Renewal in Shaw*, Jaqueline Rogers Hart interview transcript; Gilbert, *Ten Blocks from the White House*, 145.

88. "The Looter's Point of View," *Washington Evening Star*, April 6, 1968.

89. "The Looter's Point of View," *Washington Evening Star.*

90. "John D. Jackson interview," 15–16, 20, box 1, folder 6, MS 0769, 1968

District of Columbia Riot," May 20, 1968, 43, Brookings Institution, Washington, DC.

7. "Guard Call Late? Mayor Is Satisfied, but Questions Asked," *Washington Daily News*, April 6, 1968; "Growing Doubt: Why the Delay," *Washington Daily News*, April 6, 1968.

8. Gilbert, *Ten Blocks from the White House*, 100.

9. "Preliminary Action and Status Reports Relating to the Mayor, Director of Public Safety and the Police Department Relative to April 1968 Civil Disorders in the District of Columbia," *Report on Civil Disturbances in Washington, D.C., April 1968.*

10. "Operation Bandaid One," 20, 1968, box 1, folder: "April 4–8," RG 23, Office of Emergency Preparedness Records, District of Columbia Archives, Washington, DC; "Guard Call Late? Mayor Is Satisfied, but Questions Asked," *Washington Daily News.* While the White House and Capitol were not under threat, the troops' presence was intended to create a "psychological effect" to be a "strong deterrent against rioters challenging the application of force by the disturbance control troops," according to the Army's riot control doctrine, *Field Manual 19-15: Civil Disturbances and Natural Disasters: Field Manual 19-15: Civil Disturbances and Natural Disasters* (Washington, DC: Government Printing Office, 1968) 7–8, originally quoted in Price, *King to King*, 97.

11. Gilbert, *Ten Blocks from the White House*, 93. Soldiers headed out after first staging (preparing) at several centers in the city, including the U.S. Soldiers' Home in DC's Petworth neighborhood.

12. They blocked off Seventh Street NW from K Street to S Street NW.

13. Gilbert, *Ten Blocks from the White House*, 96–98, 110.

14. "Arsonists and Looters Leave Parts of Capital in Shambles" *Washington Evening Star*, April 6, 1968.

15. Gilbert, *Ten Blocks from the White House*, 82–85, 98–99.

16. "The District Fire Department's Role in the Civil Disturbances of April 4, 5, 6, 7, and 8, 1968," *Report on Civil Disturbances in Washington, D.C., April 1968.*

17. "Fireman: I Couldn't Even Tell You What Day It Was," *Daily News.*

18. "Operation Bandaid One," Office of Emergency Preparedness Records, 9. Reports of stoning firefighters even reached the desk of the president. A memo to Johnson reported that "firemen are being attacked

by sticks, stones, and crow bars." "Situation Room Information Memorandum," Friday April 5, 1968, 7:15 PM, "Situation Room Information Memos, Troop Movements and Riots 1968, Martin Luther King Jr. Assassination, Selected Civil Rights Files—James Gaither, 1968," in "Civil Rights during the Johnson Administration, 1963–1969, Part I: The White House Central Files," ProQuest History Vault: Black Freedom Struggle. See also "Situation Room Information Memorandum," April 5, 1968, 5:30 PM, "Situation Room Information Memos."

19. Gilbert, *Ten Blocks from the White House*, 51.

20. Gilbert, *Ten Blocks from the White House*, 86.

21. "4:30 PM Local Washington D.C. Status Report," "Situation Room Information Memos"; Gilbert, *Ten Blocks from the White House*, 51–52. For example, firefighters left fires at Seventh Street and Florida Avenue and at Fourteenth Street and Columbia on April 5 because of being stoned.

22. Robert Allen, "April's Black Rebellions: A Political Analysis," *The Hilltop*, April 26, 1968.

23. "4:30 PM Local Washington D.C. Status Report," "Situation Room Information Memos."

24. "Selected Racial Developments and Disturbances," April 6, 1968, time illegible, DDRS-26392, Reproduced in *Declassified Documents Reference System* (Farmington Hills, MI: Gale), 2015.

25. Lillian Wiggins, "Stores Looted, Rocks Thrown at D.C. Police," *Washington Afro-American*, April 9, 1968.

26. "Fireman: I Couldn't Even Tell You What Day It Was," *Daily News*.

27. Gilbert, *Ten Blocks from the White House*, 86.

28. Gilbert, *Ten Blocks from the White House*, 106.

29. "Preliminary Action and Status Reports Relating to the Mayor, Director of Public Safety and the Police Department Relative to April 1968 Civil Disorders in the District of Columbia," *Report on Civil Disturbances in Washington, D.C., April 1968*; "The District Fire Department's Role in the Civil Disturbances of April 4, 5, 6, 7, and 8, 1968," *Report on Civil Disturbances in Washington, D.C., April 1968*.

30. Nicholas Horrock, "D.C. Police: No Faith in Mace," *Washington Evening Star*, April 11, 1968; Price, *King to King*, 100–101.

31. *Civil Disturbances in Washington: Hearings Before the Committee on the District of Columbia House of Representatives* (hereafter referred to as *Civil*

Disorders within the Eleventh Precinct Beginning Thursday April 4, 1968, Problems Encountered, Solutions Utilized and Recommendations," 2, DC Public Library, Special Collections, Vertical Files—Riots, 1968 (April); Gilbert, *Ten Blocks from the White House*, 84. While the names of both officers are given in *Ten Blocks from the White House*, the records obtained through a FOIA request still redact the officers' names.

63. Gilbert, *Ten Blocks from the White House*, 85.

64. Gilbert, *Ten Blocks from the White House*, 83.

65. Metropolitan Police Department of the District of Columbia, "Lists of Deaths Probably/Possibly Established in Connection with Civil Disturbances in Washington, D.C. April 5–7," DC Public Library, Special Collections, Vertical Files—Riots. 1968 (April).

66. Price, *King to King*, 96; "Lists of Deaths Probably/Possibly Established in Connection with Civil Disturbances in Washington, D.C. April 5–7."

67. John Smith Oral History, 24–25, box 1, folder 4, MS 0769, 1968 Riots Oral History Collection, Kiplinger Research Library Archives, Washington, DC.

68. "Fireman: I Couldn't Even Tell You What Day It Was," *Washington Daily News*.

69. Gilbert, *Ten Blocks from the White House*, 98.

70. "Guard Call Late? Mayor Is Satisfied, But Question Asked," *Washington Daily News*, April 6, 1968.

71. "Architecture and Society Fall Midterm 1996," Ben's Chili Bowl Papers; "Press Conference," Bowl Papers; "The Shaw Community: The Impact of the Civil Rights Movement, as Told by Mrs. Virginia Ali, Owner of Ben's Chili Bowl," Ben's Chili Bowl Papers.

72. "The Shaw Community: The Impact of the Civil Rights Movement, as Told by Mrs. Virginia Ali, Owner of Ben's Chili Bowl," Ben's Chili Bowl Papers, 23.

73. "The Shaw Community: The Impact of the Civil Rights Movement, as Told by Mrs. Virginia Ali, Owner of Ben's Chili Bowl," Ben's Chili Bowl Papers, 25–26.

74. Gilbert, *Ten Blocks from the White House*, 72–73.

75. Multiple people in oral interviews recalled seeing "soul brother" signs. See *South of U Oral History Project—Life, Riots and Renewal in Shaw*, Ibrahim Mumin interview transcript, Dig DC archives, https://

dcplislandora.wrlc.org/islandora/object/dcplislandora%3A68604/pages;
Virginia Ali Interview, February 23, 2003, 15, 26, box 1, folder 1, MS 0769,
1968 Riots Oral History Collection, Kiplinger Research Library Archives,
Washington, DC.

76. Virginia Ali Interview, February 23, 2003.

77. David Holmberg, ". . . A Blue-Skied Palm Sunday," *Washington Daily News*, April 8, 1968; "Looting Was Often Selective" *Washington Daily News*, April 8, 1968

78. Richard Starnes, "D.C. Loses Its Innocence," *Washington Daily News*, April 8, 1968.

79. Ruth Jenkins, "No Busting Easter Shopping Just 'Soul' Signs, Troopers," *Washington Afro-American*, April 9, 1968.

80. "Looting Was Often Selective," *Washington Daily News*, April 8, 1968.

81. Adrienne Manns and Robert Nesnick, "Was It Riot or Insurrection?" *The Hilltop*, April 26, 1968.

82. Gerard Ivanhoe Sawyer, Diary Entry, Monday 8, 1968, Gerard Ivanhoe and Margaret Sawyer Diary Collection, Kiplinger Library, Washington, DC.

83. Starnes, "D.C. Loses Its Innocence," *Washington Daily News*.

84. "Looting Was Often Selective," *Washington Daily News*.

85. Gilbert, *Ten Blocks from the White House*, 101–102. For transcripts of the speeches see *Report on Civil Disturbances in Washington, D.C., April 1968*. By 7 a.m. the next morning, while all fires were under control, twenty-four still burned. "The District Fire Department's Role in the Civil Disturbances of April 4, 5, 6, 7, and 8, 1968," *Report on Civil Disturbances in Washington, D.C., April 1968*.

86. "Operation Bandaid One," Office of Emergency Preparedness Records, 31.

87. "The District Fire Department's Role in the Civil Disturbances of April 4, 5, 6, 7, and 8, 1968," *Report on Civil Disturbances in Washington, D.C., April 1968*.

88. Gilbert, *Ten Blocks from the White House*, 104.

89. Price, *King to King*, 91. At its peak, a total of 15,530 troops were in DC—13,682 active-duty troops and 1,848 National Guard troops. Price, *King to King*, 99.

90. "Public Works Journal," *Report on Civil Disturbances in Washington, D.C., April 1968.*

91. Gilbert, *Ten Blocks from the White House*, 111.

6

"You Have a City in Flames. . . . And so Some People Will Have to Languish in Jail": The Administration of Justice

1. Ben Gilbert, *Ten Blocks from the White House: Anatomy of the Washington Riots of 1968* (New York: Frederick A. Praeger, 1968), 122.

2. William Dobrovir, *Justice in Time of Crisis: A Staff Report to the District of Columbia Committee on the Administration of Justice under Emergency Conditions* (Washington, DC: U.S. Government Printing Office, 1969), 16; Harold Greene, "A Judge's View of the Riots," *D.C. Bar Journal*, August–October 1968; Riots Vertical Files April 4–15, 1968, Washingtoniana Collection, Martin Luther King Jr. Memorial Public Library, Washington, DC.

3. Gilbert, *Ten Blocks from the White House*, 123; Greene, "A Judge's View of the Riots," *D.C. Bar Journal*; Dobrovir, *Justice in a Time of Crisis*, 16.

4. Greene, "A Judge's View of the Riots," *D.C. Bar Journal*.

5. "Report of Arrest Procedures on and After April 4, 1968, in the District of Columbia," *Report on Civil Disturbances in Washington, D.C., April 1968*, Gelman Library Special Collections at the George Washington University, Washington, DC. Documents from this report are indicated by their title within the report as the document does not use page numbers.

6. "Justice During a Crisis," *Washington Post*, April 10, 1968; David A. Jewell, "Liberties Union's Suit Angers court," *Washington Post*, April 9, 1968. A total of 1,825 people were processed from 11 p.m. on Thursday to Monday at 9:30 p.m.

7. "Justice During a Crisis," *Washington Post*; Dobrovir, *Justice in a Time of Crisis*, 16.

8. James E. Clayton, "Riot Cases Jam Court Around Clock," *Washington Post*, April 7, 1968; Gilbert, *Ten Blocks from the White House*, 124–126.

9. Gilbert, *Ten Blocks from the White House*, 125.

10. Clayton, "Riot Cases Jam Court Around Clock," *Washington Post*; Gilbert, *Ten Blocks from the White House*, 124–126. In the coming months, over four hundred lawyers represented riot defendants in their trials. See

William Shumann, "How Courts of 2 Cities Dealt With Riot Suspects," *Washington Post*, April 28, 1968.

11. Jewell, "Liberties Union's Suit Angers Court," *Washington Post*; Clayton, "Riot Cases Jam Court Around Clock," *Washington Post*.

12. Justice System Needs Revamping, Study Finds," *Washington Post*, May 18, 1968; Gilbert, *Ten Blocks from the White House*, 126.

13. Russel Chandler, "Riot Arrest Set Up Called Paper Maze," *Washington Star*, May 18, 1968. While the Justice Department had designed simplified police forms to use in case of a civil disorder, they had not yet printed them when the upheaval began. See Gilbert, *Ten Blocks from the White House*, 122.

14. Gilbert, *Ten Blocks from the White House*, 122.

15. Gilbert, *Ten Blocks from the White House*, 127; Dobrovir, *Justice in a Time of Crisis*, 14; "Report of Arrest Procedures on and After April 4, 1968, in the District of Columbia," *Report on Civil Disturbances in Washington, D.C., April 1968*.

16. Gilbert, *Ten Blocks from the White House*, 127.

17. Gilbert, *Ten Blocks from the White House*, 129.

18. Clayton, "Riot Cases Jam Court Around Clock", *Washington Post*; James E. Clayton, "Court Struggles to Clear Jails," *Washington Post*, April 8, 1968.

19. Lawrence Speiser, Ralph J. Temple, and W.M. Warfield Ross, "The Administration of Justice," *Washington Post*, April 13, 1968; "Report of Arrest Procedures on and After April 4, 1968, in the District of Columbia," *Report on Civil Disturbances in Washington, D.C., April 1968*; Dobrovir, *Justice in a Time of Crisis*, 11. People were held in the cellblocks of the Court of General Sessions and U.S. District Court, and beginning Saturday night the Occoquan workhouse in Lorton, Virginia, while they waited. "Report of Arrest Procedures on and After April 4, 1968, in the District of Columbia," *Report on Civil Disturbances in Washington, D.C., April 1968*.

20. "Report of Arrest Procedures on and After April 4, 1968, in the District of Columbia," *Report on Civil Disturbances in Washington, D.C., April 1968*.

21. Gilbert, *Ten Blocks from the White House*, 129–130.

22. Gilbert, *Ten Blocks from the White House*, 132; "Looting Suspect 'Lost' in D.C. Jails for 4½ Days," *Washington Post*, April 28, 1968.

23. Gilbert, *Ten Blocks from the White House*, 129.

24. "Report of Arrest Procedures on and After April 4, 1968, in the District of Columbia," *Report on Civil Disturbances in Washington, D.C., April 1968*; Clayton, "Riot Cases Jam Court Around Clock," *Washington Post*; Clayton, "Court Struggles to Clear Jails," *Washington Post*.

25. Dobrovir, *Justice in a Time of Crisis*, 7.

26. Gilbert, *Ten Blocks from the White House*, 121.

27. "Report of Arrest Procedures on and After April 4, 1968, in the District of Columbia," *Report on Civil Disturbances in Washington, D.C., April 1968*; Gilbert, *Ten Bocks from the White House*, 128; Dobrovir, *Justice in a Time of Crisis*, 5, 7, 11; Hardy, "Corrections' Participation in Disturbance Commencing April 4, 1968, April 16, 1968," *Report on Civil Disturbances in Washington, D.C., April 1968*; Clayton, "Riot Cases Jam Court Around Clock," *Washington Post*; William Shumann, "Curfew Violation Trials May Be Avoided," *Washington Post*, April 18, 1968. The policy was so uniform that analyst William Dobrovir concluded, "It seems fair to say that the penalty for violation of curfew was one night in jail and a $25.00 fine."

28. "Report of Arrest Procedures on and After April 4, 1968, in the District of Columbia," *Report on Civil Disturbances in Washington, D.C., April 1968*. Forty-four defendants who remained on the morning of April 7 refused to identify themselves after giving false names when booked. Rufus "Catfish" Mayfield, an activist and former head of Pride, Inc., agreed to obtain the names of these prisoners after Judge Halleck promised to release most into Mayfield's custody on personal bond. "Catfish Gets Docket Clear," *Washington Daily News*, April 9, 1968; Jewell, "Liberties Union's Suit Angers Court," *Washington Post*; Gilbert, *Ten Blocks from the White House*, 131.

29. Dobrovir, *Justice in a Time of Crisis*, xxiv; "Report of Arrest Procedures on and After April 4, 1968, in the District of Columbia," *Report on Civil Disturbances in Washington, D.C., April 1968*.

30. Gilbert, *Ten Blocks from the White House*, 123, 127; Dobrovir, *Justice in a Time of Crisis*, 16–17, 47; Clayton, "Riot Cases Jam Court Around Clock," *Washington Post*.

31. Dobrovir, *Justice in a Time of Crisis*, 21.

32. Dobrovir, *Justice in a Time of Crisis*, 18–20; Lawrence Speiser, Ralph J. Temple, and W.M. Warfield Ross, "The Administration of Justice," *Washington Post*, April 13, 1968; Gilbert, *Ten Blocks from the White House*, 123.

33. Speiser, Temple, and Ross, "The Administration of Justice," *Washington Post*; Dobrovir, *Justice in a Time of Crisis*, 19.

34. "Three Judges Hold Night Session," *Washington Daily News*, April 6, 1968; Gilbert, *Ten Blocks from the White House*, 123–124; "Memorandum from Lloyd N. Cutler to Walter E. Washington, John N. Mitchell, David L. Bazelon, Harold H. Greene," June 18, 1969, *Justice in Time of Crisis*, *iii*, 22–25; Jewell, "Liberties Union's Suit Angers Court," *Washington Post*.

35. Dobrovir, *Justice in a Time of Crisis*, 26; Jewell, "Liberties Union's Suit Angers Court, *Washington Post*; Gilbert, *Ten Blocks from the White House*, 131; "A Time to Start Rebuilding," *Washington Daily News*, April 8, 1968.

36. Dobrovir, *Justice in a Time of Crisis*, 56–59; Gilbert, *Ten Blocks from the White House*, 124.

37. Dobrovir, *Justice in a Time of Crisis*, 27–29.

38. Gilbert, *Ten Blocks from the White House*, 124.

39. Dobrovir, *Justice in a Time of Crisis*, 32. Even as he followed restricted release, Judge Murphy stated in court that it was problematic. As he set bail for a person who was a good candidate for personal bond, he stated, "This is what's wrong with automatic bond on looters."

40. Dobrovir, *Justice in a Time of Crisis*, 39.

41. Dobrovir, *Justice in a Time of Crisis*, 35. As will be discussed later, the American Civil Liberties Union did file a lawsuit claiming, among other things, the judge's actions violated the Bail Reform Act. It was dismissed the same day.

42. Dobrovir, *Justice in a Time of Crisis*, 49–51, 68; Jim Hoagland, "86 Defendants in Riot Cases Still in Jail for Lack of Bail," *Washington Post*, April 26, 1968.

43. Dobrovir, *Justice in a Time of Crisis*, 49.

44. Gilbert, *Ten Blocks from the White House*, 130; Dobrovir, *Justice in a Time of Crisis*, 48.

45. Jewell, "Liberties Union's Suit Angers Court," *Washington Post*; Hoagland, "86 Defendants in Riot Cases Still in Jail for Lack of Bail," *Washington Post*.

46. Dobrovir, *Justice in a Time of Crisis*, 47–49; Gilbert, *Ten Blocks from the White House*, 130.

47. Dobrovir, *Justice in a Time of Crisis*, 48–49.

48. Dobrovir, *Justice in a Time of Crisis*, 26, 43; Jewell, "Liberties Union's Suit Angers Court, *Washington Post*; Gilbert, *Ten Blocks from the White House*, 131; "A Time to Start Rebuilding," *Washington Daily News*.

49. Dobrovir, *Justice in a Time of Crisis*, 26; Jewell, "Liberties Union's Suit Angers Court, *Washington Post*; Gilbert, *Ten Blocks from the White House*, 131; "A Time to Start Rebuilding," *Washington Daily News*.

50. Dobrovir, *Justice in a Time of Crisis*, xxvi.

51. Dobrovir, *Justice in a Time of Crisis*, 47; Hoagland, "86 Defendants in Riot Cases Still in Jail for Lack of Bail," *Washington Post*.

52. Dobrovir, *Justice in a Time of Crisis*, 53.

53. Jewell, "Liberties Union's Suit Angers Court," *Washington Post*.

54. Jewell, "Liberties Union's Suit Angers Court," *Washington Post*; Gilbert, *Ten Blocks from the White House*, 131; Dobrovir, *Justice in a Time of Crisis*, 55–56.

55. Speiser, Temple, and Ross, "The Administration of Justice," *Washington Post*.

56. Jewell, "Liberties Union's Suit Angers Court," *Washington Post*; Gilbert, *Ten Blocks from the White House*, 131; Dobrovir, *Justice in a Time of Crisis*, 55–56.

57. "Memorandum from Lloyd N. Cutler to Walter E. Washington, John N. Mitchell, David L. Bazelon, Harold H. Greene," June 18, 1969, *Justice in Time of Crisis: A Staff Report to the District of Columbia Committee on the Administration of Justice under Emergency Conditions* (Washington, DC: U.S. Government Printing Office, 1969), iv–viii.

58. Dobrovir, *Justice in a Time of Crisis*, 42.

59. Dobrovir, *Justice in a Time of Crisis*, 3.

60. "Bail and Riots," *Washington Post*, May 27, 1968.

61. Gilbert, *Ten Blocks from the White House*, 123.

62. Dobrovir, *Justice in a Time of Crisis*, 47, 53, 60–62.

63. Gilbert, *Ten Blocks from the White House*, 125.

64. Dobrovir, *Justice in a Time of Crisis*, 49–51, 68; Hoagland, "86 Defendants in Riot Cases Still in Jail for Lack of Bail," *Washington Post*.

65. Dobrovir, *Justice in a Time of Crisis*, 65.

66. Gilbert, *Ten Blocks from the White House*, 125.

67. Gilbert, *Ten Blocks from the White House*, 125–126, 136. Additionally, while three of the eighteen judges handling the disorders were Black, they were not present when the much-criticized bail policy was determined. One judge was sick and the other two were not on duty.

7

"Calm and Compassionate Style":
Community Aid and Restoring Normalcy

1. David Holmberg, ". . . A Blue-Skied Palm Sunday," *Washington Daily News*, April 8, 1968; "Looting Was Often Selective" *Washington Daily News*, April 8, 1968; "Game Again Put Off," *Washington Evening Star*, April 6, 1968.

2. Arsonists and Looters Leave Parts of Capital in Shambles," *Washington Evening Star*, April 6, 1968.

3. "Thousands of Spectators Pour into Violence-Hit Areas, Cause Traffic Jams," *Washington Star*, April 7, 1968.

4. "The beginning of Holy Week in Washington," *Washington Daily News*, Monday, April 8, 1968; Richard Starnes, "D.C. Loses Its Innocence," *Washington Daily News*, April 8, 1968. Historian Barrye La Troye Price also recounted the traffic jams on Sunday as "visitors and curious suburbanites glutted District streets by driving into damaged sections of the city." Barrye La Troye Price, "King to King: A Study of Civil Unrest and Federal Intervention 1968–1992" (PhD diss., Texas A&M University, 1997), 91.

5. Pamela Howard, "Cherry Blossoms and Riot Ruins," *Washington Daily News*, April 9, 1968.

6. Ben Gilbert, *Ten Blocks from the White House: Anatomy of the Washington Riots of 1968* (New York: Frederick A. Praeger, 1968), 103–104; "Thousands of Spectators Pour into Violence-Hit Areas, Cause Traffic Jams," *Washington Star*, April 7, 1968.

7. Julius Duscha, "Postscript to the Story of Seventh Street," *New York Times Magazine*, June 2, 1968.

8. Marian Burros, "City Faces Food Crisis," *Washington Daily News*, April 8, 1968; Ronald Sarro, "Panel to Begin D.C. Riot Probe," *Washington Star*, May 26, 1968.

9. Burros, "City Faces Food Crisis," *Washington Daily News*.

10. "A Time to Start Rebuilding," *Washington Daily News*, April 8, 1968.

11. Burros, "City Faces Food Crisis," *Washington Daily News*.

12. "Emergency Health Services Civil Disturbance, April 5–8, 1968," *Report on Civil Disturbances in Washington, D.C., April 1968*, Gelman Library Special Collections at the George Washington University, Washington, DC.

13. *Rehabilitation of District of Columbia Areas Damaged by Civil Disorders: Hearings Before the Subcommittee on Business and Commerce of the Committee on the District of Columbia United States Senate*, Ninetieth Cong. 332 (1968) (statement of Calvin Rolark, representative of the Washington Highlands Civic Association).

14. "Operation Bandaid One," 1968, 40–42, box 1, folder "April 4–8," RG 23, Office of Emergency Preparedness Records, District of Columbia Archives, Washington, DC.

15. "A Time to Start Rebuilding," *Washington Daily News*; "Hollering Whitey-This and Whitey-That," *Washington Daily News*, April 8, 1968.

16. "Agriculture Dept. Pouring Surplus Food into City," *Washington Daily News*, April 8, 1968; Betty James, "Emergency Food Is Available for Victims of D.C. Violence," *Washington Post*, April 7, 1968.

17. Winifred G. Thompson, "Role of the Department of Public Welfare During Civil Disturbance," *Report on Civil Disturbances in Washington, D.C., April 1968*; Burros, "City Faces Food Crisis," *Washington Daily News*.

18. "Operation Bandaid One," Office of Emergency Preparedness Records, 37.

19. John Mercer, "Students Operate Emergency Relief Center for 12 Days," *The Hilltop*, April 26, 1968.

20. "Emergency Health Services Civil Disturbance, April 5–8, 1968," *Report on Civil Disturbances in Washington, D.C., April 1968*.

21. https://en.wikipedia.org/wiki/Mutual_aid_(organization_theory)

22. The DC government estimated that 1,056 were injured, while Barrye La Troye Price estimated that there were 1,201 injuries based on the army's after-action report. This figure comes from the mayor's report. "Emergency Health Services Civil Disturbance, April 5–8" *Report on Civil Disturbances in Washington, D.C., April 1968*; Price, *King to King*, 95–96.

23. "Emergency Health Services Civil Disturbance, April 5–8," *Report on Civil Disturbances in Washington, D.C., April 1968*.

24. "Hospitals Rise to the Emergency," *Washington Evening Star*, April 6, 1968.

25. Gilbert Y. Steiner, "The Brookings Institution Seminar on the District of Columbia Riot," May 20, 1968, 22–23, Brookings Institution, Washington, DC.

26. "Emergency Health Services Civil Disturbance, April 5–8," *Report on Civil Disturbances in Washington, D.C., April 1968*.

27. James E. Clayton, "Riot Cases Jam Court Around Clock," *Washington Post*, April 7, 1968; Gilbert, *Ten Blocks from the White House*, 124–126. In the coming months, over four hundred lawyers represented riot defendants in their trials. See William Shumann, "How Courts of 2 Cities Dealt With Riot Suspects," *Washington Post*, April 28, 1968. On Friday afternoon, Judge Greene asked John E. Powell, president of the DC Bar Association, to ask lawyers to volunteer as defense attorneys. Powell refused because he was afraid volunteers would sue the Bar Association if they were injured. Greene also did not want to send out a request because he refused to admit publicly that "the court was in serious trouble." Greene neglected to consult the Washington Bar Association, the black lawyers' organization, and its president, Alexander Benton, later criticized this oversight. See Gilbert, *Ten Blocks from the White House*, 125.

28. David A. Jewell, "Liberties Union's Suit Angers Court," *Washington Post*, April 10, 1968. Clayton, "Riot Cases Jam Court Around Clock," *Washington Post*; "Justice System Needs Revamping, Study Finds," *Washington Post*, May 18, 1968; Gilbert, *Ten Blocks from the White House*, 126.

29. Gilbert, *Ten Blocks from the White House*, 126.

30. Clayton, "Riot Cases Jam Court Around Clock," *Washington Post*.

31. Gilbert, *Ten Blocks from the White House*, 128.

32. Gilbert, *Ten Blocks from the White House*, 120, 128; Clayton, "Riot Cases Jam Court Around Clock," *Washington Post*.

33. Memorandum from the director of the Office of Criminal Justice Daniel J. Freed to Attorney General Ramsey Clark, "D.C. Civil Disorder—Administration of Justice," April 11, 1968, *Report on Civil Disturbances in Washington, D.C., April 1968*. The three government lawyers were Steven Waldhorn of Department of Housing and Urban Development, Lee Saterfield of the Equal Employment Opportunity Commission, and Daniel J. Freed of the Office of Criminal Justice.

34. Gilbert, *Ten Blocks from the White House*, 128; Freed, "D.C. Civil Disorder—Administration of Justice," April 11, 1968, *Report on Civil Disturbances in Washington, D.C., April 1968*; James E. Clayton, "Court Struggles to Clear Jails," *Washington Post*, April 8, 1968.

35. "Catfish Gets Docket Clear," *Washington Daily News*, April 9, 1968, Washingtoniana Periodicals, Martin Luther King Jr. Memorial Library, Washington, D.C.; Gilbert, *Ten Blocks from the White House*, 131.

36. Robert Rogers, "Summary of Activity—D.C. Citizen Information Telephone Answering Service," *Report on Civil Disturbances in Washington, D.C., April 1968*.

37. Steiner, "The Brookings Institution Seminar on the District of Columbia Riot," 108; "Batteries of Phones Help Lift Fog of Rumor in D.C. Turmoil," *Washington Evening Star*, April 11, 1968.

38. "Murphy Meets Topkick," *Washington Daily News*, 3 April 10, 1968.

39. "City Rights Leaders Plead for Calm," *Washington Star*, April 7, 1968.

40. Gilbert, *Ten Blocks from the White House*, 97.

41. Gilbert, *Ten Blocks from the White House*, 75.

42. "Conflict in Morals," *Washington Daily News*, April 9, 1968.

43. Gilbert, *Ten Blocks from the White House*, 108.

44. Steiner, "The Brookings Institution Seminar on the District of Columbia Riot," 41–42.

45. "Radio, TV: Restraint," *Washington Daily News*, April 6, 1968.

46. "Proclamation of Emergency," April 6, 1968, *Report on Civil Disturbances in Washington, D.C., April 1968*.

47. John D. Jackson Interview, box 1, folder 6, MS 0769, 1968 Riots Oral History Collection, Kiplinger Research Library Archives, Washington, DC.

48. Gilbert, *Ten Blocks from the White House*, 109.

49. "Army Guards D.C. Streets," *The Hilltop*, April 26, 1968.

50. Gilbert, *Ten Blocks from the White House*, 109.

51. For a vivid representation of this, see Gilbert, *Ten Blocks from the White House*, 70–71.

52. Ruth Jenkins, "No Bustling Easter Shopping Just 'Soul' Signs, Troopers," *Washington Afro-American*, April 9, 1968.

53. Richard Starnes, "D.C. Loses Its Innocence," *Washington Daily News*, April 8, 1968.

54. "A Time to Start Rebuilding," *Washington Daily News*, April 9, 1968.

55. John D. Jackson Interview, 17.

56. Holmberg, ". . . A Blue-Skied Palm Sunday," *Washington Daily News*, April 8, 1968.

57. "A Time to Start Rebuilding," *Washington Daily News*, April 9, 1968.

58. "The Beginning of Holy Week in Washington," *Washington Daily News*, April 8, 1968.

59. "The District Fire Department's Role in the Civil Disturbances of April 4, 5, 6, 7, and 8, 1968," *Report on Civil Disturbances in Washington, D.C., April 1968.*

60. "Preliminary Action and Status Reports Relating to the Mayor, Director of Public Safety and the Police Department Relative to April 1968 Civil Disorders in the District of Columbia," 6, *Report on Civil Disturbances in Washington, D.C., April 1968.*

61. "A Time to Start Rebuilding," *Washington Daily News*, April 9, 1968.

62. "Troops Made Home in Schools," *Washington Post*, April 9, 1968; Joy Manson, "Children Reflect Confused Society: What 'Soul' Is All About," *Washington Post*, April 10, 1968.

63. "Preliminary Action and Status Reports Relating to the Mayor, Director of Public Safety and the Police Department Relative to April 1968 Civil Disorders in the District of Columbia," 6, *Report on Civil Disturbances in Washington, D.C., April 1968.*

64. "Operation Bandaid One," Office of Emergency Preparedness Records, 75.

65. Price, *King to King*, 91.

66. "Troops Made Home in Schools," *Washington Post.*

67. "District Eases Curfew, Liquor Rules Further," *Washington Evening Star*, April 11, 1968.

68. Steiner, "The Brookings Institution Seminar on the District of Columbia Riot," 33.

69. Memo from J. Edgar Hoover to President Lyndon Johnson, "Selected Racial Developments and Disturbances," April 7, 1968, DDRS-26392,

reproduced in *Declassified Documents Reference System* (Farmington Hills: MI: Gale, 2015).

70. "Selected Racial Developments and Disturbances," 4, April 8, 1968, DDRS-26392, reproduced in *Declassified Documents Reference System*.

71. S. Oliver Goodman, "Bulk of Washington Firms to Close in King Tribute," *Washington Post*, April 9, 1968.

72. For example, see ads from Ida's Department Store, Perpetual Building Association, and various grocery stores in the *Washington Daily News*, April 9ᐧ 1968; *Washington Evening Star*, April 9, 1968.

73. Display Ad 27—No Title, *Washington Post*, April 9, 1968; Display Ad No 13—No Title, *Washington Post*, April 9, 1968.

74. Display Ad 32—No Title, *Washington Post*, April 9, 1968.

75. Display Ad No 6—No Title, *Washington Post*, April 9, 1968. As an exception, an ad for SCAN furniture read: "In Memoriam: Rev. Dr. Martin Luther King, Jr., I refuse to accept the view that mankind is so tragically bound to the starless midnight of racism and war that the bright daybreak of peace and brotherhood can never become a reality."

76. Display Ad 39—No Title, *Washington Post*, April 9, 1968.

77. "Bulk of Washington Firms to Close in King Tribute," *Washington Post*, April 9, 1968.

78. *Washington Evening Star*, April 11, 1968.

79. "District Eases Curfew, Liquor Rules Further," *Washington Evening Star*, April 11, 1968; "Game Again Put Off," *Washington Evening Star*, April 6, 1968.

80. "Batteries of Phones Help Lift Fog of Rumor in D.C. Turmoil," *Washington Evening Star*, April 11, 1968.

81. "Proclamation of Emergency," April 10, 1968, *Report on Civil Disturbances in Washington, D.C., April 1968*; "D.C. Eases the Curfew Even Further (10 p.m.) and Opens Up the Bars," *Washington Daily News*, April 10, 1968.

82. "Help Plans Growing," *Washington Daily News*, April 12, 1968.

83. "Preliminary Action and Status Reports Relating to the Mayor, Director of Public Safety and the Police Department Relative to April 1968 Civil Disorders in the District of Columbia," *Report on Civil Disturbances in Washington, D.C., April 1968*; Price, *King to King*, 93–94.

8

"A Vacuum and an Opportunity": Creating a Framework for Reconstruction

1. "Sees City's Chance for New Identity," *Washington Afro-American*, April 16, 1968.

2. Mary E. Briggs, letter to William Calomiris, July 17, 1968, box 287, file 17: "Riots of 1968—Comments, Aftermath, Reactions," Greater Washington Board of Trade Records, Gelman Library Special Collections Research Center, George Washington University, Washington, DC.

3. Historians such as Thomas Sugrue, Michael Flamm, Kevin Kruse, Matt Lassiter, Lisa McGirr, and Robert O. Self have documented how white suburbanites reshaped American politics as they rejected the civil rights movement and Great Society agendas. For more, see Thomas J. Sugrue, "Crabgrass-Roots: Race, Roots, and the Reaction Against Liberalism in the Urban North, 1940–1964," *Journal of American History* 82, no. 2 (September 1995): 551; Thomas J. Sugrue, *The Origins of the Urban Crisis: Race and Inequality in Postwar Detroit* (Princeton, NJ: Princeton University Press, 1996); Robert O. Self, *American Babylon: Race and the Struggle for Postwar Oakland* (Princeton, NJ: Princeton University Press, 2003); Kevin Kruse, *White Flight: Atlanta and the Making of Modern Conservatism* (Princeton, NJ: Princeton University Press, 2005); Lisa McGirr, *Suburban Warriors: The Origins of the New American Right* (Princeton, NJ: Princeton University Press, 2001); Matthew D. Lassiter, *The Silent Majority: Suburban Politics in the Sunbelt South* (Princeton, NJ: Princeton University Press, 2005); Michael Flamm, *Law and Order: Street Crime, Civil Unrest, and the 1960s* (New York: Columbia University Press, 2005); Michael Flamm, *In the Heat of the Summer: The New York Riots of 1964 and the War on Crime* (Philadelphia: University of Pennsylvania Press, 2017).

4. Flamm, *Law and Order*, 97.

5. Flamm, *Law and Order*, 10.

6. Clay Risen, *A Nation on Fire: America in the Wake of the King Assassination* (Hoboken, NJ: John Wiley & Sons, Inc., 2009), 4–5.

7. Peniel Joseph, ed., *Neighborhood Rebels: Black Power at the Local Level* (New York: Palgrave Macmillan, 2010), 1–9.

8. *Rehabilitation of District of Columbia Areas Damaged by Civil Disorders. Hearings Before the Subcommittee on Business and Commerce of*

the Committee on the District of Columbia United States Senate (hereafter referred to as *Rehabilitation of District of Columbia Areas Damaged by Civil Disorders*), Ninetieth Cong. 109 (1968) (statement of Walter E. Washington, mayor of Washington, DC).

9. *Rehabilitation of District of Columbia Areas Damaged by Civil Disorders*, Ninetieth Cong. 149–150 (1968) (statement of Carroll Harvey, executive director of Pride, Inc.).

10. Jonathon Cottin, "Senate Report Finds: Rioting 'Indorsed' Here," *Washington Daily News*, July 31, 1968.

11. "Hollering Whitey-This and Whitey-That," *Washington Daily News*, April 8, 1968.

12. "Report of the City Council Public Hearings on the Rebuilding and Recovery of Washington, D.C. from the Civil Disturbances of April, 1968," 2, P1614, Kiplinger Research Library Archives, Washington, DC.

13. "Report of the City Council Public Hearings on the Rebuilding and Recovery of Washington, D.C. from the Civil Disturbances of April, 1968," 2; *Rehabilitation of District of Columbia Areas Damaged by Civil Disorders*, 129–130 (statement of John W. Hechinger, chairman of the DC City Council).

14. For examples, see the transcript of community hearings testimony in "District of Columbia City Council Public Hearings on the Rebuilding and Recovery of the City," *Civil Disturbances in Washington: Hearings Before the Committee on the District of Columbia House of Representatives* (hereafter referred to as *Civil Disturbances in Washington*), Ninetieth Cong. (1968).

15. "Report of the City Council Public Hearings on the Rebuilding and Recovery of Washington, D.C. from the Civil Disturbances of April, 1968," 6.

16. "Booker, Reginald H. (1941), Chairman, Washington (D.C.) Construction Area Industry Task Force. July 24, 1970," 13, Ralph J. Bunche Oral Histories Collection (formerly the Civil Rights Documentation Project), Moorland-Spingarn Research Center, Howard University; Peniel E. Joseph, *Stokely: A Life* (New York: Basic Civitas, 2014), 235; Minutes of the Black United Front, February 13, 1968, box 16, folder 14 "Black Empowerment, Black United Front, April–May 1968," MS 2070, Walter Fauntroy Papers, Gelman Library Special Collections at the George Washington University, Washington, DC.

17. Memo from the Black United Front to "All members of the Black

United Front," April 23, 1968, box 4, folder "Black United Front," DC Community Archives, Washingtoniana Collection, Martin Luther King Jr. Memorial Library, Washington, DC.

18. "Report of the City Council Public Hearings on the Rebuilding and Recovery of Washington, D.C. from the Civil Disturbances of April, 1968," 22.

19. "Report of the City Council Public Hearings on the Rebuilding and Recovery of Washington, D.C. from the Civil Disturbances of April, 1968," 4-6.

20. "Report of the City Council Public Hearings on the Rebuilding and Recovery of Washington, D.C. from the Civil Disturbances of April, 1968," 15, 27.

21. "Report of the City Council Public Hearings on the Rebuilding and Recovery of Washington, D.C. from the Civil Disturbances of April, 1968," 28, 35.

22. "Report of the City Council Public Hearings on the Rebuilding and Recovery of Washington, D.C. from the Civil Disturbances of April, 1968," 15, 27.

23. *Civil Disturbances in Washington*, Ninetieth Cong. 337 (1968) (statement of Rev. Phillip Newell of the Urban Institute, Father Geno Baroni of the Office of Urban Affairs of the Catholic Archdiocese of Washington, and Rabbi Eugene J. Lipman of the Urban Problems Subcommittee of the Jewish Community Council).

24. "Report of the City Council Public Hearings on the Rebuilding and Recovery of Washington, D.C. from the Civil Disturbances of April, 1968," 2-3.

25. *Civil Disturbances in Washington*, Ninetieth Cong. 150-52 (1968) (statement of Marion Barry, director of operations of Pride, Inc.).

26. *Civil Disturbances in Washington*, Ninetieth Cong. 433 (1968) (statement of Theodore Thalis).

27. *Civil Disturbances in Washington*, Ninetieth Cong. 382 (1968) (statement of Charles L. Cassell, vice chairman of the Emergency Committee on Transportation Crisis).

28. R.H. Booker described the board of conveners as the "steering committee" and leadership of the Black United Front. "Booker, Reginald H. (1941), Chairman, Washington (D.C.) Construction Area Industry Task

Force. July 24, 1970," 13, Ralph J. Bunche Oral Histories Collection on the Civil Rights Movement, Moorland Spingarn Research Center, Howard University, Washington, DC; "Minutes of the Black United Front March 19, 1968," box 4, folder "Black United Front," Julius Hobson Papers, 1960–1977, DC Community Archives, Washingtoniana Collection, Martin Luther King Jr. Memorial Library, Washington, DC.

29. *Civil Disturbances in Washington*, statement of Marion Barry, 313.

30. *Rehabilitation of District of Columbia Areas Damaged by Civil Disorders*, Ninetieth Cong. 149–151 (1968) (statement of Marion Barry of Pride, Inc.).

31. *Civil Disturbances in Washington*, statement of Marion Barry, 313–315.

32. "Partnership Seen as Goal," *Washington Afro-American*, April 16, 1968.

33. *Rehabilitation of District of Columbia Areas Damaged by Civil Disorders*, statement of Marion Barry, 150–154.

34. *Civil Disturbances in Washington*, statement of Marion Barry, 313. Specifically, Barry requested that the Small Business Administration wait to write disaster relief loans. Further, the city should not grant licenses to rebuild until "the total community has been involved in a plan."

35. *Civil Disturbances in Washington*, statement of Marion Barry, 313.

36. *Civil Disturbances in Washington*, Ninetieth Cong. 384–89 (1968) (statement of R.H. Booker, chairman of the Emergency Committee on the Transportation Crisis).

37. "Black movement leaders seek right to rebuild," *Washington Afro-American*, May 7, 1968.

38. "Rebuilding of Black Neighborhoods," 1968, folder 29, May 3, 1968, Walter E. Washington Papers, Moorland Spingarn Research Center, Howard University, Washington, DC; "Black Movement Leaders Seek Right to Rebuild," *Washington Afro-American*, May 7, 1968.

39. Heather Long and Andrew Van Dam, "The Black-White Economic Divide Is as Wide as It Was in 1968," *Washington Post*, June 4, 2020.

40. "Report of the City Council Public Hearings on the Rebuilding and Recovery of Washington, D.C. from the Civil Disturbances of April, 1968," 3.

41. *Rehabilitation of District of Columbia Areas Damaged by Civil Disorders*, statement of John W. Hechinger, 131.

42. "Statement by John W. Hechinger, Chairman of the City Council at a News Conference on Rebuilding and Recovery of the City," in "Report of the City Council Public Hearings on the Rebuilding and Recovery of Washington, D.C. from the Civil Disturbances of April, 1968."

43. "Report of the City Council Public Hearings on the Rebuilding and Recovery of Washington, D.C. from the Civil Disturbances of April, 1968," 7.

44. "Report of the City Council Public Hearings on the Rebuilding and Recovery of Washington, D.C. from the Civil Disturbances of April, 1968," 5.

45. "Report of the City Council Public Hearings on the Rebuilding and Recovery of Washington, D.C. from the Civil Disturbances of April, 1968," 15–18.

46. "Report of the City Council Public Hearings on the Rebuilding and Recovery of Washington, D.C. from the Civil Disturbances of April, 1968," 15–18.

47. "Report of the City Council Public Hearings on the Rebuilding and Recovery of Washington, D.C. from the Civil Disturbances of April, 1968," 19–20.

48. "Report of the City Council Public Hearings on the Rebuilding and Recovery of Washington, D.C. from the Civil Disturbances of April, 1968," 15–18.

49. "Report of the City Council Public Hearings on the Rebuilding and Recovery of Washington, D.C. from the Civil Disturbances of April, 1968," 19–20.

50. "Report of the City Council Public Hearings on the Rebuilding and Recovery of Washington, D.C. from the Civil Disturbances of April, 1968," 27–30.

51. "Report of the City Council Public Hearings on the Rebuilding and Recovery of Washington, D.C. from the Civil Disturbances of April, 1968," 38–40; Richard M. Cohen, "Pool Formed for Ghetto Insurance: Insurance Firms Form Pool to Cover Ghetto Merchants," *Washington Post*, September 27, 1968.

52. "Report of the City Council Public Hearings on the Rebuilding and Recovery of Washington, D.C. from the Civil Disturbances of April, 1968," 8.

53. "Report of the City Council Public Hearings on the Rebuilding and

Recovery of Washington, D.C. from the Civil Disturbances of April, 1968," 36–37.

54. "Report of the City Council Public Hearings on the Rebuilding and Recovery of Washington, D.C. from the Civil Disturbances of April, 1968," 5.

55. Elsie Carper, "To Rebuild," *Washington Post*, May 21, 1968. Prior to giving this speech, Mayor Washington sent a copy of his planned remarks to Chuck Stone, another member of the BUF's board of conveners, to solicit his comments and "to give him an opportunity to suggest changes." See "The B.U.F. Task Force Meeting," May 23, 1968, box 16, folder "Black Empowerment: Black United Front, April–May 1968," Walter Fauntroy Papers.

56. Wolf Von Eckardt, "City Pushes to Meet Deadline on Plan to Rebuild Riot Areas—25 Days to Go," *Washington Post*, July 23, 1968; "Mayor Unveils 1st Plans to Rebuild Riot Areas," *Washington Post*, August 29, 1968.

57. Von Eckardt, "City Pushes to Meet Deadline on Plan to Rebuild Riot Areas—25 Days to Go," *Washington Post*; "Minutes of the Black United Front Board of Conveners Meeting, May 15, 1968" and "Minutes of the Black United Front, May 22, 1968, " box 16, folder 14 "Black Empowerment, Black United Front, April–May, 1968," MS 2070, Walter Fauntroy Papers.

58. "Minutes of the Black United Front May 22, 1968," Walter Fauntroy Papers.

59. "Minutes of the Black United Front May 22, 1968," Walter Fauntroy Papers.

60. "The B.U.F. Task Force Meeting," Walter Fauntroy Papers; "Minutes of the Black United Front May 22, 1968," Walter Fauntroy Papers.

9

"The Troublemakers . . . Will Be Dealt With Severely":
The Backlash to Restraint

1. "While Washington Burned," *Washington Daily News*, April 9, 1968.

2. "The Face of the City," *Washington Daily News*, April 6, 1968.

3. Elsie Carper, "Hill Wants Troops to Stay; Police-Aid Pacts Suggested: Arrest Powers Planned," *Washington Post*, April 9, 1968.

4. Jesse W. Lewis Jr., "Baltimore Troubles Follow Washington Pattern," *Washington Post*, April 8, 1968.

5. "The Mindless Mob Spurns Dr. King's Creed," *Sunday Star*, April 7, 1968.

6. Tom Donnelly, letter to the editor, *Washington Daily News*, April 9, 1968.

7. Carper, "Hill Wants Troops to Stay; Police-Aid Pacts Suggested: Arrest Powers Planned," *Washington Post*.

8. "Congress's Reactions Split over Violence in Big Cities," *Washington Afro-American*, April 16, 1968.

9. Letter from Joseph H. Deckman to O.L. Weird, April 8, 1968, box 284a, folder 34: "Special TF: Civil Disturbances, Correspondence, March–June 1968," Greater Washington Board of Trade Records.

10. Advertisement, "Ben Brown Is Dead," *Washington Post*, May 7, 1968.

11. David Lawrence, "To Defy Law Is to Invite Violence," *Washington Evening Star*, April 8, 1968.

12. Lawrence, "To Defy Law Is to Invite Violence," *Washington Evening Star*.

13. John Fialka, "Businessmen See Riots Planned by Outsiders," *Washington Star*, May 1, 1968.

14. "Federation of Citizens Associations of District of Columbia Bill of Particulars Relative to the District of Columbia Riots of April 1968," *Civil Disturbances in Washington: Hearings Before the Committee on the District of Columbia House of Representatives* (hereafter referred to *Civil Disturbances in Washington*), Ninetieth Cong. 57 (1968).

15. Jonathon Cottin, "Byrd Wants Troops to Stay Indefinitely," *Washington Daily News*, April 9, 1968.

16. *Civil Disturbances in Washington*, Ninetieth Cong. 6 (1968) (statement of Patrick V. Murphy, director of the Office of Public Safety of the District of Columbia).

17. *Civil Disturbances in Washington*, statement of Patrick V. Murphy, 5.

18. Letter from the Association of the Oldest Inhabitants of Washington to Attorney General Ramsey Clark, May 13, 1968, box 284a, folder 34: "Special TF: Civil Disturbances, Correspondence, March–June 1968," Greater Washington Board of Trade Records.

19. Letter from the Association of the Oldest Inhabitants of Washington to Attorney General Ramsey Clark.

20. Joseph Deckman, letter to William Calomiris from Washington Suburban Mortgage, Inc., April 29, 1968, box 284a, folder 34: "Special TF: Civil Disturbances, Correspondence, March–June 1968," Greater Washington Board of Trade Records.

21. "Federation of Citizens Associations of District of Columbia Bill of Particulars Relative to the District of Columbia Riots of April 1968," *Civil Disturbances in Washington*, Ninetieth Cong. 57 (1968).

22. Arthur J Howe, letter to the editor, *Washington Star*, May 11, 1968.

23. "Strong Man," *Washington Post*, April 14, 1968.

24. *Civil Disturbances in Washington*, statement of Patrick V. Murphy, 18–20.

25. *Civil Disturbances in Washington*, statement of Patrick V. Murphy, 39.

26. *Civil Disturbances in Washington*, statement of Patrick V. Murphy, 51.

27. "Congress' Reactions Split over Violence in Big Cities," *Washington Afro-American*, April 16, 1968.

28. "Congress's Reactions Split over Violence in Big Cities," *Washington Afro-American*.

29. "Minutes: Special Meeting, Board of Directors, April 11, 1968," box 42, folder 10 "Board of Directors Executive Committee 4/11/68," MS 2029, Greater Washington Board of Trade Records.

30. "An Editorial Broadcast by WMAL—The Evening Star Broadcasting Company," April 14, 1968, box 284A, folder 36 "TF: Civil Disturbances—Clippings," MS 2029, Greater Washington Board of Trade Records.

31. Carper, "Hill Wants Troops to Stay; Police-Aid Pacts Suggested: Arrest Powers Planned," *Washington Post*.

32. William Dobrovir, *Justice in Time of Crisis: A Staff Report to the District of Columbia Committee on the Administration of Justice under Emergency Conditions* (Washington, DC: U.S. Government Printing Office, 1969), xxiv. The Lemberg Center for the Study of Violence reported that 8,236 people were arrested in this time period (Lemberg Center for the Study of Violence, Riot Data Review (Ann Arbor, MI: University of Michigan, 1968), 62, 227). I use Dobrovir's numbers since he specifies that 6,230 people were arrested in connection to the disorders. Additionally, Dobrovir's report was more deeply researched over a greater period of time.

33. William Raspberry, "Punish, Don't Destroy Looters," *Washington Post*, April 15, 2015. It also created a maximum sentence of ninety days imprisonment for "rioting," defined as engaging in "a public disturbance involving an assemblage of five or more persons which by tumultuous and violent conduct" damages people or property. Rioting could be tacked onto felony charges of looting or could be a stand-alone misdemeanor charge. William Shumann, "Looting Suspects Held for Grand Jury as Court Tackles Riot Cases," *Washington Post*, April 18, 1968.

34. Dobrovir, *Justice in a Time of Crisis*, xxiv, 14–15. After the city was restored to order, Bress and the U.S. Attorney's Office created guidelines to "break down" second-degree burglary charges in exchange for a plea to a misdemeanor with a lesser sentence such as petty larceny, attempted burglary, unlawful entry, or destruction of private property. Although the U.S. Attorney's Office developed the criteria to reduce charges, many felonies were not reduced for several reasons. First, the U.S. Attorney's Office marked the guidelines as "confidential" and distributed them to few people, so many defense attorneys were not aware that their client's charges could be broken down. Further, some of the volunteer lawyers representing the accused only had experience in civil law so they were not aware or were unsure of the possibility of plea bargaining. Additionally, many defendants refused to plead guilty to a lesser charge that still risked imprisonment. Defendants and their lawyers often determined that the evidence against them was "thin," so they preferred a trial and possible acquittal. Due to such limitations, all but 104 of the 121 defendants eligible to reduce their charges for looting while coming or going from a store declined to do so. Thus, despite the desire of the U.S. Attorney's Office to avoid felony trials, many accused of looting were still charged with a felony.

35. Dobrovir, *Justice in a Time of Crisis*, 86.

36. David Jewell, "Huge Backlog of Cases Jams U.S. District Court," *Washington Post*, August 4, 1968. This is based in a comparison to the backlog in April 1968 prior to the upheaval.

37. David Jewell, "25 Riot Cases of 452 Due Felony Trial," *Washington Post*, October 10, 1968.

38. Dobrovir, *Justice in a Time of Crisis*, 81–82, 86.

39. Jewell, "25 Riot Cases of 452 Due Felony Trial," *Washington Post*.

40. "Jury 'Acquits' 2 in First Riot Trial," *Washington Post*, July 12, 1968.

41. In the few cases where individuals were convicted of second-degree burglary, court records suggest that the judges were fairly lenient as they commonly suspended jail sentences. In a sample of fourteen individuals convicted of second-degree burglary, only four served jail time."32 Offenders Sentenced in U.S. District Court," *Washington Post*, December 7, 1968; "Sentences Meted Out in District Court," *Washington Post*," March 22, 1969; "Sentences Given by District Court," *Washington Post*, March 15, 1969.

42. Jewell, "25 Riot Cases of 452 Due Felony Trial," *Washington Post*.

43. Dobrovir, *Justice in a Time of Crisis*, 86–89. When convicted, only 18 percent of those sentenced in District Court actually served time in prison; 14 percent of those sentenced in the Court of General Sessions served time.

44. "Bonds for Parade Permits, and Removal of Destroyed Buildings," *Civil Disturbances in Washington*, Ninetieth Cong. 1 (1968). This section of the publication is hereafter referred to as *Bonds for Parade Permits, and Removal of Destroyed Buildings*.

45. *Bonds for Parade Permits, and Removal of Destroyed Buildings*, 80 (statement of Richard O. Haase, chairman of the Legislation and Taxation Committee of the Washington Board of Realtors).

46. *Riots, Civil and Criminal Disorders: Hearings Before the Permanent Subcommittee on Investigations of the Committee on Government Operations, United States Senate* (hereafter referred to as *Riots, Civil and Criminal Disorders*), Ninety-First Cong. 141 (1969) (statement of Hilliard Schulberg, executive director of the Washington DC Retail Liquor Dealers Association).

47. *Bonds for Parade Permits, and Removal of Destroyed Buildings*, statement of Richard O. Haase, 100.

48. *Bonds for Parade Permits, and Removal of Destroyed Buildings*, statement of Richard O. Haase, 81.

49. Paul W. Valentine, "Merchants to Sue City for Riot Related Losses," *Washington Post*, May 10, 1968.

50. Thomas W. Lippman, "Insurance Firm Sues for D.C. Riot Losses," *Washington Post*, April 26, 1969.

51. Sanford J. Ungar, "4 Damaged in Riots Ask $3 Million; 4 Ask $3 Million in Riot Damages," *Washington Post*, August 21, 1970.

52. Ungar, "4 Damaged in Riots Ask $3 Million; 4 Ask $3 Million in Riot Damages," *Washington Post*.

53. Sanford J. Ungar, "Court Absolves D.C. in Riot Damage Suit," *Washington Post*, October 14, 1970.

54. "Minutes: Washington, D.C. Riot and Future Planning," May 7, 1968, "Washington, D.C. Civil Rights Issues Including Riot Prevention, Poor People's Campaign, and Urban Renewal, 1968–1969," found in "Civil Rights During the Johnson Administration, 1963–1969, Part I: The White House Central Files;" ProQuest History Vault: Black Freedom Struggle.

55. Fred Bohen, Memo to Joe Califano, April 6, 1968, "Civil Rights Issues, Including Martin Luther King, Jr. Assassination, Urban Disturbances and Use of Army Units, and Situation in Baltimore, April 1968," found in "Civil Rights During the Johnson Administration, 1963–1969, Part I: The White House Central Files;" ProQuest History Vault: Black Freedom Struggle.

56. George Reedy, "Memorandum for the President," April 6, 1968, "Civil Rights Issues, Including Martin Luther King, Jr. Assassination, Urban Disturbances and Use of Army Units, and Situation in Baltimore, April 1968," found in "Civil Rights During the Johnson Administration, 1963–1969, Part I: The White House Central Files;" ProQuest History Vault: Black Freedom Struggle.

57. Flamm, *Law and Order*, 147–148.

58. "Civil Rights Bill Stirs Mixed emotions," *Washington Afro-American*, April 16, 1968.

59. Flamm, *Law and Order*, 132–141; Elizabeth Hinton, *From the War on Poverty to the War on Crime: The Making of Mass Incarceration in America* (Cambridge, MA: Harvard University Press, 2016), 135–142.

60. Hinton, *From the War on Poverty to the War on Crime*, 154–155; Flamm, *Law and Order*, 141–146; Lyndon Johnson, letter to John W. McCormack, July 3, 1968; George Christian, "Memorandum for the President," June 10, 1968, "Washington, D.C. Civil Rights Issues Including Riot Prevention, Poor People's Campaign, and Urban Renewal, 1968–1969," found in "Civil Rights During the Johnson Administration, 1963–1969, Part I: The White House Central Files," ProQuest History Vault: Black Freedom Struggle.

61. Lyndon Johnson, letter to John W. McCormack, July 3, 1968; George Christian, "Memorandum for the President," June 10, 1968, "Washington, D.C. Civil Rights Issues Including Riot Prevention, Poor People's Campaign,

and Urban Renewal, 1968–1969," found in "Civil Rights During the Johnson Administration, 1963–1969, Part I: The White House Central Files;"
ProQuest History Vault: Black Freedom Struggle.

62. "Memorandum from Joe Califano to President Lyndon B. Johnson,
"Minutes: Washington, D.C. Riot and Future Planning," April 17, 1968,
found in "Civil Rights During the Johnson Administration, 1963–1969, Part
I: The White House Central Files," ProQuest History Vault: Black Freedom
Struggle.

63. Warren Christopher, deputy attorney general, "Improvement of Civil
Disorder Intelligence Capabilities for Washington Metropolitan Area,"
May 4, 1968, found in "Civil Rights During the Johnson Administration,
1963–1969, Part I: The White House Central Files," ProQuest History Vault:
Black Freedom Struggle.

64. Undersecretary of the Army David E. McGiffert, letter to Walter
E. Washington, June 6, 1968; letter to David E. McGiffert from Walter E.
Washington, June 7, 1968; box 47, folder 9: Metropolitan Police Records,
1968, Walter E. Washington Papers, Mooreland-Spingarn Research Center,
Howard University Library, Washington, DC.

65. William Raspberry, "News Satire Misconstrued," *Washington Post*,
May 26, 1968.

66. Raspberry, "News Satire Misconstrued," *Washington Post*.

67. For a full history of the Poor People's Campaign, read Gordon
Mantler, *Power to the People: Black-Brown Coalition and the Fight for
Economic Justice, 1960–1974* (Chapel Hill: University of North Carolina
Press, 2013).

68. Ben Gilbert, *Ten Blocks from the White House: Anatomy of the Washington Riots of 1968* (New York: Frederick A. Praeger, 1968), 196–201; Lauren Pearlman, *Democracy's Capital: Black Political Power in Washington,
D.C. 1960s–1970s* (Chapel Hill: University of North Carolina Press, 2019),
124–127.

69. Pearlman, *Democracy's Capital*, 128–133; Gilbert, *Ten Blocks from
the White House*, 200–202.

70. Pearlman, *Democracy's Capital*, 129–133; Gilbert, *Ten Blocks from
the White House*, 202–207.

71. For an excellent examination of these contradictory policies, see
Hinton, *From the War on Poverty to the War on Crime*.

10

"We Want to Rebuild. . . . What Do You Want?":
Community Control and Reconstruction

1. *Civil Disturbances in Washington: Hearings Before the Committee on the District of Columbia House of Representatives* (hereafter referred to as *Civil Disturbances in Washington*), Ninetieth Cong. 114–116 (1968).

2. *Civil Disturbances in Washington*, Ninetieth Cong. 116–117, 23–36 (1968).

3. *Civil Disturbances in Washington*, Ninetieth Cong. 154–155 (1968) (statement of Walter Washington, commissioner of the District of Columbia).

4. Elsie Carper, "To Rebuild," *Washington Post*, May 21, 1968. Prior to giving this speech, Mayor Washington sent a copy of his planned remarks to Chuck Stone, another member of the BUF's board of conveners to solicit his comments and "to give him an opportunity to suggest changes." See "The B.U.F. Task Force Meeting," May 23, 1968, box 16, folder: "Black Empowerment: Black United Front, April–May 1968," MS 2070 Walter Fauntroy Papers, Gelman Library Special Collections at the George Washington University, Washington, DC.

5. DC Office of the Mayor, *Ten Years Since April 4, 1968: A Decade of Progress for the District of Columbia*, 7, F 200.T 46, Kiplinger Research Library Archives, Washington, DC.

6. "Report of the City Council Public Hearings on the Rebuilding and Recovery of Washington, D.C. from the Civil Disturbances of April, 1968," 30–33, P1614, Kiplinger Research Library Archives, Washington, DC.

7. *Riots, Civil and Criminal Disorders: Hearings Before the Permanent Subcommittee on Investigations of the Committee on Government Operations, United States Senate* (hereafter referred to as *Riots, Civil and Criminal Disorders*), Ninety-First Cong. 3,242 (1969) (testimony of Thomas W. Fletcher, Lt. Col. Sam Starobin, and John G. Stone III).

8. *Riots, Civil and Criminal Disorders*, testimony of Thomas W. Fletcher, Lt. Col. Sam Starobin, and John G. Stone III, 3,237–38; Peter Braestrup, "Fletcher: Riot Area Rebuilding on Target," *Washington Post*, April 13, 1969.

9. Vincent Paka, "Shaw Area Results Show," *Washington Post*, February 8, 1970.

10. Jim Hoagland, "Negro Team to Survey Shaw," *Washington Post*, May 2, 1968; Braestrup, "Fletcher: Riot Area Rebuilding on Target," *Washington Post*.

11. Letter to Fauntroy from Melvin Mister, March 3, 1972, box 24, folder 36: "Correspondence, D.C. Redevelopment Land Agency, 1971–1972, 1974, n.d.," Walter Fauntroy Papers, Gelman Library Special Collections at George Washington University, Washington, DC.

12. Richard M. Cohen, "Pool Formed for Ghetto Insurance: Insurance Firms Form Pool to Cover Ghetto Merchants," *Washington Post*, September 27, 1968.

13. "Pride Gets $3.8 Million to Open Two Work Projects," *Washington Afro-American*, August 13, 1968.

14. Robert Samuelson, "Bleak Facts Slow 'Black Capitalism,'" *Washington Post*, August 31, 1969.

15. DC Office of the Mayor, *Ten Years Since April 4, 1968*, 7.

16. DC Office of the Mayor, *Ten Years Since April 4, 1968*, 7.

17. Martin Austermuhle, "Norton Decries 'Shocking' Threat from Republicans to Repeal D.C. Home Rule," NPR, February 17, 2022.

18. Chris Meyers Asch and George Derek Musgrove, *Chocolate City: A History of Race and Democracy in the Nation's Capital* (Chapel Hill: University of North Carolina Press, 2017), 380.

19. DC Office of the Mayor, *Ten Years Since April 4, 1968*.

20. Leon Dash and Phil McCombs, "New Kind of City Emerging out of Ruins of '68 Riot," *Washington Post*, April 2, 1978.

21. Peter Braestrup, "Fletcher: Riot Area Rebuilding on Target," *Washington Post*, April 13, 1969; Eugene Meyer, "City Asks Funds for Riot Areas," *Washington Post*, June 26, 1970; "Shaw School Urban Renewal Area," box 27, folder 1: "Map, Shaw School Urban Renewal Area, n.d." Walter Fauntroy Papers, Gelman Library Special Collections at George Washington University, Washington, DC.

22. "MICCO and You," box 24, folder 5: "Brochure, MICCO and You, n.d." Walter Fauntroy Papers, Gelman Library Special Collections at the George Washington University, Washington, DC.

23. Elaine Barber Todd, "Urban Renewal in the Nation's Capital: A History of the Redevelopment Land Agency in Washington, D.C., 1946–1973" (PhD Diss, Howard University, 1986), 200–201.

24. Eugene Meyer, "RLA Sets Bidding on Shaw Land," *Washington Post*, November 11, 1971; Todd, "Urban Renewal in the Nation's Capital," 209, 229–230.

25. Todd, "Urban Renewal in the Nation's Capital," 221.

26. "14th Street Development," 1973, box 35, folder 1: "14th Street Development," Walter E. Washington Papers, Mooreland-Spingarn Research Center, Howard University Library, Washington, DC; "The Shaw Urban Renewal Area Urban Renewal Plan and Annual Action Program," box 27, folder 4: "Plan, the Shaw Urban Renewal Area, c. 1969," Walter Fauntroy Papers, Gelman Library Special Collections at George Washington University, Washington, DC; "Annual Report 1970," box 27, folder: "Annual Report 1970," Walter Fauntroy Papers, Gelman Library Special Collections at George Washington University, Washington, DC.

27. "Results of the MICCO Questionnaire," box 25, folder 16: "Questionnaire, MICCO Community Results, c. 1968," Walter Fauntroy Papers, Gelman Library Special Collections at George Washington University, Washington, DC.

28. Braestrup, "Fletcher: Riot Area Rebuilding on Target," *Washington Post*.

29. George Day, "Urban Renewal: A Slow, Painful Process," *Washington Post*, July 2, 1969.

30. "Status Report: First Action Year," box 26, folder 1: "Report, First Action Year, c. 1968," Walter Fauntroy Papers, Gelman Library Special Collections at George Washington University, Washington, DC.

31. "The Shaw Urban Renewal Area Urban Renewal Plan and Annual Action Program," box 27, folder 4: "Plan, the Shaw Urban Renewal Area, c. 1969," Walter Fauntroy Papers, Gelman Library Special Collections at George Washington University, Washington, DC.

32. *Riots, Civil and Criminal Disorders*, Ninety-First Cong. 3,159–3,169 (1969) (testimony of Edward C. Hromanik); "The Shaw Urban Renewal Area Urban Renewal Plan and Annual Action Program," Walter Fauntroy Papers. The Redevelopment Land Agency would administer the loan.

33. "The Shaw Urban Renewal Area Urban Renewal Plan and Annual Action Program," Walter Fauntroy Papers.

34. "Annual Report 1971," box 25, folder 20: "Report, Annual Report, 1971," Walter Fauntroy Papers.

35. "Statement of the Model Inner City Community Organization, Inc. The Reverend Walter E. Fauntroy, President/Director at the D.C. Council Public Hearings on the Proposed Second Urban Renewal Action Year for Shaw June 3, 1970," box 26, folder 8: "Statement, 2nd Urban Renewal Action Year, June 30, 1970," Walter Fauntroy Papers.

36. "2nd Action Year for Shaw," box 25, folder 10: "Pamphlet, '2nd Action Year for Shaw,' n.d.," Walter Fauntroy Papers.

37. Eugene L. Meyer, "Renewal Plan Cuts Foreseen," *Washington Post*, June 22, 1970. The plan was that the National Capital Housing Authority would subsidize the leases for those one thousand units.

38. Letter to Terry C. Chisholm from Melvin Mister, June 4, 1971, box 35, folder 1: "14th Street Development," Walter E. Washington Papers, Mooreland-Spingarn Research Center, Howard University Library, Washington, DC.

39. Letter to Terry C. Chisholm from Melvin Mister, Walter E. Washington Papers.

40. Letter to Walter Fauntroy from Melvin Mister, box 24, folder 36: "Correspondence, D.C. Redevelopment Land Agency, 1971–1972, 1974, n.d.," Walter Fauntroy Papers.

41. Robert J. Samuelson, "Low, Moderate Income Housing Stalls," *Washington Post*, June 15, 1969.

42. "5 Years Later: Riot Areas Not Rebuilt," *Washington Post*, April 8, 1973.

43. Letter to Walter Fauntroy from Melvin Mister, box 24, folder 36: "Correspondence, D.C. Redevelopment Land Agency, 1971–1972, 1974, n.d.," Walter Fauntroy Papers.

44. Eugene L. Meyer, "Build More Costly Housing First in Shaw, Advisors Say," *Washington Post*, December 14, 1970.

45. Letter to "MICCO Board Member" from James Woolfork, box 24, folder 36: "Correspondence, D.C. Redevelopment Land Agency, 1971–1972, 1974, n.d.," Walter Fauntroy Papers.

46. "5 Years Later: Riot Areas Not Rebuilt," *Washington Post*.

47. Eugene L. Meyer, "RLA Sets Bidding on Shaw Land," *Washington Post*, November 11, 1971.

48. Meyer, "RLA Sets Bidding on Shaw Land," *Washington Post*; letter from Walter Fauntroy to Melvin Mister, July 12, 1971, Walter Fauntroy

NOTES 269

Papers; letter to Walter Fauntroy from Robert E. Tracey, August 30, 1971, box 24, folder 32: "Correspondence, Melvin Mister, July 12, 1971," Walter Fauntroy Papers.

49. Letter to Melvin Mister from Walter Fauntroy, August 31, 1971, Walter Fauntroy Papers; letter to Walter Fauntroy from Robert E. Tracey, August 30, 1971, box 24, folder 32: "Correspondence, Melvin Mister, July 12, 1971," Walter Fauntroy Papers.

50. Meyer, "RLA Sets Bidding on Shaw Land," *Washington Post*; Howard Gillette Jr., *Between Justice and Beauty: Race, Planning, and the Failure of Urban Policy in Washington, D.C.* (Philadelphia: University of Pennsylvania Press, 1995), 185.

51. Gillette, *Between Justice and Beauty*, 185–188.

52. Letter to Walter Fauntroy from Melvin Mister, March 3, 1972, Walter Fauntroy Papers.

53. Braestrup, "Fletcher: Riot Area Rebuilding on Target," *Washington Post*.

54. William Greider, "President Orders Aid to Riot Areas," *Washington Post*, April 9, 1968.

55. Peter Braestrup and Carl Bernstein, "President Nixon . . . Has Promised Me a . . . Timetable Under Which the Construction in These Areas Would Begin Next Fall," *Washington Post*, April 10, 1969.

56. Peter Braestrup, "Even Messy 'Model Cities' Programs Beat a Riot," *Washington Post*, June 29, 1969; Kirk Scharfenberg, "Model Cities' Aid Revised," *Washington Post*, March 1, 1972.

57. After Nixon's urging, by mid-April 1969, the NCPC approved a "concept plan" for rebuilding H Street. The Model Cities Commission, however, urged the city to delay its approval of the plan because it felt that citizens did not have enough involvement in it. The RDC had only started canvassing in February and received a mere one thousand surveys. By the summer of 1970, no plans had been officially approved for the H Street area due to the extended debates over the lack of community involvement. See Peter Braestrup, "Building Commission Backs Rebuilding Plan for H Street," *Washington Post*, April 19, 1969; Braestrup, "H Street Renewal Scored," *Washington Post*; Braestrup and Bernstein, "President Nixon . . . Has Promised Me a . . . Timetable Under Which the Construction in These Areas Would Begin Next Fall," *Washington Post*; Braestrup, "Even Messy 'Model Cities' Programs Beat a Riot," *Washington Post*;

15. "Law and Order in the National Capital Parks," June 21, 1968, Federation of Citizens Association Records, series: Office Files, box 2, folder: "Office Files: 1968–1969," Washingtoniana Collection, Martin Luther King Jr. Memorial Library, Washington, DC.

16. *Rehabilitation of District of Columbia Areas Damaged by Civil Disorders: Hearings Before the Subcommittee on Business and Commerce of the Committee on the District of Columbia United States Senate* (hereafter referred to as *Rehabilitation of District of Columbia Areas Damaged by Civil Disorders*), Ninetieth Cong. 316 (statement of John R. Immer, president of the Federation of Citizens Associations of the District of Columbia and acting chairman of Independent Democrats).

17. "Resume of Minutes, Special Meeting, Board of Directors, May 10, 1968," box 42, folder 12 "Board of Directors Executive Committee, May 19, 1968," Greater Washington Board of Trade Records.

18. Jonathon Cottin, "Byrd Wants Troops to 'Stay Indefinitely,'" *Washington Daily News*, April 9, 1968.

19. "Troops in Washington," editorial broadcast by WMAL, May 12, 1968, 65–66, *Civil Disturbances in Washington*, Ninetieth Cong. 58 (1968).

20. "WMAL Editorial June 10, 1968," box 297, folder: "Law and Order—Restoration—Correspondence, April 1968–Jan 1969," Greater Washington Board of Trade Records.

21. "WMAL Editorial June 10, 1968," Greater Washington Board of Trade Records.

22. *Civil Disturbances in Washington*, Ninetieth Cong. 74 (1968) (statement of George Kalavitinos).

23. Susan Jacoby, "Fairfax School's Field Trips into City Banned After Riots," *Washington Post*, April 19, 1968.

24. "Resume of Minutes, Special Meeting, Board of Directors," May 10, 1968, box 42, folder 12 "Board of Directors Executive Committee, May 10, 1968," Greater Washington Board of Trade Records.

25. Elise Carper, "Visitors Bureau Reports Sharp Drop in Tourism," *Washington Post*, June 1, 1968.

26. Reuben M. Jackson Interview, 18, box 1, folder 2, MS 0769, 1968 Riots Oral History Collection, Kiplinger Library, Washington, DC.

27. Brookland Citizen's Association, letter to George Brady, October 7, 1968, collection 28: Federation of Citizens Associations, box 2, folder: "FCADC 1967–1968 Office Files," Washingtoniana Collection, MLK Library.

28. Eleanor Bartlett, "Annual Reports 1968–1969," Records of the Public Library of the District of Columbia, Washingtoniana Collection, Martin Luther King Jr. Library, Washington DC.

29. Bartlett, "Annual Reports 1968–1969," Records of the Public Library of the District of Columbia, Washingtoniana Collection, Martin Luther King Jr. Library, Washington DC.

30. "The Shaw Community: The Impact of the Civil Rights Movement, as Told by Mrs. Virginia Ali, Owner of Ben's Chili Bowl," Ben's Chili Bowl Papers.

31. "How Race, Crime, Affect Life Today in Washington," *Washington Afro-American*, January 28, 1969.

32. John Hechinger Sr. and Gavin Taylor, "Black and Blue: The D.C. City Council vs. Police Brutality, 1967–69," *Washington History Journal* 11, no. 2 (Fall/Winter 1999/2000): 4–23.

33. James McNeirney, "Husband Killed by Police, Wife Grief Stricken," *Washington Afro-American*, July 9, 1968; "Urge Better Police Community Efforts," *Washington Afro-American*, July 23, 1968.

34. "A Move to Improve Community Relations," *Washington Afro-American*, August 27, 1968; "Statement of Council Chairman John W. Hechinger Concerning Police-Community Relations at the City Council Meeting July 16, 1968," "Report of the City Council Public Safety Committee on Police-Community Relations," P 2341, Kiplinger Research Library Archives, Washington, DC.

35. "Transmittal and Summary of Report on Police-Community Relations," August 5, 1968, P 2341, "Report of the City Council Public Safety Committee on Police-Community Relations." Kiplinger Research Library Archives, Washington, DC.

36. "Introductory Statement by Councilman William S. Thompson on the Booklet Concerning City Council Action on Police-Community Relations," *Report on City Council Actions to Improve Police-Community Relations* (Government of the District of Columbia City Council, 1968), P 2342, Kiplinger Library Archives.

37. "Status Chart of Council Actions," ii, *Report on City Council Actions to Improve Police-Community Relations*, (Government of the District of Columbia City Council, 1968), P 2342, Kiplinger Library Archives.

38. "Coalition Demands Civilian Control of Police Officers," *Washington Afro-American*, October 15, 1968; "Crowds Block Street," *Washington Afro-American*, October 15, 1968. For his part, Mayor Washington then

created an ad hoc committee on public safety to address the issue. The committee suggested "radical changes in the handling of homicide cases involving policemen," according to the *Washington Afro-American*. These included ending the coroner's power to declare a homicide "justifiable" or not, ending the US Attorney's power to present homicide cases to a grand jury since they believed they were too close to the police (a civil rights attorney from the Justice Department would do it instead), and more citizen control over police discipline and police use of firearms. See "Mayor's Safety Committee Asks for Sweeping Changes," *Washington Afro-American*, October 29, 1968.

39. "Mayor's Safety Committee Asks for Sweeping Changes," *Washington Afro-American*.

40. Later drafts of the bill also added lawyers for both the police and citizens making the complaints. "Statement of Mr. Thompson," November 21, 1968, 32, 34–42, *Report on City Council Actions to Improve Police-Community Relations* (Government of the District of Columbia City Council, 1968), P 2342, Kiplinger Library Archives.

41. *Report on City Council Actions to Improve Police-Community Relations*, 46–53.

42. Darrel W. Stephens, Ellen Scrivner, and Josie F. Cambareri. "Civilian Oversight of the Police in Major Cities" (Washington, DC: Office of Community Oriented Policing Services).

43. "Statement of William S. Thompson, November 21, 1968, Chairman of the District of Columbia Public Safety Committee," *Report on City Council Actions to Improve Police-Community Relations* (Government of the District of Columbia City Council, 1968), P 2342, Kiplinger Library Archives.

44. "Council Slaps Stiff Gun Rules on Cops," *Washington Afro-American*, December 28, 1968.

45. Statement of William S. Thompson, December 17, 1968: Chairman of the District of Columbia Public Safety Committee," *Report on City Council Actions to Improve Police-Community Relations* (Government of the District of Columbia City Council, 1968), P 2342, Kiplinger Library Archives.

46. John Layton, memo, November 30, 1968, *Report on City Council Actions to Improve Police-Community Relations* (Government of the District of Columbia City Council, 1968), P 2342, Kiplinger Library Archives.

47. "Statement to D.C. Council's Public Safety Committee on Its Report on Police-Community Relations," August 16, 1968, Federation of Citizens

Associations Records, collection 28, box 2, folder: "FCADC Office Files 1968–1969," Martin Luther King, Jr. Memorial Library, Washington, DC.

48. "Status Chart of Council Actions," ii, *Report on City Council Actions to Improve Police-Community Relations* (Government of the District of Columbia City Council, 1968), P 2342, Kiplinger Library Archives.

49. Walter Washington, letter to Walter Fauntroy, December 28, 1968, 15; "Statement of Mr. Hechinger," January 6, 1969, 16–17; *Report on City Council Actions to Improve Police-Community Relations* (Government of the District of Columbia City Council, 1968), P 2342, Kiplinger Library Archives.

50. "Statement of Mr. Hechinger," January 14, 1969, 18, *Report on City Council Actions to Improve Police-Community Relations* (Government of the District of Columbia City Council, 1968), P 2342, Kiplinger Library Archives.

51. "Status Chart of Council Actions," ii, *Report on City Council Actions to Improve Police-Community Relations* (Government of the District of Columbia City Council, 1968), P 2342, Kiplinger Library Archives.

52. Hechinger and Taylor, "Black and Blue: The D.C. City Council vs. Police Brutality, 1967–69," 4–23.

53. Robert C. Albright, "Nixon Blasts Administration on Attitudes Toward Crime," *Washington Post*, August 1, 1968.

54. Don Oberdorfer, "Nixon Hits D.C. Crime: Vows to Stem Lawlessness, Criticizes HHH," *Washington Post*, September 28, 1968.

55. Chalmers M. Roberts, "Nixon Hits Rise in Crime," *Washington Post*, May 9, 1968.

56. "Nixon on D.C. Crime: 'Disgrace,'" *Washington Post*, September 28, 1968.

57. William Raspberry, "Crime Capital? Let's Look at the Record," *Washington Post*, September 27, 1968.

58. Oberdorfer, "Nixon Hits D.C. Crime: Vows to Stem Lawlessness, Criticizes HHH," *Washington Post*; Robert L. Asher, "Nixon Labels D.C. a 'Crime Capital,' Blames Johnson," *Washington Post*, June 23, 1968; "Nixon on D.C. Crime: 'Disgrace,'" *Washington Post*.

59. Oberdorfer, "Nixon Hits D.C. Crime: Vows to Stem Lawlessness, Criticizes HHH," *Washington Post*.

60. Roberts, "Nixon Hits Rise in Crime," *Washington Post*.

61. Asher, "Nixon Labels D.C. a 'Crime Capital,' Blames Johnson," *Washington Post*.

62. Raspberry, "Crime Capital? Let's Look at the Record," *Washington Post*.

63. "Mayor Washington Hits Back on Crime," *Washington Post*, September 29, 1968.

64. "Mr. Nixon's Simple Solution," *Washington Post*, June 29, 1968.

65. "BUF Hits Nominees to Council," *Washington Afro-American*, February 18, 1968.

66. "Congress Clears Controversial D.C. Crime Control Bill." In *CQ Almanac 1970*, 26th ed., Washington, DC:

67. Elizabeth Hinton, *From the War on Poverty to the War on Crime: The Making of Mass Incarceration in America* (Cambridge, MA: Harvard University Press, 2016), 154–159.

68. Hinton, *From the War on Poverty to the War on Crime*, 141.

69. Hinton, *From the War on Poverty to the War on Crime*, 153–158.

70. "Congress Clears Controversial D.C. Crime Control Bill," *CQ Almanac*.

71. Hinton, *From the War on Poverty to the War on Crime*, 153–158.

72. "'Probably' Unconstitutional," *Washington Afro-American*, February 18, 1969.

73. "Roy Wilkins Speaks," *Washington Afro-American*, August 11, 1970.

74. Jerry V. Wilson, *The War on Crime in the District of Columbia 1955–1975* (Washington, DC: National Institute of Law Enforcement and Criminal Justice, Law Enforcement Administration, United States Department of Justice, 1978), 22–23.

75. Wilson, *Crime in the District of Columbia*, 22–24.

76. Wilson, *Crime in the District of Columbia*, 22–24. Additionally, Nixon invited DC police officers who won awards for valor and merit to the White House to thank them in 1972.

77. Wilson, *Crime in the District of Columbia*, 22–24.

78. Foreman, *Locking Up Our Own*, 48–52.

79. Hinton, *From the War on Poverty to the War on Crime*, 158.

80. Hinton, *From the War on Poverty to the War on Crime*, 158.

81. Hinton, *From the War on Poverty to the War on Crime*, 11. For more on the rise of mass incarceration and its impacts, see Michelle Alexander, *The New Jim Crow: Mass Incarceration in the Age of Colorblindness* (New York: The New Press, 2012).

Epilogue

1. Marisa M. Kashino, "The Reinvention of 14th Street: A History," *Washingtonian*, April 4, 2018.

2. Paul Schwartzman and Robert E. Pierre, "From Ruin to Rebirth in D.C.," *Washington Post*, April 6, 2008.

3. For more on neoliberalism and gentrification, see Sabiyha Prince, *African Americans and Gentrification in Washington, D.C.: Race, Class and Social Justice in the Nation's Capital* (New York: Routledge, 2014); Brandi Thompson Summers, "H Street, Main Street, and the Aesthetics of Cool," in *Capital Dilemma: Growth and Inequality in Washington, D.C.*, eds. Derek Hyra and Sabiyha Prince (New York: Routledge, 2016).

4. Schwartzman and Pierre, "From Ruin to Rebirth in D.C.," *Washington Post*.

5. Rene Sanchez and Liz Spayd, "U Street, New Street?" *Washington Post*, April 11, 1995.

6. Linda Wheeler, "A Whole New U: Businesses Spring Up Along Historic Street in NW," *Washington Post*, December 26, 1995.

7. "A Revitalization for Washington's U Street Corridor," *New York Times*, June 12, 2005.

8. Howard Gillette, "Introduction," in *Capital Dilemma*, 2.

9. Derek Hyra, *Race, Class, and Politics in the Cappuccino City* (Chicago: University of Chicago Press, 2017), 8.

10. Gillette, "Introduction," in *Capital Dilemma*, 5; Derek Hyra and Sabiyha Prince, "Forward," in *Capital Dilemma*, xiv; Prince, *Gentrification in Washington, D.C.*, 3.

11. Hyra and Prince, "Forward," in *Capital Dilemma*, xiv.

12. Hyra, *Race, Class, and Politics in the Cappuccino City*, 12–13.

13. *South of U Oral History Project—Life, Riots and Renewal in Shaw*, Kenneth Tolliver interview transcript, Dig DC archives, https://dcplislandora.wrlc.org/islandora/object/dcplislandora%3A68528/pages.

14. *South of U Oral History Project—Life, Riots and Renewal in Shaw*, Elizabeth Williams Frazier interview transcript, April 2012, Dig DC archives, https://dcplislandora.wrlc.org/islandora/object/dcplislandora%3A68545/pages.

15. See Sabiyha Prince, *African Americans and Gentrification in Washington, D.C.: Race, Class and Social Justice in the Nation's Capital* (New

Publishing in the Public Interest

Thank you for reading this book published by The New Press; we hope you enjoyed it. New Press books and authors play a crucial role in sparking conversations about the key political and social issues of our day.

We hope that you will stay in touch with us. Here are a few ways to keep up to date with our books, events, and the issues we cover:

- Sign up at www.thenewpress.com/subscribe to receive updates on New Press authors and issues and to be notified about local events
- www.facebook.com/newpressbooks
- www.twitter.com/thenewpress
- www.instagram.com/thenewpress

Please consider buying New Press books not only for yourself, but also for friends and family and to donate to schools, libraries, community centers, prison libraries, and other organizations involved with the issues our authors write about.

The New Press is a 501(c)(3) nonprofit organization; if you wish to support our work with a tax-deductible gift please visit www.thenewpress.com/donate or use the QR code below.